Studies in
Aurangzib's Reign

Studies in
Aurangzib's Reign

(Being Studies in Mughal India, First Series)

By

SIR JADUNATH SARKAR, Kt., C.I.E.

GYAN

Published by

GYAN

Gyan Publishing House
5, Ansari Road
Daryaganj, New Delhi-110002
Phone: 011-47034999, 9811692060
E-mail: books@gyanbooks.com

Distribution Network
gyanbooks.com
India, USA, Canada, UK, Australia, France

ISBN : 978-81-212-6802-8 (PB)
First Published, 1933

2nd Impression 2022

Printed at: Gyan Press, Delhi.

STUDIES IN AURANGZIB'S REIGN
Author: SIR JADUNATH SARKAR

STUDIES IN
AURANGZIB'S REIGN

(Being *Studies in Mughal India, First Series*)

SIR JADUNATH SARKAR, Kt., C.I.E.,
Honorary Member, Royal Asiatic Society of Great Britain.

1933

WORKS OF SIR JADUNATH SARKAR

		Rs.	A.
1.	*History of Aurangzib,*		
	Vols. 1 & 2 in one, 2nd ed.	5	0
	Vol. 3, 3rd. ed	3	8
	,, 4, 2nd. ed.	4	0
	,, 5, ...	4	0
2.	*Shivaji and His Times,* 3rd ed. (rewritten) ...	5	0
3.	*A Short History of Aurangzib*	5	0
4.	*Mughal Administration,* 2nd ed.	3	0
5.	*Anecdotes of Aurangzib,* Eng. tr., 2nd ed. ...	1	8
6.	*Ahkam-i-Alamgiri,* Persian text, 2nd ed. ...	1	0
7.	*Chaitanya*: His Life and Teachings, 3rd ed.	2	0
8.	*Fall of the Mughal Empire,* Vol. I (1739—54)	5	0
9.	*Bihar & Orissa during the Fall of the Mughal Empire,* paper cover	2	0
10.	*India through the Ages*	1	8
11.	*Studies in Aurangzib's Reign*	2	8
12.	*Studies in Mughal India* (excluding the Reign of Aurangzib) 2nd series ...		
13.	*Documents and Studies on the House of Shivaji (in prep)*		
14.	*India of Aurangzib*: statistics, topography and roads *(out of pr.)*		
15.	*Economics of British India (out of pr.)* ...		

CONTENTS

[* First included in the present edition.]

BIBLIOGRAPHICAL NOTE

In 1912 was published the first edition of my *Historical Essays* (ten studies), bound up with my English translation of the *Anecdotes of Aurangzib.* Thereafter the two works have been separated. In 1919 the second edition, with 12 essays added, was published under the title of *Studies in Mughal India.* In the present or third edition (1933), the number of my later writings has made it necessary to divide this book into two volumes or series,—one on the reign of Aurangzib and the second dealing with other periods. These will be followed by a third containing original documents and studies in Maratha history, never collected before.

In the present volume, twelve of the essays of the second edition have been included, besides six altogether new ones. In addition, all the earlier essays have been thoroughly revised and more or less rewritten, three of them being greatly enlarged. One paper of the second edition, *viz.*, that on the Revenue Regulations of Aurangzib, it has been decided to exclude from the *Studies* henceforth and to reprint only as a chapter of my *Mughal Administration.*

The following nine essays published in the old one-volume *Studies* of 1919 have been placed in the new second series, which includes several other papers now collected for the first time: Daily Life of Shah Jahan, Wealth of Ind, Companion of an Empress, Who Built the Taj? William Irvine, Khuda Bakhsh the Indian Bodley, Art in Muslim India, Education in Muhammadan India, and Oriental Monarchies.

Jadunath Sarkar.

I

AURANGZIB, HIS LIFE AND CHARACTER

(A sketch)

EARLY LIFE.

Muhiuddin Muhammad Aurangzib, the third son of the Emperor Shah Jahan and his famous consort Mumtaz Mahal, was born on 24th October, 1618, at Dohad, now a town in the Panch Mahal *taluq* of the Bombay Presidency and a station on the Godra-Rutlam railway-line. The most notable incident of his boyhood was his display of cool courage when charged by an infuriated elephant, during an ELEPHANT COMBAT under his father's eyes on the bank of the Jamuna outside Agra Fort, (28 May, 1633). The victorious beast, after putting its rival to flight, turned fiercely on Aurangzib, who firmly kept his horse from running away and struck the elephant on the forehead with his spear. A sweep of the brute's tusk hurled the horse on the ground ; but Aurangzib leaped down from the saddle in time and again faced the elephant. Just then aid arrived, the animal ran away, and the prince was saved. The Emperor rewarded the heroic lad with his weight in gold.

On 13th December, 1634, Aurangzib, then 16 years of age, received his first appointment in the imperial army as a commander of ten thousand cavalry (nominal rank), and next September he was sent out to learn the art of war in the campaign against Jhujhar Singh and his son Vikramajit, the Bundela chiefs of Urchha, who were finally extirpated at the end of the year.

From 14th July 1636 to 28th May 1644, Aurangzib served as VICEROY OF THE DECCAN,—paying several visits to Northern India during the period to see the Emperor. This, his first governorship of the Deccan, was marked by the conquest of Baglana and the final extinction of the Nizam-Shahi dynasty of Ahmadnagar. He was married, first to Dilras Banu, the daughter of Shah Nawaz Khan Safawi, (8th May, 1637), and at some later but unknown date to Nawab Bai, and began to have children by them, his eldest offspring being Zeb-un-nisa, the gifted poetess, (born 15th February, 1638)

In May, 1644 the prince gave up his duties and took to a life of retirement as a protest against Dara Shukoh's jealous interference with his work and Shah Jahan's partiality to his eldest son. At this the Emperor was highly displeased, and at once deprived him of his governorship, estates, and allowances. For some months the prince lived at Agra in disgrace. But on 25th November, when Jahanara, the eldest and best-beloved daughter of Shah Jahan, recovered from a terrible burn, her joyful father could refuse her nothing, and at her entreaty Aurangzib was restored to his rank. On 16th February, 1645, the viceroyalty of Gujrat was given to him ; his vigorous rule suppressed lawlessness in the province and won rewards from the Emperor.

From Gujrat Aurangzib was recalled two years later and SENT TO CENTRAL ASIA to recover Balkh and Badakhshan, the cradle of the royal house of Timur. Leaving Kabul on 7th April, 1647, he reached Balkh on 25th May, and battled long and arduously with the fierce enemy. The bravest Rajputs shed their blood in the van of the Mughal army in that far-off soil ; immense quantities of stores, provisions and treasure were wasted ; but the Indian army merely held the ground on which it encamped ; the hordes of Central Asia, "more numerous than ants and locusts," and all of them born horsemen,—swarmed on all sides and could not be crushed once for all. The barren and distant conquest could have been retained only at a ruinous cost. So, a truce was patched up : Nazar Muhammad Khan, the ex-king of Balkh, was sought out with as much eagerness as Sir Lepel Griffin displayed in getting hold of the late Amir Abdur Rahman, and coaxed into taking his throne back, and the Indian army beat a hurried retreat to avoid the dreaded winter of that region. Many *krores* of Rupees of Indian revenue were thus wasted for absolutely no gain ; the abandoned stores alone had cost several *lakhs*, and much property too had to be sacrificed by the rearguard for lack of transport.

During this campaign Aurangzib did an act which made his fame ring throughout the Islamic world. While the Mughal army was fighting desperately with the vast legions of Abdul Aziz Khan, king of Bukhara, the time for the evening prayer (*zuhar*) arrived. Disregarding the prohibitions of his officers, Aurangzib dismounted from his elephant, knelt down on the ground, and deliberately and peacefully went through all the ceremonies of the prayer, in full view of both the armies. Abdul Aziz on hearing of it cried out, 'To fight with such a man is to court one's own ruin,' and suspended the battle.

From Balkh, Aurangzib returned to Kabul on 27th October, 1647, and was afterwards appointed viceroy of Multan (15th March, 1648). This post he held till July, 1652, being in the meantime twice called away from his charge to BESIEGE QANDAHAR (16th May—5th September, 1649, and 2nd May—9th July, 1652). This fort had been wrested from Shah Jahan by the Persians, and these two huge and costly sieges and a third and still greater one under Dara (28th April—27th September, 1653) failed to recover it.

With his SECOND VICEROYALTY OF THE DECCAN (to which he was sent off on 17th August, 1652), began the most important chapter of Aurangzib's early life. What Gaul was to Julius Cæsar as a training-ground for the coming contest for empire, the Deccan was to Aurangzib. Many hundreds of his letters, preserved in the *Adab-i-Alamgiri*, give us much interesting information about his life and work during the next six years,—how he overcame his recurring financial difficulties, how he gathered a picked band of officers round himself, how ably and strenuously he ruled the country, maintaining order and securing the happiness of the people. By constant inspection and exercise he kept his army in good condition. He must have been often out on tour, as he admits in one of his letters that he was a hard rider and keen sportsman in those days. Thus the year 1658 found him beyond doubt the ablest and best equipped of the sons of Shah Jahan in the ensuing War of Succession.

At this period, too, occurred the only romance of his life, his PASSION FOR HIRA BAI, (surnamed ZAINABADI), whom he took away from the harem of his maternal uncle. It was a case of love at first sight, and Aurangzib's infatuation for the beautiful singer knew no bound: to please her he consented to drink wine! Their union was cut short by her death in the bloom of youth, which plunged her lover into the deepest grief.

After a long intrigue he seduced from the king of Golkonda his *wazir* Mir Jumla, one of the ablest Persians who have ever served in India. At Aurangzib's recommendation Shah Jahan enrolled Mir Jumla among his officers and threw the mantle of imperial protection over him. To force the Golkonda king to give up Mir Jumla's family and property, Aurangzib made a RAID ON HAIDARABAD (24th January, 1656); the king fled to Golkonda where he was forced to make a humiliating peace with immense sacrifices. Mir Jumla joined Aurangzib (20th March), was summoned to Delhi and created *wazir* (7th July), and then on 18th January, 1657, returned to the Deccan to reinforce Aurangzib.

A year after his unprovoked attack on Golkonda, Aurangzib with his father's sanction INVADED Bijapur on the death of its king Muhammad Adil Shah, captured the forts of Bidar and Kaliani (29th March and 1st August, 1657 respectively), and was looking forward to annexing a good deal of the territory, when the whole scene changed in the most unexpected and sudden manner.

The Emperor Shah Jahan had now reached his 66th year, and was evidently declining in health. His eldest son and intended heir-apparent, Dara Shukoh, who lived with him and conducted much of the administration, induced him to recall the additional troops sent to Aurangzib for the Bijapur war, on the very reasonable ground that the Bijapur king had thrown himself on the Emperor's mercy and offered a large indemnity and piece of territory as the price of peace. But this peremptory order to Aurangzib to come to terms with Bijapur gave him a sharp check when flushed with victory and cut short his schemes of aggression. Besides, the depletion of his army left him too weak to hold the Bijapuris to their promises, and thus the fruits of his victory were lost to him.

WAR OF SUCCESSION.

On 6th September, 1657, Shah Jahan was taken severely ill at Delhi. For some time his life was despaired of. Dara attended him day and night with extreme filial piety, but he also took steps to secure his own succession. He stopped the couriers on the roads and prevented his brothers from getting true news of Court affairs. But this only aggravated the evil: the wildest rumours prevailed all over the country; the Emperor was believed to be already dead; the officers in the provinces were distracted by the prospect of an empty throne; lawless men in all parts raised their heads without fear of punishment. Two of the princes, Murad and Shuja, openly crowned themselves in their governments, Gujrat and Bengal respectively. Aurangzib after a short period of gnawing anxiety and depressing uncertainty, decided to play a subtler game. He denounced Dara as an apostate from Islam, proclaimed his own design to be merely to free the old Emperor from Dara's domination and to purge the State from non-Islamic influences, and lastly he made an alliance with Murad Bakhsh swearing on the *Quran* to give him all the Mughal territory from the Panjab westwards.

Meanwhile Dara had despatched two armies, one under his son Sulaiman Shukoh and Mirza Rajah Jai Singh against Shuja who was advancing from Bengal, and the other under Maharajah Jaswant Singh and Qasim Khan against Aurangzib and Murad. The first army surprised and routed Shuja at Bahadurpur, opposite Benares, (14th February, 1658), and pursued him to Mungir. But Aurangzib and Murad effected a junction outside Dipalpur and crushed Jaswant's army after a long and terribly contested BATTLE AT DHARMAT, 14 miles south of Ujjain (15th April). Dara sent off urgent orders recalling his son from Bengal. But his division of his forces had been a fatal mistake: Sulaiman returned from far-off Bihar too late to help his father or even to save himself. Aurangzib had the immense advantage of crushing his enemies piecemeal, while his own armed strength was doubled by the league with Murad.

From Ujjain the victorious brothers pushed on to the capital. AT SAMUGARH, 10 miles east of Agra, DARA who had issued from the city with a second army, attacked them on a frightfully hot day (29th May), was signally DEFEATED, and fled from Agra towards Delhi and the Panjab. Aurangzib now marched on Agra, compelled his old father to surrender the fort by stopping the supply of drinking water from the Jamuna, and kept Shah Jahan strictly confined in the harem for the remainder of his life. Then, at Mathura he treacherously MADE MURAD PRISONER at a banquet (25th June), and advancing to Delhi crowned himself Emperor (21st July, 1658). Dara was chased through the Panjab and Sindh to Tatta, whence he fled to Gujrat over the Rann of Cutch, undergoing terrible hardships on the way. A second army which he raised was destroyed near Ajmir (14th March, 1659) and he was hunted by Aurangzib's generals from place to place, till he reached Dadar, at the Indian mouth of the Bolan Pass, whose chief betrayed him to Aurangzib. The captive DARA was brought to Delhi, paraded with insult through the bazar, and MURDERED by some slaves of Aurangzib, (30th August, 1659), who had got the Mullas to issue a sentence that according to Islamic Law Dara deserved an apostate's death. MURAD BAKHSH was BEHEADED in Gwalior prison as a judicial punishment, on the accusation of a man whose father he had slain in Gujrat, (4th December, 1661). Dara's eldest son, Sulaiman Shukoh, was secretly done to death in the same State-prison, (May, 1662).

Meantime SHUJA had gathered together a new army and advanced beyond Allahabad to make a second attempt for the throne. But he was signally DEFEATED at KHAJWA, (5th January, 1659), and driven back to

Bengal, whence after a sixteen months' struggle on land and river he was forced to flee miserably to ARRACAN for refuge (12th May, 1660). Here he was MASSACRED with his whole family for a plot against the Burmese king on whose hospitality he was living.

Thus all his rivals being removed from his path, Aurangzib became the undisputed sovereign of India.

AURANGZIB'S REIGN IN NORTHERN INDIA.

The new monarch now enjoyed a long period of comparative peace: he received grand embassies from Persia (22nd May, 1661), Bukhara (19th November, 1661), Mecca, Abyssinia (1665), and Arabia, sent to congratulate him on his accession; and the envoys were treated to a sight of the lavish splendour of the Mughal Court,—a splendour which dazzled the eyes of Bernier, Tavernier and other European travellers of the time. He had a sharp attack of illness (12th May—24th June, 1662), which threatened to shake his newly established throne; but he recovered and paid a visit to Kashmir (1st May—29th September, 1663).

Though peace reigned in the heart of the empire, there was WAR ON THE FRONTIERS: ambitious and enterprising officers tried to extend their master's dominion; Daud Khan, the governor of Bihar, conquered Palamau (April—December, 1661). Mir Jumla, the governor of Bengal, overran Kuch Bihar and Assam, capturing their capitals on 19th December, 1661 and 17th March, 1662; but famine and pestilence destroyed his army, and he sank down under disease before reaching Dacca on return (31st March, 1663). Shaista Khan, the next governor of Bengal, wrested Chatgaon (Chittagong) from the Portuguese and Burmese pirates (26th January, 1666), and also captured the island of Sondip in the Bay of Bengal. An expedition from Kashmir forced the ruler of Greater Tibet to be a feudatory of the Emperor and to "submit to Islam" (November, 1665). To crown all, the able and astute general Jai Singh tamed Shivaji, the daring and hitherto invincible Maratha chief, annexed two-thirds of his forts, (Treaty of Purandar, 11th June, 1665), and induced him to do homage to the Emperor by a visit to Agra (12th May, 1666). Aurangzib's lack of statesmanship in dealing with Shivaji and the latter's romantic escape from prison (19th August) are a familiar tale all over India. True, the Mughal arms did not gain any conspicuous success in Jai Singh's invasion of Bijapur (first half of 1666), but these expeditions were of the nature of raids for extortion, and not deliberate schemes of conquest.

A more formidable but distant trouble was the revolt of the Yusufzai clan and their allies on the Afghan frontier, (began in 1667). The war against these sturdy hillmen dragged on for many years; successive Mughal generals tried their hands and buried their military reputation there, and at last peace was purchased only by paying a large annual subsidy from the Indian revenue to these "keepers of Khaibar gate."

A state of war also continued against the Bijapur

king and Shivaji for many years ; but the Mughal generals were bribed by the former to carry on the contest languidly, and the latter was more than able to hold his own. These operations present us with nothing worthy of note. The Muhammadan kings of the Deccan, in fear of the Mughals, courted the alliance of Shivaji, who rapidly grew in wealth, territory, armed strength, and prestige, and had made himself the foremost power in the Deccan when death cut his activity short at the age of 52, (4th April, 1680).

Meantime Aurangzib had begun to give free play to his RELIGIOUS BIGOTRY. In April, 1669 he ordered the provincial governors to "DESTROY THE TEMPLES and schools of the infidels and to utterly put down their teaching and religious practices." The wandering Hindu saint Uddhav Bairagi was confined in the police lock-up. The Vishwanath temple at Benares was pulled down in August, 1669. The grandest shrine of Mathura, Kesav Rai's temple, built at a cost of 33 lakhs of Rupees by the Bundela Rajah Birsingh Dev, was razed to the ground in January, 1670, and a mosque built on its site. "The idols were brought to Agra and buried under the steps of Jahanara's mosque that they might be constantly trodden on" by the Muslims going in to pray. About this time the new temple of Somnath on the south coast of the Kathiawar peninsula was demolished, and the offering of worship there ordered to be stopped. The smaller religious buildings that suffered havoc were beyond count. The Rajput War of 1679-80 was accompanied by the destruction of 240 temples in Mewar alone, including the famous one of Someshwar and three grand ones at Udaipur. In the loyal State of Jaipur 67 temples were demolished by his order. On 2nd April, 1679, the JAZIYA or poll-tax on non-Muslims was REVIVED. The poor Hindus who appealed to the Emperor and blocked a road abjectly crying for its remission, were trampled down by elephants at his order and dispersed. By another ordinance (March, 1695), "all Hindus except Rajputs were forbidden to carry arms or ride elephants, *palkis*, or Arab and Persian horses." "With one stroke of his pen he dismissed all the Hindu clerks from office." Custom duties were abolished on the Muslims and doubled on the Hindus.

The discontent provoked by such measures was an ominous sign of what their ultimate political consequence would be, though Aurangzib was too blind and obstinate to think of the future. A rebellion broke out among the peasantry in the Mathura and Agra districts, especially under Gokla Jat (1669), and the Satnamis or Mundias rose near Narnol (May 1672), and it taxed the imperial power seriously to exterminate these 5,000 stubborn peasants fighting for church and home. The Sikh Guru Tegh Bahadur was tortured in prison till he courted death as a release (1675), but his followers thereafter gave no rest to the Panjab officers.

At last Aurangzib threw off all disguise and openly ATTACKED THE RAJPUTS. Maharajah Jaswant Singh of Jodhpur died in the Emperor's service at Peshawar (10th December, 1678). Immediately Aurangzib sent out officers to take possession of his kingdom and himself marched to Ajmir to overawe opposition. Two wives of the Maharajah delivered two sons after reaching Lahor in the following February. Aurangzib sold the Jodhpur throne (May, 1679) for 36 lakhs of Rupees to a worthless nephew of Jaswant and ordered the late Maharajah's widows and new-born babes to be seized and detained in his Court till the latter should come of age. But thanks to the devotion of their Rathor guards, most of whom died like heroes, and the sagacity and loyalty of Durgadas, (one of the noblest characters in Rajput history), Ajit Singh, the surviving infant of Jaswant and the future hope of Marwar, was safely conveyed to Jodhpur (23rd July, 1679). But Aurangzib was up to any trick: he proclaimed Ajit Singh to be a counterfeit prince, and for many years cherished a beggar boy in his Court under the significant name of Muhammadi Raj, as the real son of Jaswant! All Rajputana (except ever-loyal Jaipur) burst into flame at this outrage to the head of the Rathor clan. The Maharana, Raj Singh, chivalrously took up the defence of the orphan's rights. The war dragged on with varying fortune; the country was devastated wherever the Mughals could penetrate; the Maharana took refuge in his mountain fastnesses. At last PRINCE AKBAR, the fourth son of Aurangzib, REBELLED (January, 1681), joined the Rajputs, and assumed the royal title. For a few days Aurangzib was in a most critical position, but his wonderful cunning saved him: by a false letter he sowed distrust of Akbar in the minds of the Rajputs, the prince's army melted away, and he fled, leaving all his family and property behind and reaching the Maratha Court after a perilous journey under the guidance of the faithful Durgadas (May, 1681). The Emperor patched up a peace with the Maharana (June, 1681), both sides making concessions. But henceforth the Rajputs ceased to be supporters of the Mughal throne; we no longer read of large Rajput contingents fighting under the imperial banner; he had to depend more on the Bundelas. The Rathors continued the war till the close of Aurangzib's life. Here ends the first and stable half of Aurangzib's reign—the period passed in Northern India.

AURANGZIB'S REIGN IN THE DECCAN.

We next enter on a scene of unceasing but fruitless exertion for 26 years,—the war with the "slim" Marathas, which ruined the Emperor's health, the *morale* of his army, and the finances of his State,—a war of which all saw the futility and all were heartily tired, all save Aurangzib, who pursued one policy with increasing obstinacy, till at last the old man of 90 sank into the grave amidst despair, darkness, and chaos ready to overwhelm his family and empire.

Shivaji's eldest son Shambhu was a more daring raider than his father and deterred by no fear of consequences. With Akbar as his pensioner, what might he not do against the Mughal crown? Moreover, all of Aurangzib's generals and even his sons sent against the kingdoms of the Deccan had failed of conquest, and were rightly suspected of corruption. So there was nothing left for Aurangzib but to conduct the war in person. With this object he left Ajmir for the Deccan (8th

September, 1681, never again to return to Northern India alive or dead. The capital Aurangabad was reached on 22nd March, 1682. Thence, on 13th November, 1683, he arrived at Ahmadnagar, a town to which he was destined to return 23 years afterwards only to die. Two of his sons and some nobles were despatched against the Bijapuris and the Marathas, but they effected nothing decisive, though many of Shambhu's forts were captured. A large force which penetrated through the Ramghat pass into Southern Konkan under Prince Muazzam, returned with failure and heavy loss (September, 1683—May, 1684).

Fierce as was Aurangzib's hatred of the Hindus (the vast majority of his subjects), it was equalled by his AVERSION FOR THE SHIAS,—who supplied him with some of his best generals and all his ablest civil officers. To him the Shia was a heretic (*rāfizi*) ; in one of his letters he quotes with admiration the story of a Sunni who escaped to Turkey after murdering a Shia at Isfahan, and draws from it the moral, "Whoever acts for truth and speaks up for truth, is befriended by the True God." In another letter he tells us how he liked the naming of a dagger as the 'Shia-slayer' (*Rāfizi-kush*), and ordered some more of the same name to be made for him. In his correspondence he never mentions the Shias without an abusive epithet: 'corpse-eating demons' (*ghul-i-bayābāni*), 'misbelievers' (*bātil mazhabān*), are among his favourite phrases. Indeed, even the highest Shia officers had such a bad time of it in his Court that they often played the hypocrite to please him! Aurangzib threw the cloak of Sunni orthodoxy over his aggressive conquest of Bijapur and Golkonda, of which the rulers were Shias. The Chief Qazi Shaikh-ul-Islam (one of the purest characters of the age,) tried to dissuade the Emperor from these "wars between Muslims" as opposed to Islam. But Aurangzib grew displeased at the opposition; the honest and manly Shaikh resigned his post, left the Court, and for the rest of his life rejected the Emperor's repeated solicitations to resume his high office.

On 1st April, 1685 the SIEGE OF BIJAPUR was begun by Ruhullah Khan and Khan-i-Jahan Bahadur. The Emperor advanced to Sholapur (24th May) to be near the seat of war. A terrible famine desolated the besiegers; but reinforcements soon arrived with provisions, though scarcity of a kind continued in a chronic state in the Mughal camp. The relieving armies of Berads and Marathas were beaten back and the siege pressed on. The garrison fought with the heroism of despair. Aurangzib himself arrived in the environs of the city to superintend the siege operations (3rd July, 1686). At last, on 12th September, Sikandar, the last of the Adil-Shahi kings, surrendered, and his kingdom was annexed.

Meantime another force had been sent under Prince Muazzam or Shah Alam (28th June, 1685) against Golkonda to prevent aid from coming from that quarter to Bijapur. It captured the rich city of Haidarabad, making an immense loot (October). The king, Abul Hasan, a worthless voluptuary and the exact counterpart of Wajid Ali of Oudh, helplessly SHUT himself UP in the FORT OF GOLKONDA. But his chiefs were seduced by the Mughals; there was discontent among his Muhammadan officers at the power of his Brahman minister Mādanna Pant. Aurangzib himself arrived near Golkonda on 28th January, 1687, and laid siege to it. The besiegers had a hard time of it before that impregnable fort: a terrible famine raged in Haidarabad, but the rains and swollen rivers rendered the transport of grain impossible, and the most ghastly scenes were acted by the sufferers. At an immense cost the Mughals filled the moat and also erected a huge barrier wall of wood and clay completely surrounding the fort and preventing ingress and egress. But mining and assault failed, and it was only the treachery of a Golkonda officer that opened the gate of the fort to the Mughals at midnight (21st September, 1687). The king was dragged out and sent to share the captivity of his brother of Bijapur. His kingdom was annexed. Two years later, SHAMBHUJI, the brave but dissolute Maratha king, was surprised by an energetic Deccani officer (Muqarrab Khan), ignominiously paraded through the imperial camp like a wild beast, and EXECUTED with prolonged and inhuman tortures (11th March, 1689). His capital Raigarh was captured (19th October) and his entire family, "mothers, wives, daughters, and sons" made prisoner by the Mughals. His eldest son, Shahu, was brought up at the imperial Court in gilded fetters.

All seemed to have been gained by Aurangzib now, but in reality all was lost. It was THE BEGINNING OF HIS END. The saddest and most hopeless chapter of his life now opened. The Mughal empire had become too large to be ruled by one man or from one centre. Aurangzib, like the boa constrictor, had swallowed more than he could digest. It was impossible for him to take possession of all the provinces of the newly annexed kingdoms and at the same time to suppress the Marathas. His enemies rose on all sides, he could defeat but not crush them for ever. As soon as his army marched away from a place, the enemy who had been hovering round occupied it again, and Aurangzib's work was undone! Lawlessness reigned in many places of Northern and Central India. The old Emperor in the far-off Deccan lost control over his officers in Hindustan, and the ADMINISTRATION grew SLACK and corrupt; chiefs and zamindars defied the local authorities and asserted themselves, filling the country with tumult. In the province of Agra in particular, there was chronic disorder. Art and learning decayed at the withdrawal of imperial patronage,—not a single grand edifice, finely written manuscript, or exquisite picture commemorates Aurangzib's reign. The endless war in the Deccan exhausted his treasury; the Government turned bankrupt; the soldiers, starving from arrears of pay, mutinied; and during the closing years of his reign the revenue of Bengal, regularly sent by the faithful and able diwan Murshid Quli Khan, was the sole support of the Emperor's household and army, and its arrival was eagerly looked forward to. Napoleon I used to say, "It was the Spanish ulcer which ruined me." The Deccan ulcer ruined Aurangzib.

To resume the narrative, imperial officers were despatched to all sides to take over the forts and provinces of the two newly annexed kingdoms from their local officers, many of whom had set up for themselves. The

Berads, a wild Kanarese tribe, whom Col. Meadows Taylor has described in his fascinating *Story of My Life,* were the first to be attacked. Their country, situated between Bijapur and Golkonda, was overrun, their capital Sagar captured (28th Nov., 1687), and their chief Pam Naik, a strongly built uncouth black savage, brought to the Court. But the brave and hardy clansmen rose under other leaders and the Mughals had to send two more expeditions against them.

A desolating epidemic of BUBONIC PLAGUE broke out in Bijapur (early in November, 1688), sparing neither prince nor peasant. The imperial household paid toll to Death in the persons of Aurangabadi Mahal (a wife of the Emperor), Fazil Khan the *Sadr,* and the bogus son of Jaswant Singh. Of humbler victims the number is said to have reached a *lakh.*

After Shambhu's capture, his younger brother Rajaram made a hair-breadth escape to the fort of Jinji, (Gingee in the S. Arcot district of Madras), which was besieged by the Mughal general Zulfiqar Khan Nusrat Jang (September, 1690), and fell on 7th January, 1698. Two years afterwards Rajaram, the last king of the Marathas, died. But the MARATHA captains, each acting on his own account, incessantly raided the Mughal territory and did the greatest possible injury by their GUERILLA WARFARE. The two ablest, most successful, and most dreaded leaders of this class were Dhana Singh Jadav and Santa Ghorparé (and latterly Nima Sindhia), who dealt heavy blows at some important Mughal detachments. They seemed to be ubiquitous and elusive like the wind.

The movable columns frequently sent from the imperial headquarters to "chastise the robbers", only marched and countermarched, without being able to crush the enemy. When the Mughal force had gone back the scattered Marathas, like water parted by the oar, closed again and resumed their attack, as if nothing had happened to them.

THE LAST PHASE.

After moving about almost every year between Bijapur in the south and the Manjira river in the north, Aurangzib (21st May, 1695) finally made Brahmapuri on the Bhima river, 20 miles south-east of Pandharpur, his Base CAMP, and named it ISLAMPURI. Here a city sprang up from his encampment, and it was walled round in time. Here his family was lodged when he went forth on campaigns.

On 19th October, 1699, after a four years' stay at Islampuri, Aurangzib, now aged 81 years, set out to BESIEGE THE MARATHA FORTS IN PERSON. The rest of his life is a repetition of the same sickening tale: a hill fort captured by him after a great loss of time men and money, the fort recovered by the Marathas from the weak Mughal garrison after a few months, and the siege begun again after a year or two! The soldiers and camp-followers suffered unspeakable hardships in marching over flooded rivers, muddy roads, and broken hilly tracks; porters disappeared, transport beasts died of hunger and overwork; scarcity of grain was ever presentt in the camp. His officers all wearied of this labour of Sisyphus; but Aurangzib would burst into wrath at any suggestion of retreat to Hindustan and taunt the unlucky counsellor with cowardice and love of ease! The mutual jealousies of his generals, Nusrat Jang and Firuz Jang, Shujaet Khan and Muhammad Murad Khan, Tarbiyat Khan and Fathullah Khan, spoiled his affairs as thoroughly as the French cause in the Peninsular War was damaged by the jealousies of Napoleon's marshals. Therefore, the Emperor must conduct every operation in person, or nothing would be done!

A bare RECORD OF HIS SIEGES will suffice here:

BASANTGARH (siege, 22nd—25th November, 1699).

SATARA (siege, 8th December, 1699—21st April, 1700).

PARLIGARH near Satara (siege, 30th April—9th June).

Halt at Khawaspur for the rainy season of 1700 (30th August—16th December).

PANHALA (siege, 9th March—28th May, 1701), also Pavangarh captured.

Halt at Khatav for the rainy season of 1701, (29th May—7th November).

Capture of Wardhangarh (6th June, 1701), Nandgir, Chandan and Wandan (6th October) by Fathullah Khan.

KHELNA (siege, 26th December, 1701—4th June, 1702).

The rainy season of 1702 spent in a most painful march (10th June—13th Nov.) from Khelna to Bahadurgarh, with a month's halt at Vadgaon in August.

KONDANA (siege, 27th December, 1702—8th April, 1703).

Halt at Puna for the rainy season of 1703, (1st May—10th November).

RAJGARH (siege, 2nd December, 1703—16th February, 1704).

TORNA (siege, 23rd February—10th March).

Halt at Khed for the rainy season of 1704 (17th April—22nd October).

WAGINGERA (siege, 8th February—27th April, 1705).

Halt at Devapur, 6 miles from Wagingera, *for the rainy season* of 1705, (May—23rd October).

This was the last of his sieges, for here he got a warning of what was to come. At Devapur a severe illness attacked him, which was aggravated by his insistence on transacting business as usual. The whole camp was thrown into despair and confusion: who would extricate them from that gloomy mountainous region if the Emperor died? At last Aurangzib yielded to their entreaty and probably also to the warning of approaching death, and RETREATED TO Bahadurgarh (6th December, 1705), whence he reached AHMADNAGAR (20th January, 1706), to die a year later.

The last years of his life were inexpressibly sad. On its public side there was the consciousness that his long reign of half a century had been a colossal failure. "After me will come the deluge!" this morose foreboding of Louis XV was repeated by Aurangzib almost word for word (*Az mā-st hamah fasād-i-bāqi*). His domestic life, too, was loveless and dreary, and wanting in the benign peace and hopefulness which throw a halo round old age. A sense of unutterable loneliness haunted the heart of Aurangzib in his last years. One daughter, Zinat-un-nisa, already an old maid, looked after his household, and his youngest concubine, Udaipuri, bore him company. But he had, at one time or other, to imprison all his five sons except one! By his own conduct in the War of Succession he had raised a spectre which relentlessly pursued him: what if *his* sons should treat him in his weak old age as he had treated Shah Jahan? This fear of Nemesis ever haunted his mind, and he had no peace while his sons were with him! Lastly, there was the certainty of a deluge of blood when he would close his eyes, and his three surviving sons, each supported by a provincial army and treasury, would fight for the throne to the bitter end. In two most pathetic letters written to his sons when he felt the sure approach of death, the old Emperor speaks of the alarm and distraction of his soldiery, the passionate grief of Udaipuri, and his own bitter sense of the futility of his life, and then entreats them not to cause the slaughter of Musalmans by engaging in a civil war among themselves. A paper, said to have been found under his pillow after his death, contained a plan for the peaceful partition of the empire among his three sons. Meantime death was also busy at work within his family circle. When Gauharārā, the last among Aurangzib's brothers and sisters, died, (about March, 1706), he felt that his own turn would come soon. Some of his nephews, daughters, and grandsons, too, were snatched away from him in the course of his last year. In the midst of the darkness closing around him, he used to hum the pathetic verses:—

By the time you have reached your 80th or 90th year,
You will have felt many a hard blow
from the hand of Time;
And when from that point you reach the
stage of a hundred,
Death will put on the form of your life.

And also,—

In a twinkle, in a minute, in a breath,
The condition of the world changes.

His last illness overtook him at Ahmadnagar, early in February 1707; then he rallied for 5 or 6 days, sent away his two sons from his camp to their provincial governments, and went through business and daily prayers regularly. But that worn-out frame of 90 years had been taxed too much. A severe fever set in, and in the morning of Friday, 20th February, 1707, he gradually sank down exhausted into the arms of death, with the Muslim confession of faith on his lips and his fingers on his rosary.

His corpse was despatched to Khuldabad, six miles from Daulatabad, and there buried in the courtyard of the tomb of the saint Shaikh Zainuddin, in a plain red sandstone sepulchre built by Aurangzib in his lifetime. The tombstone, 9 feet by 7, is only a few inches high, and has a cavity in the middle which is filled with earth for planting fragrant herbs in.

Aurangzib's wife DILRAS BANU BEGAM, the daughter of Shah Nawaz Khan Safavi, died on 8th October, 1657, after bearing him Zeb-un-nisa, Azam and Akbar. A secondary wife (*mahal*) NAWAB BAI, the mother of Sultan and Muazzam, does not seem to have been a favourite, as her husband seldom sought her society after his accession. Of his three concubines (*parastār*), Hirā Bai or ZAINABADI, with whom he was infatuated almost to madness, died very young; AURANGABADI, the mother of Mihr-un-nisa, died of the plague in November, 1688; UDAIPURI, the favourite companion of Aurangzib's old age and the mother of his pet son Kam Bakhsh, entered his harem after his accession. She is said to have been a Circassian slave-girl of Dara, gained by Aurangzib among the spoils of victory. But another account which describes her as a Kashmiri woman, is more likely to be true, because the *Masir-i-Alamgiri* calls her *Bai,* a title which was applied to Hindu women only . Her descent from the royal house of Mewar is a fanciful conjecture of some modern writers.

Aurangzib's eldest son, Muhammad SULTAN, chafing under the restraints of his father's officers, during the war of succession in Bengal, fled to Shuja and married his daughter, but in a few months returned to his father. The foolish youth, then only 20 years old, was kept in prison for the rest of his life. (Died 3rd December, 1676).

His second son, MUAZZAM, (also *Shah Alam*), who in 1707 succeeded his father on the throne as Bahadur Shah I., incensed Aurangzib by intriguing with the besieged kings of Bijapur and Golkonda, and was placed in confinement (21st February, 1687). After his spirit had been thoroughly tamed, his captivity was relaxed little by little (in a rather amusing fashion), and at last, on 9th May, 1695, he was sent to the Panjab as governor, (afterwards getting Afghanistan also to govern).

The third prince, AZAM, stepped into the vacant place of the heir-apparent (*Shah-i-alijah*) during Muazzam's disgrace, and was made much of by his father. But he was extremely haughty, prone to anger, and incapable of self-restraint.

The fourth, AKBAR, rebelled against his father in 1681, and fled to Persia where he died an exile in November, 1704. His presence at Farah, on the Khurasan frontier, was long a menace to the peace of India.

The youngest, KAM BAKHSH, the spoilt child of his father's old age, was worthless, self-willed, and foolish. For his misconduct during the siege of Jinji he was put under restraint, and again confined for his fatuous attachment to his foster-brother, a wretch who had tried to assassinate an excellent officer. The third and fifth brothers fell fighting in the struggle for the throne which followed Aurangzib's death, (1707 and 1709).

AURANGZIB'S CHARACTER.

So lived and so died Aurangzib, surnamed Alamgir Padishah, the last of the Great Mughals. For, in spite of his religious intolerance, narrowness of mind, and lack of generosity and statesmanship, he was great in the possession of some qualities which might have gained for him the highest place in any sphere of life except the supremely difficult one of rule over men. He would have made a successful general, minister, theologian, or school-master, and an ideal departmental head. But the critical eminence of a throne on which he was placed by a freak of

Fortune, led to the failure of his life and the blighting of his fame.

Pure in his domestic relations, simple and abstemious like a hermit, he had a passion for work and a hatred of ease and pleasure which remind one of George Grenville, though with Grenville's untiring industry he had also Grenville's narrowness and obstinacy. European travellers observed with wonder the greyheaded Emperor holding open Court every day, reading every petition and writing orders across it with his own hand. Of the letters dictated by him, those that are known to exist in Europe and India number about two thousand. I have secured copies of all of them as far as known to me. Many more must have perished.

In matters of official discipline and Court etiquette he was a martinet and enforced the strictest obedience to rules and established usages: "If I suffer a single regulation to be violated, all of them will be disregarded," was his frequent remark. But this punctilious observance of the form must have led to neglect of the spirit of institutions and laws.

His passion for doing everything himself and dictating the minutest particulars to far-off governors and generals, robbed them of all self-reliance and power of initiative, and left them hesitating and helpless in the face of any unexpected emergency. His suspicious policy crushed the latent ability of his sons, so that at his death they were no better than children though turned of fifty years of age. Alike in his passion for work, distrust of the men on the spot, preference for incompetent but servile agents, and religious bigotry, he resembled his contemporary in Europe, Louis XIV .

His coolness and courage were famous throughout India: no danger however great, no emergency however unlooked for, could shake his heart or cloud the serene light of his intellect. Indeed, he regarded danger as only the legitimate risk of greatness. No amount of exertion could fatigue that thin wiry frame. The privations of a campaign or forced ride had no terror for him. Of diplomacy he was a past master, and could not be beaten in any kind of intrigue or secret manipulation. He was as much a "master of the pen" as a "master of the sword."

From the strict path of a Muslim king's duty as laid down in the Quranic Law nothing could make him deviate the least. And he was also determined not to let *others* deviate too! No fear of material loss or influence of any favourite, no tears or supplication could induce him to act contrary to the *Shara* (Canon Law). Flatterers styled him "a living saint," (*Alamgir zinda pir*). Indeed, from a very early age he had chosen "the strait gate and narrow way which leadeth unto life"; but the defects of his heart made the gate straiter and the way narrower.

He lacked that warm generosity of the heart, that chivalry to fallen foes, and that easy familiarity of address in private life, which made the great Akbar win the love and admiration of his contemporaries and of all posterity. Like the English Puritans, Aurangzib drew his inspiration from the old law of relentless punishment and vengeance and forgot that mercy is an attribute of the Supreme Judge of the Universe.

His cold intellectuality, his suspicious nature, and his fame for profound statecraft, chilled the love of all who came near him. Sons, daughters, generals, and ministers, all feared him with a secret but deep-rooted fear, which neither respect nor flattery could disguise.

Art, music, dance, and even poetry (other than "familiar quotations") were his aversion, and he spent his leisure hours in hunting for legal precedents in Arabic works on Jurisprudence.

Scrupulously following the rules of the *Quran* in his own private life, he considered it his duty to enforce them on everybody else; the least deviation from the strict and narrow path of Islamic orthodoxy in any part of his dominions, would (he feared) endanger his own soul. His spirit was therefore the narrow and selfish spirit of the lonely recluse, who seeks his individual salvation, oblivious of the outside world. A man possessed of such ideas may have made a good *faqir*,—though Aurangzib lacked the *faqir's* noblest quality, charity;—but he was the worst ruler imaginable of an empire composed of many creeds and races, of diverse interests and ways of life and thought.

"The nature of man is intricate; the objects of society are of the greatest possible complexity; and therefore no simple disposition or direction of power can be suitable either to man's nature, or to the quality of his affairs......Political reason is a computing principle; adding, subtracting, multiplying, and dividing true moral denominations......The true lawgiver ought to have an heart full of sensibility. He ought to love and respect his kind, and to fear himself. Political arrangement is to be only wrought by social means. There mind must conspire with mind." (*Burke*).

Aurangzib utterly lacked sympathy, imagination, breadth of vision, elasticity in the choice of means, and that warmth of the heart which atones for a hundred faults of the head. These limitations of his character completely undermined the Mughal empire, so that on his death it suddenly fell in a single downward plunge. Its inner life was gone, and the outward form could not deceive the world long. Time relentlessly sweeps away whatever is inefficient, unnecessary, or false to Nature.

II

AURANGZIB'S DAILY LIFE.

I shall now present to the reader an account of Aurangzib's daily life at Delhi at the beginning of his reign, as supplied by the contemporary Persian history *Alamgirnamah.* He was a strict Muhammadan, a veritable Puritan in the purple. Hence his life was marked by greater seriousness, religious devotion, and aversion to amusement than his father's. He scorned delights and lived laborious days.

AURANGZIB'S ROUTINE OF WORK.

A.M.

5 ...Wakes—Morning Prayer—Devotional reading.

7-30...Justice in Private Chamber.

8-30...*Darshan*—Review—Elephant fights.

9-15...Public Darbar.

11 ...Private Audience.

11-50...Harem—Siesta.

P.M.

2 ...*Zuhar* Prayer.

2-30...Private Chamber—Study—Business—*Asar* Prayer—State affairs.

5-30...Evening salute in the Private Audience Hall—Sunset Prayer.

6-40...*Soiree* in the *Diwan-i-khas.*

7-40...Court dismissed—*Isha* Prayer.

8 ...In the Harem—Religious meditation and reading—Sleep.

MORNING PRAYER.

Rising from his bed some time before dawn, the Emperor performed his morning ablutions, went from the *harem* to the mosque attached to the Hall of Private Audience (*Diwan-i-khas*), and sat there facing the west, waiting for the time of the morning prayer as indicated by the *Hadis* (or Muhammad's Traditions). After performing this religious rite, he read the *Quran* and the Prophet's *Traditions* till the breakfast hour, (say 7-30 A.M.).

COURT OF JUSTICE IN CHAMBER.

Then he went to his private chamber (*khilwatgah*), to which only a few confidential officers and his personal attendants were admitted, and sat on the throne dispensing justice, the first duty of an eastern king. The superintendents of the law-courts presented to him all aggrieved persons, who had come either from the capital or from the provinces to seek justice at its fountain head. Their plaints were reported, and then the Emperor personally examined them to find out the truth.

On the basis of the facts so ascertained, all cases coming under Canon Law were decided according to the *Quranic* injunctions. Common-law cases were tried according to the customary procedure and regulations of the Empire, evidently at the Emperor's own discretion. Needy and miserable plaintiffs were helped with money from the public treasury.

DARSHAN.

Next, he entered the bed-chamber and showed his face at one of its windows, called 'the window of *darshan*,' which overlooked the broad sandy beach of the Jamuna. A vast and varied crowd filled this plain at the foot of the fort, in expectation of the Emperor's appearance. Here the army was often reviewed, and here too were paraded the retainers of the nobles who accompanied the Emperor when he rode out in procession to perform the Friday prayer in the vast Jama Masjid of Delhi. Elephant combats, the training of war-elephants to charge cavalry without fear, and the parade of newly captured untamed elephants, took place in this plain, as was also the case under Shah Jahan.

PUBLIC DARBAR.

After passing some three quarters of an hour at the *darshan* window, the Emperor, at about 9-15 A.M., took his seat in the alcove overlooking the floor of the *Diwan-i-am*, and transacted public affairs of the same kind and in the very same way that Shah Jahan had done. This took nearly two hours.

PRIVATE AUDIENCE.

Some time before noon he withdrew to the *Diwan-i-khas*, and held a private or select audience, conducting confidential business and bestowing gifts till noon. Here were admitted a few nobles, clerks, servants, mace-bearers, the imperial retinue, his special watchmen (*Khas-chauki*), many slaves, the standard-bearers and such other necessary persons only. At this audience his business and pleasure were identical with those of Shah Jahan, as described by me in another essay. The despatches of the provincial viceroys and governors of towns were either read by the Emperor or reported in brief abstracts by the Grand *Wazir*. The Emperor's orders were taken, and their purport dictated by the Wazir to the secretaries (*munshis*), who drafted the replies. Many of these were looked over and revised by the Emperor ; then they were copied out fair and placed before His Majesty for being signed and sealed. Sometimes he wrote in his own hand the beginnings of the letters to the high grandees, either to do them greater honour, or to declare the orders as very urgent, or to remove all doubt as to their genuineness.

HAREM.

It was now about noon, and the Emperor retired to the *harem* to take his well-earned rest. After eating his meal, he slept for an hour to refresh his body and spirits.

PRAYER.

But shortly before the *Zuhar* prayer (about 2 P.M.) he was up again, washed himself, and waited in the palace mosque reciting God's names and telling his beads. This prayer was performed in company, as recommended by the Prophet. The congregation privileged to join the Emperor in his devotions, consisted of *ulema* (theologians), Sayyids, Shaikhs, *faqirs*, and a few of His Majesty's close attendants and *khawases*.

IN THE PRIVATE CHAMBER.

Thereafter the Emperor went to his Private Chamber, situated between the *harem* and the Hall of Private Audience (popularly called the *Ghusal-khanah*), and engaged in works of piety, such as, reading the *Quran*, copying it, collating his transcipt of it, hunting through books on Arabic jurisprudence for precedents in Canon Law, &c. Or, His Majesty read the books and pamphlets of the Islamic pious men and saints of all ages. Then, urgent affairs of State forced themselves on his attention. The petitions of aggrieved parties rich enough to buy the mediation of the favourite courtiers, were now submitted. On some days, work being over, His Majesty visited the *harem* again for an hour, heard the petitions of poor women, widows, and orphans, and satisfied them with gifts of money, lands, or ornaments.

By this the time for the *Asar* prayer (4 P.M.) arrived. It was performed in company in the mosque close to the Hall of Private Audience; afterwards the Emperor returned to his Private Chamber and spent the short remainder of the day in the work of administration.

EVENING SALUTE AND PRAYER.

About half an hour before sunset, His Majesty visited the Hall of Private Audience again and sat on the throne. A little work was done. The courtiers made their bows. The nobles and officers, who had sentry duty that night, presented themselves in full accoutrement, and were marshalled by the Mir Tuzuk and the sergeants according to their ranks on the two sides of the imperial standard of cows' tails and balls. The chief men formed a line in front ; the rear ranks were made up by the subordinates. The Paymasters made them salute, according to the imperial regulations.

The sun was now setting. Piercing the evening air came the loud cry,—

God is most great! God is most great! I testify that there is no deity except God and that Muhammad is His Apostle! Come to prayer! Come to prayer! Come to salvation!

It was the *muazzin* or crier of the mosque, chanting the call to prayer from the church-spire. What the *angelus* is to the French peasantry, the *azan* is to the Muslim world. All work was at once suspended. The Emperor withdrew his mind from earthly affairs, and listened with great reverence to the call. At every pause in the crier's voice, he interjected, like a pious Musalman, these responses :—

Yes, God is most great! I testify that there is no deity except God and that Muhammad is the Apostle of God! I have no power or strength save from God! What He willeth shall be, and what He willeth not shall not take place.

Then he rose from the throne, went to the mosque in full congregation and performed the evening prayer and certain non-obligatory extra rites of devotion (*viz.*, the *sunnah* and the *nafl*). These acts of piety occupied more than half an hour.

SOIREE IN THE DIWAN-I-KHAS.

The *Diwan-i-khas* (or Hall of Private Audience) was lit up with camphorated candles and torches, and golden lanterns, making it rival the vault of the sky spangled with myriads of twinkling stars. The Emperor arrived here from the mosque and occupied the throne. The *Wazir* reported on all affairs of the revenue department, both general and particular, and took his orders. Other kinds of State business were also done. There was no music or dance, as Aurangzib had banished these mundane vanities from his Court in the 11th year of his reign (1668 A.D.). The assembly continued for more than an hour; and shortly before 8 P.M., the call to the *Ishq* prayer was heard; the Court was dismissed.

The Emperor prayed in the adjoining mosque with only his close attendants and *khawases,* and then retired to the *harem,* but not to sleep. Several hours were here spent in prayer and religious meditations, before his tired frame sank into the necessary repose.

This routine was varied on three days of the week. On Friday, the Islamic Sabbath, no Court was held. WEDNESDAY was sacred to justice, and no public darbar was then held, but the Emperor went straight from the *darshan* to the Private Audience Hall, thronged with the law officers, *qazis, muftis,* scholars, theologians (*ulema*), judges, and the prefect of police for the City. None else was admitted unless his presence was needed. The Emperor went on personally judging cases till noon.

On THURSDAY he gave his Court a half-holiday, as we get on Saturday in British India. The usual routine was followed up to noon; but there was no afternoon Court, nor any assembly in the *Diwan-i-khas* at night.

The whole evening was spent in prayer and sacred reading, and the world and its distractions were kept out.

If we may believe the Court historian, Aurangzib slept only three hours out of twenty-four. It was a very strenuous life that this Emperor led. All work and no play gave to his Court a cold, sombre and dreary aspect. He seems to have taken for his motto the following words of Louis XIV, whom he greatly resembled in his aggressive foreign policy, religious intolerance, love of centralised government, unbounded egotism, and tireless industry,—"One must work hard to reign, and it is ingratitude and presumption towards God, and injustice and tyranny towards man, to wish to reign without hard work."

III

THE EDUCATION OF A MUGHAL PRINCE.

I

Some letters of Aurangzib preserved in the Persian work *Adab-i-Alamgiri,* give us interesting information about the way in which Mughal princes were educated and the ideas of etiquette and decorum held in the seventeenth century. In October, 1654, Aurangzib was viceroy of the Deccan and his eldest son, Muhammad Sultan, then in his 15th year, was marching towards Ajmir to be presented to the Emperor Shah Jahan. The father was naturally anxious that his boy should make a good impression at the imperial Court. Minute directions were sent to the prince regulating every act of his life and prescribing a strict routine for every hour of his day.

This is how the prince was commanded to spend his time:—

"Whether you are in residence or on a march, get up from bed 72 minutes before sunrise. After spending 48 minutes in bathing and getting ready, come out of your rooms for the morning prayer. After saying the prayer and reciting set passages, read one section of the *Quran*. Breakfast in the inner apartments comes next. If you are on a march, take horse 48 minutes after sunrise. Should you hunt on the way, take care to reach the halting place appointed for that day punctually. Arriving there, if you are so inclined or have the necessary time, read something in Arabic ; otherwise take rest. About 24 minutes after noon, when the sun begins to decline, come out of your tent for the *zuhar* prayer which should be performed in full congregation. The principal meal and some repose—(evidently the siesta or afternoon nap so popular in the hot countries of Europe and Asia alike) will fill your time till two hours before sunset, when the *asar* prayer should be said. But if the meal alone suffices to refresh you, spend the interval in improving your handwriting, composing letters, or reading Persian prose and poetry. After the *asar* prayer, read Arabic for a short time, and then, some 24 minutes before sunset, hold a 'select audience,' at which you should sit till 48 minutes after nightfall. Then leave the chamber and read a section of the *Quran*, and retiring to the inner apartments, go to bed at 9 P.M.

"If you are on a journey, but it is a day of halt, do the other works mentioned above at the stated time, but (in the place of riding) spend 48 minutes of the morning in archery and musketry practice, and one hour and twenty-four minutes after sunrise hold a public Court for about 48 minutes or more as the business may require. Then, if there is important work to be done, hold a private council for about an hour with your chief officers. Otherwise this period (four *gharis*) should be spent in reading Arabic.

"On a day of march read two sections and on a day of halt three of the *Quran*. If the stage to be covered is a long one, take horse immediately after performing the morning prayer and eat your breakfast on the way, otherwise you should break your fast before starting. No march should be begun at such an unseasonable time as the morning twilight or after 9 A.M. If you want to hunt on the way, send your army to the halting-place by the shortest route in charge of the Paymaster of the Forces, and go to the hunting ground with a few attendants only."

II

The Mughal government of India was essentially of the nature of a military occupation and the stability of the throne depended on the efficiency of the army and the military capacity of the princes. Aurangzib, therefore, advises his son, "Gradually make yourself perfect in the habit of wearing arms. Let your sweat dry before you take off your coat and lie down, lest you should fall ill." Strict discipline was to be maintained in the army, and every one taught to keep his station. The prince is thus instructed on the subject:

"Don't allow any of my officers except Muhammad Tahir (the prince's guardian), or any servant of the Emperor below a commander of 2,000 horse, to ride in front of your army, (where the prince himself marched.)" Certain specified officers were to be posted right and left of him and therefore in the van of the army, but they were to be accompanied by not more than two valets. The prince is commanded to see to this rule strictly, "as the crowding of the vulgar in front of the army destroys its order and discipline."

The commander should not make himself too affable,

lest familiarity should breed contempt. "At all times,—whether marching or holding court,—speak just as many words as are necessary. As for those who are not high enough to be personally spoken to by you, contrive to evade them politely. This sort of behaviour keeps fear and reverence alive (in their hearts.) A sketch plan is sent herewith to show how you should marshal the officers at the public and private *darbars* that you hold."

This prince seems to have been too fond of hunting and rather averse to study. His father complains, "I regret very much that I took him out with myself to hunt at too early an age, for after once tasting the delights of sport, he has got a dislike for reading, writing and similar accomplishments and given up cultivating them." To the study of the Turkish language,—so necessary for the Mughal emperors who entertained large numbers of Turkish soldiers and generals,—Muhammad Sultan had a rooted aversion. The prince is censured for leaving his Turki tutor behind him when setting out for Northern India. He pleads in excuse that the tutor was too old and weak to bear the fatigue of a march! Aurangzib angrily retorts that the prince had shunned his tutor even when in residence at Aurangabad. "He has been engaged for a year's time and drawn a lot of money as his salary, but you never tried to study with him." The prince is now ordered to call the tutor to himself and converse with him in Turki to learn the language. The father remarks indignantly, "You refuse to learn the accomplishments of (gentle) men and kings. What does it matter to *me*? You are now old enough to know good from evil."

III

As might be expected in a noble Muhammadan family, the highest importance is attached to etiquette. The prince is told whom to admit to his 'select audience' and whom to keep out, how to arrange the *mansabdars* at court, and whom to address and whom not. He must be particular about his dress. "Your father has been shocked to hear that you sometimes go to prayer in undress, wearing a waist-coat and trousers only. This is a matter of surprise, as you have lived long enough with him and watched his (decorous) habits and manners."

Special attention is directed to style. "Read the *Akbarnamah* at leisure, so that the style of your conversation and writing may become pure and elegant. Before you have thoroughly mastered the meanings of words and the proper connection in which they may be used, do not employ them in your speeches or letters. Ponder carefully on what you speak or write."

This advice had a most comic effect. The *Akbarnamah* is the despair of readers and the rage of critics, by reason of its extravagant, involved and pedantic style. It is the worst possible literary model for a slow-witted lad of fourteen to imitate. Muhammad Sultan's next letter to his father made him open his eyes wide in astonishment. The poor child had written to his father an exact copy of one of the letters of Akbar to his subjects as drafted by Abul Fazl! It began with Akbar's favourite motto *Allahu akbar! Jall-i-jalaluhu!* in the place of the orthodox *Bismillah,* and the writer had applied to himself the imperial phrases and epithets of Akbar's letter though addressing his own princely father.

In deep vexation Aurangzib wrote back, "I had advised you to study the *Akbarnamah* of Abul Fazl, to make you follow its style and not to make you adopt the author's creed, who had changed the orthodox Sunni practices by his heretical innovations. You designate your letter as 'my imperial letter' (*nishan-i-wala*) and your seal as 'His Majesty's seal' (*muhar-i-khas*). In what terms will you then describe the Emperor's letter and seal?"

However, in spite of this poor success in improving Sultan's style and literary knowledge, he was very graciously received by his imperial grandfather at Hindun (in December next), and loaded with gifts and other marks of favour.

IV

The reader may be interested in the later history of this unpromising scholar. Three years after this journey, when the war for the throne of Delhi broke out, he accompanied his father's army to the North and often acted as his lieutenant, as we should expect of an eldest son. At the great battles of Dharmat, Samugarh, and Khajwa he commanded his father's vanguard. Indeed, his firm stand is said to have snatched victory out of the jaws of defeat at Khajwa. When Shah Jahan helplessly surrendered, Muhammad Sultan was sent to see him in Agra Fort and arrange about his confinement. Thereafter he was sent under the guardianship of Mir Jumla to chase

Shuja back to Bengal. Here, during the operations round Rajmahal he resented the control of his guardian and his father's treatment, and listened eagerly to Shuja's emissaries who offered him marriage with Shuja's daughter Gulrukh Banu Begam, to whom he is said to have been betrothed in childhood. The infatuated young man deserted his army and fled to his uncle's camp one dark night (8 June, 1659) and was married to his beloved. Eight months later, Shuja was hopelessly defeated, and Sultan left him to return to Mir Jumla. Stern was the punishment meted out by Aurangzib to the deserter. He was taken to Delhi under strong guard and confined in the Gwalior State prison for the rest of his life. While there his portrait was occasionally taken and sent to the Emperor for inspection. Thus only did the father know of his erring son's health! Death put an end to his miseries on 3rd December, 1676, when he was about to complete his 37th year. Only four years before his death was he brought closer to his father, by being removed to the fortress of Salimgarh (Delhi), and restored to favour in a small degree—being thrice married in this short period.

IV

BAHADUR SHAH I.

I

The tragedy of Aurangzib's life lay in the conduct of his sons. He was a good husband and a good father; no harem scandal was associated with his name, if we exclude his youthful passion for Hira Bai; he always treated his wives with due consideration and fidelity. As a father, too, he loved his children, anxiously provided for their education according to the best ideas of that age, looked after their morals in early life, and gave them practical training in administration and war by placing them in youth in charge of armies or provinces, under the guardianship of some trusty old noble.

But he was a busy man, and could give little of his society to his sons, or seldom personally caress them as Shah Jahan used to do. Distant campaigns often kept him away from his family for long periods before his accession to the throne, and the pressure of official work left him little time for visiting the harem and nursery even when his wives were with him. Thus, his sons, in one sense, grew up in isolation from him. Their intellectual isolation was still greater. He was a methodical, hard-working man, with an alert and aspiring mind and a heart and temper under perfect control. He never spared himself and could see no reason why others should expect to be spared. He was what the English call "a heavy Pa."

Hence, he was unhappy in his sons. Not that they were vicious or cowardly; their personal courage was indisputable,—two of them died fighting and two others openly challenged his power in battle; their harems did not assume unusual magnitude; and under the orthodox Aurangzib no Mughal prince was allowed to besot himself with drink, as the sons of the latitudinarian Akbar had been.

But Aurangzib's sons were unworthy cubs of such a lion among men. They were either slack, "feckless" youths, or (as in the case of Muhammad Azam) fiery undisciplined souls, impetuous unpractical and therefore futile in their endeavours. A strict businessman and disciplinarian like Aurangzib was the last person to tolerate such conduct in anybody, least of all in the future guardians of his people. He had frequent recourse to grave sermons and sharp reprimands, and watchful spying on the actions of his sons. But these only widened the gulf between father and son. Even after they had grown to mature manhood, wide temperamental differences separated him from them. Finally, their plots and advance preparations in expectation of the contest for the throne after his death made the situation at his Court extremely complex and deepened the gloom of the closing years of his life.

II

Muhammad Muazzam (born 4th October 1643) naturally took the eldest son's place during the captivity of Muhammad Sultan. But in 1670 he came under a cloud. It was reported to the Emperor that this prince, at the instigation of evil counsellors, was aiming at independence in the Deccan. His mother Nawab Bai was sent from Court to bring him back to the path of obedience, and a noble was also deputed to deliver to him a stern reprimand on behalf of the Emperor. The charge was ultimately admitted by Aurangzib to be groundless. The public, however, believed that Muazzam's plan of rebellion against his father was a mere pretence, contrived in collusion with the Emperor in order to induce Shivaji to come to his camp so that he might be easily arrested.

In fact, Muazzam was not born with the spirit to rebel. As Manucci, who saw him most intimately, remarks, "Aurangzib had more confidence in Shah Alam than in any of the other [princes], for he knew him down to the ground, and had tested his not having enough boldness to try rebellion. When this prince was very young, ...a young rat passed in front of him. He was so frightened that he came out shouting......His father, on being told what had happened, exclaimed that it was an astonishing thing that in the race of Taimur should be born a prince who was such a poltroon." [*Storia*, ii.395. Cf. 465.] And, again, "Adopting another style of life, he gave himself up to pleasure, but only in secret, his occupation being drinking and other pastimes. His father heard nothing of all that, for the son knew his father's disposition, and his love of seeing his children imitate his feigned strictness. Thus, to gain his approval, the prince displayed as many signs of devoutness as ever he could. As he perceived that humility was also much to the taste of the old fellow, he showed the greatest contempt for the riches of this world......His children were just as great hypocrites as he was, and all to propitiate their grandfather." [ii. 392.]

Aurangzib's favourite officer, Hamid-ud-din Khan, narrates many anecdotes illustrating the Emperor's low opinion of the courage and sagacity of Muazzam and severe reprimand for breach of official regulations. [*Ahkam-i-Alamgiri* § 10-16, translated by me in *Anecdotes of Aurangzib.*]

At the end of 1676 Muazzam was restored to full confidence and high power and placed at the head of an independent army with the title of *Shah Alam.*

III

Shah Alam lacked his father's remorseless ambition and tireless energy. He was timid and slow, but at the same time affable, kind-hearted, generous in his instincts, and regardful of the sanctity of his word. These good qualities, however, brought about the greatest calamity of his life by making him run counter to his father's deep-laid statecraft.

When, in January 1687, Aurangzib unexpectedly invaded the Qutb Shahi kingdom and laid siege to its fort of Golkonda, Shah Alam protested against the act as a breach of faith. Early in October 1685, the prince at the head of a Mughal army had captured the city of Haidarabad, and forced its king to make peace on terms dictated by him, which the Emperor had subsequently ratified. And now that Aurangzib, in his greed of territory, broke this solemn treaty, "the prince complained to his father. He said the world would wonder that so great a king should pay no heed to the promises made by his son and heir. He, therefore, entreated him to abandon this intention of his." [*Storia*, ii. 302.]

Aurangzib's constant fear was lest his son should send aid to Qutb Shah and enable him to escape from the beleaguered fort. Shah Alam, on his part, did not wish to see a brother sovereign utterly ruined. Abul Hasan (the king of Golkonda) knew it and worked on the prince's feelings. His agents secretly visited Shah Alam with costly presents, begging him to use his influence with the Emperor to save Abul Hasan's throne and dynasty. The prince gave encouraging replies. For some time envoys and letters continued to pass between the two.

In thus negotiating behind the Emperor's back and with an enemy beyond hope of the Emperor's pardon, Shah Alam was playing a dangerous game. His rival Azam's partisans in the camp revealed to the Emperor these secret communications with the enemy. A false tale was spread that Shah Alam's favourite wife Nur-un-nisa had visited the fort in disguise to assure Abul Hasan that Shah Alam would come over to him if the Emperor rejected the peace proposed by him. At last the prince's letters to the enemy were intercepted and shown to the Emperor (20th February 1687.)

Aurangzib acted promptly. Next morning the prince and his four sons were invited to the Emperor's tent for consultation and on their arrival were sent to the side-room which served as a chapel, to receive some secret instructions from the wazir. Here they were politely asked to consider themselves as prisoners and deliver their swords. Shah Alam readily submitted ; but his eldest son Muizzuddin angrily laid his hand on the hilt of his sword and looked at his father for a signal to draw it and make a dash for liberty. But Shah Alam's only reply was a frown and a stern order to obey. The prince's entire family was imprisoned, his property attached, his troops distributed among the other commands, his favourite wife Nur-un-nisa was insulted and rebuked by eunuchs at the Emperor's bidding and deprived of her liberty, her chief officer was tortured to make him reveal the suspected disloyal acts of his master and the complicity of his mistress in them.

Aurangzib's mortification at this stern necessity was extreme. His eldest son had been put in prison and had died a captive. His eldest daughter, the gifted poetess Zeb-un-nisa, had been doomed to lifelong confinement in Delhi fort. His fourth son Akbar was a fugitive in a far off foreign land. And now his eldest surviving son had to be punished with strict imprisonment. After the arrest of the prince, the Emperor hurriedly broke up his Court, ran to his wife Aurangabadi Mahal, and kept slapping his knees and moaning "Alas ! alas ! I have razed to the ground what I had been rearing up for the last forty years." [*M.A.* 294.]

The more the prince protested his innocence, the more did the Emperor's anger flame up ; he increased the rigours of Shah Alam's captivity and ordered that he should not have his hair cut or his nails pared, nor be supplied with any delicate food, cooling drink or his customary dress.

IV

At first the Emperor boiled over with rage against his son, and no courtier durst put in a word for the unhappy prince. Only Nazir Khidmat Khan, the old *naib* of Shah Jahan, on the strength of a life spent in the royal service and the memories of Aurangzib's boyhood, entreated the Emperor to the utmost to set Shah Alam free, but without avail. Six months passed in this state. Then the force of imperial anger began to abate and the father's natural love to return gradually. At times he sent to the captive written Arabic prayers by the hand of a servant, with instructions to recite them in order that God in His grace might incline Aurangzib's heart to release him. Khidmat Khan seized the opportunity to whisper, "It is in your Majesty's power to set him free." But Aurangzib replied, "Yes, but the King of Kings has made me a ruler on earth in order that victims of oppression everywhere may complain to me and secure justice. This man [meaning Shah Alam] has been chastised by me, but the time for his release has not come yet. He has no refuge save the Court of God." [*M.A.* 341-342.]

When 14 months had passed away, Aurangzib, in April 1688, offered to release Shah Alam; but that prince generously declined his own liberty unless the Emperor also liberated Abul Hasan, because he (the prince) had been instrumental in the ruin of that king, having formerly engaged his word that neither the Mughal Emperor nor he would ever come with forces to trouble him, and that he (Shah Alam) would rather choose to lose his life than break his faith and word with the king of Golkonda, which had been confirmed by the oath taken on the Quran. [Letter from M. Chardin at Golkonda, quoted in *Fort St. George Diary,* 6 May 1688.] In June 1689, the prince's harem was sent to Delhi, while he was kept, as before, a captive * in the Emperor's moving camp in the Deccan. [*M.A.* 330.]

V

Time softened the Emperor's rigour. He began to test his son's fidelity with a view to setting him free. One day he sent him a pen-casket with a pen-knife within it, telling the bearer to observe and report faithfully his instinctive gesture, looks and words when he would look at it. Shah Alam, on opening the casket and glancing at the knife, betrayed no look or cry of delight, but gravely drew his hand back and remarked that it had been sent to him by some mistake, as it was against the rules to send any sort of steel weapon, however small, to political prisoners. It was only after the servant had assured him

* Manucci writes (ii. 305): "But afterwards food was so sparingly supplied that it was grievous to see princes of such high lineage treated in such a manner. When they marched with the camp, they appeared like shadows, devoid of all ornament and without spirit, shut up in litters put on elephants, and without retinue, just like ordinary prisoners". Their rooms (tents) were close to the Emperor's audience hall.

of the Emperor's special command, that he approached the casket again, made his bow of thanks-giving and took it up. On hearing this report, Aurangzib remarked, "I know the honourable spirit of my sons. The least disfavour shown to me by my father had embittered all my life."

After some days the Emperor copied and sent to the prince a tradition of the Prophet which says, "A man who has committed the Word of God to his memory should not be kept in perpetual durance even when he deserves imprisonment." The prince replied, "A memoriser of the *Quran* has not been doomed to eternal captivity, but a father can confine his son for life, in spite of the latter having memorised the *Quran*." This reply pleased the Emperor. [K. K. iii. 397-398.] Very cautiously he began to make a gradual and systematic relaxation of Shah Alam's captivity. The prohibition of shaving and paring the nails had been withdrawn long ago. In February 1690, the prince and his sons were presented with five maunds of rose-water and two maunds of the essence of *bid-mishk*. [*M.A.* 335.]

Then the Emperor ordered (May 1690) that when he marched away from his halting-place (Badri on the Krishna), his Court-tent should be kept standing with all its royal furniture and the prince brought there from his prison-tent, shown all the places and allowed to sit down there for some time, "for the exhilaration of his limbs and senses." The prince remarked to the Court steward (*mahafiz*), "I ought to be granted an interview. How can my thirst for the Emperor's presence be slaked by the mere view of his residence?" This speech pleased Aurangzib still more.

Early next year, when Shah Alam's mother Nawab Bai died at Delhi, Aurangzib paid his son a visit and condoled with him. At last, on 20th July 1691, the prince was brought to his father's Court and granted an interview. He was ordered to perform the evening prayer with the Emperor, and allowed to visit the royal baths situated within the fort of Bijapur and the imperial garden and tank in the suburb Shahabad. "In short, by gradual progression, the veil was removed. A eunuch was deputed to bring Shah Alam's wives from Delhi to his side. His sons were granted high *mansabs*, and on 26th April 1692 four of his grandsons were publicly received in audience and granted increase of their daily stipends, robes, jewels and other marks of favour." [*M.A.* 342-344.]

On 8th May, Muizzuddin, the eldest son of Shah Alam, was given an army and sent off against the enemy, and two of his younger brothers were promoted. (*Ibid.* 346.) Next month another son, Muhammad Azim, was married from the Court with great splendour (*Ibid.* 347.) Thereafter the prince and his sons made frequent visits to the imperial *darbar* and mosque. In October, Shah Alam was taken out of his prison-enclosure and sent to occupy a separate camp furnished in a style worthy of a prince, which was set up for him by order at some distance from the Emperor's own quarters. His full establishment of chamberlain, harem-superintendent, &c. was restored. [*Ibid.* 351.]

VI

Two events in 1693 drove Aurangzib to make a final decision about Shah Alam's future. Muhammad Azam fell seriously ill and was brought to death's door by his childish refusal to obey his doctors and submit to a strict regimen. Kam Bakhsh for his incredible folly at the siege of Jinji had to be arrested and kept in detention. His only other son, Akbar, was a rebel and a refugee in Persia. Therefore, Shah Alam alone remained as the future successor to the imperial throne. [*M.A.* 354-359; *Dil.* 117 *a*. Another motive is mentioned by Manucci, ii. 318.]

But the Emperor had to move cautiously. During the years of Shah Alam's captivity, his younger brother Muhammad Azam, who had been elevated (1681) to the title of *Shah-i-alijah*, naturally regarded himself as the heir apparent. He could not bear the thought of Shah Alam's release and restoration to power. An attack from him upon his rival, or even his rebellion in despair of getting the succession, was to be feared, and Aurangzib watched and meditated how to avert such a civil war. In this way the year 1694 passed away and also the first four months of 1695.

Shah Alam became fully free in May 1695. The Emperor sent to him one of his own robes by the hands of two eunuchs and had him brought to the public Court. The prince offered a two-fold thanksgiving to God, and was permitted to kiss his Majesty's toes. The Emperor kissed his forehead, and presented him with a diamond-crest worth one lakh of Rupees, a sword, two horses, and an elephant with costly accoutrements. The prince was now on the high road to imperial favour and restoration to his birth-right. [*M.A.* 371.]

This could not be effected without a conflict with his rival, which, however, was cut short by Aurangzib's imperious force of character. We narrate the incident in the words of the official historian, Mustad Khan:

On the day of *Id-ul-fitr* (5th May 1695) the Emperor was to go with all his sons to pray in the Grand Mosque at Bijapur, where he was then staying. As the eldest son of the Emperor always sits on the right hand of His Majesty, and during Shah Alam's captivity his younger brother Azam had been given this seat of honour, the eldest prince now asked, "What are your Majesty's orders about my rightful position on the day of *Id?*" Aurangzib replied, "Go to the *Idgah* before my cortege and you will sit on my right hand." He did so. When the imperial party reached the steps, Shah Alam advanced, met the Emperor, and kissed his toes. His Majesty after shaking hands with him, took his left hand in his own right hand, and entered the mosque. Thus the eldest prince was placed on the right of the Emperor. Azam, who was walking behind, touched the sleeve of his elder brother, signing to him to move away and make room for him on the Emperor's right. It caught his Majesty's eyes. With his right hand he grasped the skirt of Azam and dragged him away to his left side . . . . When the prayers were said and the *khatib* ascended the pulpit (to proclaim the Emperor's titles), His Majesty rose from his seat, holding the hand of Azam, and went out by the second gate, making a signal to Shah Alam to issue with his sons by the third gate. [*M.A.* 372.]*

Four days later (9th May 1695), Shah Alam was given his public farewell and sent off to Agra, accompanied by his two younger sons, while the two elder were left with the Emperor. [*M.A.* 373.] On 13th July 1696, he left Agra for Multan, which province was now placed in his charge. On the death of Amir Khan (28th April 1698), the viceroyalty of Kabul was given to the prince, and Lahor was added to his government on 31st January 1700. [*M.A.* 382, 394, 423.]

In Afghanistan, Shah Alam's chief duty was to watch the movements of his rebel brother Akbar, who was then residing at Farah on the eastern frontier of Persia, with a Persian force, intending to invade India at the first opportunity. His presence there spread alarming rumours through the Indian bazars. But Shah Alam showed no enterprise in counteracting Akbar's designs by force or diplomacy, and for this neglect and certain other faults he was repeatedly censured by his father. [India Office Pers. MS. 3301, letters No. 67, 70, also 25 and 134. *Storia* ii. 318.]

VII

As governor of Kabul, Shah Alam was hardly any

---

* Also *Storia,* ii. 318. The advice which Aurangzib gave to Shah Alam at the time of his release is detailed in Hamid-ud-din's *Ahkam* § 10 of my edition. We have no reason to doubt the authenticity of this passage, though the *Masir-i-Alamgiri* is silent on the point.

more his own master than when in captivity. He was constantly censured by his father for infringing this royal prerogative or that, or for not observing some official regulation or rule of etiquette.* All his acts were jealously watched by Aurangzib's spies, both male and female. Even in the harem he could not enjoy freedom and ease. The female superintendent (*mahaldar*) of his seraglio kept a sharp eye on him, and secured an order that the prince was never to be given pen and ink in the harem, while in the outer apartments, whenever he had an occasion to sign his name, his office superintendent (*nazir*) should produce the writing-case and take it back from the prince as soon as his signature was finished. "Tell my foolish son," the angry Emperor added, "that his many years' captivity has not made him wiser, seeing that he is taking such audacious steps. Even now the matter has not gone out of my hands. Distance cannot prevent me from punishing him." [*Anecdotes*, § 16.]

Aurangzib's constant fear was lest Shah Alam should make himself practically independent, raise an army, march on Delhi, and usurp the throne, as Aurangzib himself had done in Shah Jahan's old age. Hence, when he heard that Shah Alam was raising troops in Afghanistan, he wrote a most ironical letter of warning to him to this effect: "I hear that you are raising an army. Evidently you mean to employ it in wresting Qandahar from the Persians. May God assist you! But I cannot understand the reason of your present request to be permitted to come

* *Anecdotes of Aurangzib*, § 12-15.

to Lahor. I degrade [your deputy] Nasir Khan by five hundred and dismiss your Hindu counsellor. (*Verse*) *All troubles spring from me!*" And in another letter, "His late Majesty Shah Jahan was eager to conquer Balkh, Badakhshan &c., the ancient heritage [of our fore-father Timur], and repeatedly sent expeditions to that region. But . . . the conquests were lost . . . On the principle that where the father failed the son will accomplish it, I wish to send you, the grandson of Shah Jahan, with an army there. What else can I do? And yet, in spite of my urging, you have not yet taken Qandahar. How then can you achieve this (Balkh) business? It is clear that my work cannot be done by you." Some time later, learning that Shah Alam used to hold public court with a saffron-coloured turban on his head and a short-sleeved wrestler's jacket on his back, Aurangzib wrote to him tauntingly, "Honoured Sir, your age is six and forty, and [yet] you flaunt this gaudy turban and tunic!" [*Ruqat-i-Alamgiri,* Nos. 4, 1 and 6.[

It should be remembered that at this time (1703), Shah Alam was more than sixty years of age and already a grand-father. It is difficult to imagine a treatment more likely than his father's as described above, to utterly unman him and render him unfit for ruling a kingdom and commanding armies. The intellectual and moral bankruptcy of the later Mughals was the logical consequence of the education given them by Aurangzib.

V

PRINCE MUHAMMAD AZAM SHAH,
1653—1707.

Muhammad Azam was the only one among Aurangzib's five sons who escaped the prison or exile. Indeed, for many years he was his father's special favourite, if we except the Emperor's unreasoning dotage on Kam Bakhsh, the spoilt child of his old age.

Azam (born in 1653) was the son of Dilras Banu, a lady of the Persian royal family, and, therefore, after the rebellion and flight of his younger full brother Akbar, he remained as the only son of Aurangzib who could boast of the purest blood, because his half brothers, Muazzam and Kam Bakhsh* were the sons of Hindu mothers. Azam had a profound contempt for Muazzam and used to call him a grocer (*bania*) and a coward. Kam Bakhsh was beneath his notice. For, Azam had a haughty and imperious spirit and an impetuous rage which made him despise all obstacles and rush blindly into every danger, throwing sober advice and prudent consideration to the winds. When roused to anger he used to roll up his sleeves like a wrestler. [*Iradat Kh.*]

In his boyhood he had been petted by his aunt Raushanara, and after his marriage with Dara's daughter

* Kam Bakhsh's mother, Udaipuri Begam, was a Circassian, according to one account. *Storia*, ii. 394.

he became the favourite of his other aunt, Jahanara, who had brought up his wife as her foster-child. Aurangzib, too, liked him above his other sons, for his manliness, courage, intelligence (when not clouded by passion), and power of command. In January 1669, Azam, then 15½ years of age, was married to Jahanzeb Banu, the daughter of Dara Shukoh, amidst the most splendid rejoicings. Aurangzib throughout life showed marks of exceptional love to these two and to their eldest son Bidar Bakht,—a gallant, discreet, and ever successful general,—on all three of whom he used to lavish gifts. He probably hoped thus to atone for his cruelty to his murdered elder brother, Dara.

From the age of twenty-two, Azam was trained in war and administration by being sent away to govern provinces, such as Multan (1676), Bihar (1677) and Bengal (1678). From the last of these he was recalled next year to aid his father in the Rajput war. The prince responded to the call with his resistless ardour. Leaving Dacca on 12th October 1679, he travelled day and night. "After midnight the prince entered a *palki* and slept in it [while it was being carried]. His chief officers attended him by turns. From dawn to midday he rode on horseback, so that not more than two or three of his retinue could keep up with him when he arrived at the camping-ground ; the rest dropped in afterwards. At Patna he left his baggage, harem and stores with orders to follow him slowly. His chief wife, Jahanzeb, accompanied him from Patna to Benares, which was traversed in seven days. But here she too was left behind to be escorted to Delhi, while Azam and Bidar Bakht, slenderly attended, made a rapid march in light kit and reached Mandal (in Mewar) from Benares in twelve days, having done 140 miles in the last day (16th December 1679). Only twelve troopers, four footmen, one *chobdar*, one surveyor, and two time-keepers had been able to keep with him." [*M.A.* 182; *Ft. St. George Diary,* 22nd October 1679.]

This rapid journey across the breadth of Northern India was not without adventures, one of which we describe in the words of the Court historian: "One day while the prince and Bidar Bakht were riding on bamboo litters, with no other escort than God, the Shahzada felt very thirsty. When they reached a well near a village, a water-carrier offered him a pot of water, for which the prince gave him two gold coins. The wretch, on seeing him, thought that he was a mace-bearer of the Court carrying a quantity of gold coins . . . . Then he shouted and barred the road and rushed up threatening violence to the prince, who was about to ride past him in disregard. The prince shot him through the heart with an arrow and passed on with his porters. When one of his officers reached the place sometime after, he recognised the arrow as his master's, cut off the villain's head and took the arrow away with himself. . . . . After this incident the prince ordered some bits of uncoined gold and small gold coins as well as copper pice and *kowris* to be always kept in his pocket. . . . Nowhere was there time to cook a regular meal for him during his short halts, except one day at a qazi's house. He usually lived on dry bread and fruits and fried barley. One day the Shahzada expressed a desire for *khichri.* The attendants went to a serai, cooked it, and served it on an old used dish of wood. Both father and son were hungry, but the prince after looking at the dirty plate refused to taste it and passed it on to his son, who also rejected it. The prince consoled him by saying that, God willing, they would get food from the Emperor's own table in a few days." [*M.A.* 183-185.]

Thereafter, Muhammad Azam commanded an independent army in Rajputana and the Deccan, being his father's righthand man in these wars, as Muazzam was too tame in spirit and a failure in all his military undertakings.

In January 1680, when the Emperor marched towards Udaipur, Azam went in advance of him from the Debari pass and occupied the Sisodia capital. In March he left the city with the Emperor and returned to Ajmir, from which city he was sent to take charge of the army in the Chitor district, relieving Akbar who was transferred to Marwar (end of June). Here he was joined by Dilir Khan from the Deccan. A year later, while Azam was encamped near the Raj-samudra lake, the new Maharana, Jai Singh, interviewed him and made peace with the Emperor through his mediation. [*M.A.* 193, 208-209.]

Soon afterwards (26th July 1681) he was married to Shahar Banu (Padishah Bibi), the sister of the Bijapur king, Sikandar Adil Shah.

On 31st July 1681 Azam was sent from Rajputana to the Deccan in advance of his father, after being invested with the high title of *Shah-i-ali-jah* (King of Exalted Dignity) and given many rich presents. [*M.A.* 211.] Next year, after the Emperor himself had reached

Aurangabad, Prince Azam was sent southwards first to Ahmadnagar and then (14th June 1682) to invade Bijapur territory. The struggle was long and desultory, and he could achieve nothing as his forces were insufficient for dealing a crushing blow at the Adil Shahi monarchy. Leaving Ahmadnagar late in May, the prince invaded Bijapur and took the city of Dharur. Then he entered Shambhuji's territory, and leaving his wife Jahanzeb Banu with a strong Rajput guard under Anurudh Singh Hada, he advanced further into the enemy country. The Marathas sent off one division to keep Azam engaged, while another came upon the Begam's camp by rapid marches and threatened it in overwhelming force. The heroic daughter of Dara Shukoh mounted her elephant and advanced two miles from her camp to oppose the enemy on the way. Although Anurudh and other officers, as well as her eunuchs, tried to dissuade her from leaving the shelter of the camp, she did not listen, but urged them to advance, saying, "The situation is critical. Leave off talking and turn to the work."

Calling Anurudh Singh to her elephant, she addressed him *in her own voice* from within her covered litter, "To the Rajputs the honour of the Chaghtai dynasty is equal to their own honour. I call you my son." Giving the Rajput officers some spears with her own hand, she told them, "If God gives us victory with this small force, well. Otherwise you may rest assured about me ; I shall do my work (*i.e.*, suicide to avoid capture.)" Then a great battle was fought. Nine hundred Rajputs fell on Anurudh's side, and many of the Marathas also. During the fight Jahanzeb continually sent her eunuchs to present packets of betel leaf to every one of the Rajput captains individually in order to cheer them. At last Anurudh Singh gained the victory, though he was wounded. After the battle she called him to her side, comforted him, gave him her own necklace of pearls worth Rs. 40,000 (a gift from Aurangzib), and placed it round his neck with her own hands. Azam too defeated his own opponents and rejoined her after some days. At the end of June 1683 he was summoned by the Emperor, and arrived at Aurangabad from the bank of the Nira very promptly by making another of his favourite forced marches in light kit and slender escort, regardless of rain, mud and the privations of such a journey. A grand welcome was accorded to him on his arrival. The whole Court was assembled to do him honour; his overjoyed father gave him room in his own tent and food from his own table, and heaped upon him jewels and other gifts. [*M.A.* 230.]

Two months afterwards (20th August 1683) Azam was sent away to lead an army against the Bijapur frontier, and after another visit to the Emperor at the end of October, he was transferred to the command of the Nasik district. It was probably during this interval that he passed under a temporary cloud of suspicion.

From Ishwardas's memoirs, a rather late and partly traditional authority for such early events, we learn that in 1670 Mir Khan, then governor of Allahabad, became a partisan of Prince Muhammad Azam and incited him to futile plans [of rebellion], and that the Emperor punished the Khan with dismissal and attachment of his property

(61*b*). The official record is silent about the incident; it only mentions Mir Khan's removal from his governorship (August 1671) without stating the reason for it. [*M.A.* 110.] The removal could hardly have been by way of punishment, as Mir Khan was given the more important viceroyalty of Malwa next year. [October 1672, *M.A.* 120.] This Mir Khan is better known as Amir Khan, the most successful Mughal governor of Afghanistan.

Equally incredible is the story told by the gossipy Manucci (*Storia do Mogor*, ii. 394) that Azam was arrested and locked up in the palace and there he remained a whole year getting no wine to drink, and that he was released after his marriage with Dara's daughter, (which, as we know, took place in January 1669.)

Ishwardas (*f.* 87) tells another tale of a projected rebellion in 1683 which probably had some element of truth in it, as it is mentioned by some other contemporary writers too. He says that the prince paid a midnight visit to the tent of Dilir Khan, his chief general, and spent four hours in private talk with him. Spies reported the fact to the Emperor whose suspicion was roused, so that he removed the prince from the command of the expedition and summoned all his officers to Court. Azam in anger resigned all his posts, disbanded his troops, and shut himself up in his house, refusing to see anybody. Then the Emperor visited him and pacified his mind with soothing speeches. Dilir Khan took poison to avoid the Emperor's wrath. Bhimsen (i. 180) more briefly says: "The Emperor felt a suspicion against Prince Azam (then at Ahmadnagar) and summoned him and Dilir Khan, but they delayed coming. Dilir fell under the royal punishment."

Much of the above account is mere bazar gossip. We only know for certain that in August 1683, Muhammad Hadi (a son of the famous Amir Khan) was brought under arrest from Azam's camp to the Emperor's and, after some days spent in the custody of two police officers (probably in investigation and torture), was thrown into prison. [*M.A.* 237.]* Dilir Khan died about 20th September, by poison as the vulgar believed ; and Azam came to his father's Court, for the second time in two months, towards the end of October. [*M.A.* 230, 239.] If he was under any suspicion at the time, it must have been promptly removed.

The Emperor reached Ahmadnagar in November 1683. Azam was transferred from Nasik in the north to Bahadurgarh on the Bhima river in the south (February 1684). From this base he invaded Bijapur territory, and was checked for a long time by the brave Deccani general Sharza Khan, who is said to have inflicted a severe defeat on the prince's troops in August. But during the earlier months of the next year (1685), Azam penetrated into the south-western province of Bijapur, i.e., Western Karnatak,

---

* On 17 Sep. 1681, this Md. Hadi (now entitled Mir Khan), the diwan of Prince Azam, was reduced in rank as complaints against him (probably of extortion) had reached the Emperor's ears.

and there captured Gokak, Hubli, Dharwar, Gadak, Kopal, and even Bankapur and Karwar.

When the siege of Bijapur began in April 1685 the prince took post on the Tungabhadra river to prevent any relief coming to the enemy from the south. Here he defeated a Bijapuri attack in April. He was next placed in supreme command of the siege, and arrived before Bijapur fort, dismounting at the Begam Hauz south of it, on 14th June 1685. A fortnight later he came nearer the city and began to advance his trenches, raise gun platforms, and lay mines.

But the Bijapuris offered an able and obstinate defence. In addition, a severe famine broke out in the Mughal camp, as the roads were closed to grain convoys by the Maratha allies of Bijapur and the flooded streams. "Grain sold at Rs. 15 a seer, and that too in small quantities. . . . . No food came from any side. The soldiers were greatly weakened and many of them died."

Aurangzib (then at Sholapur) saw no other means of saving his son than to order him to retire from Bijapur. The prince held a council of war, at which all his officers voted for a retreat. But Azam had inherited from his father the bravery and firmness of the victor of Khajwa. Turning to his officers he exclaimed, "You have spoken for yourselves. Now listen to me. Muhammad Azam and his two sons and Begam will not retreat from this post of danger so long as he has life left to him. After my death His Majesty may come and order my corpse to be removed for burial. You, my followers, may stay or go away as you like." Then the council of war cried out with one voice "Our opinion is the same as your Highness's." [*M.A.* 263-264.]

On hearing of this Spartan resolution of his son, Aurangzib sent 5,000 pack-oxen laden with grain under escort of Firuz Jang, who successfully fought his way to the famished camp before Bijapur (October 1685), and thus saved the prince. The Mughal position now improved. [*M.A.* 265-266 ; K.K. ii. 317.]

Azam was the leading commander at the siege of Bijapur, though its final capitulation was negotiated by Firuz Jang. He also joined the siege of Golconda (1687) in its later stages and was the first Mughal general to enter that fort on its fall. He was next employed in conquering the possessions of the late Bijapur dynasty in the Bombay Karnatak. Here he captured Belgaon, the leading fort of the province (about April 1688), which was named Azamnagar in honour of him. [*M.A.* 315.]

In December he was again sent against Shambhuji into the North Puna district (Chakan), but achieved nothing decisive there. Then, when Kam Bakhsh was sent to the Madras Karnatak, Azam was posted for a year (December 1691 to December 1692) in the Berad country to overawe the chief of Wagingera. On the disastrous retreat of the Mughals from before Jinji (January 1693) Azam was pushed on to Kadapa, to guard the line of communication of this army in Madras.

Here, in 1693, he had a severe illness. Three years earlier his physician, Masum Khan, had warned him that he would develop dropsy unless he took medicine regularly, followed a strict regimen, and abstained from the things which caused that disease. But the prince had paid no heed to his advice, and in April 1693 he was attacked by dropsy and his limbs went on swelling to an alarming extent. His doctors plied all their art, the prince regulated his diet strictly ; but it was too late, and nothing seemed to be able to arrest the disease. As he tells the story, "One night all gave up the hope of my recovery and expected my skin to burst. My wife, eldest son and daughters and some attendants of the harem, who were surrounding my couch, were half dozing like me, when the luminous vision of a man with wheat-coloured beard and moustaches appeared at the foot of my bed and facing me said, 'Up to this time the disease has not abated at all. Repent sincerely, vowing never to relapse into sin, and God will give you quick recovery' . . . . I repented in the terms dictated by him and immediately felt ease of body, and he vanished. I then awoke the Begam and the other people and gave them the glad news of my recovery. . . . . By the next morning I was greatly relieved and nearly all the swelling (literally, seven parts of it) had disappeared. . . . . On the second day I received a letter from a darvish of Adoni that he had had a vision of the Khalif Ali,* who had told him 'To-night

* Azam was afterwards suspected of being a Shia. We learn from Khafi Khan (ii. 439) that Mustafa Khan Kashi, who had the greatest influence over this prince, was ordered by Aurangzib to be expelled from Azam's camp and afterwards sent to Mecca. On his return he lived at Aurangabad like a faqir and wrote an index to the Quran, but failed to regain the Emperor's good graces. Was it on a suspicion of heresy? Some of the highest Shia nobles of Aurangzib's reign were in this prince's entourage.

I have given the prince (holy) dust and begged of God for his recovery. He will speedily recover. Have no doubt about it.' . . . . [*M.A.* 362—364.]

Meantime, the Emperor on hearing of his son's illness, had sent a *palki* with glass windows to bring him with comfort and care, and his Court physician and a high grandee to attend on him during the journey. The prince accompanied by two of his sons was brought to his father's camp at Galgala on 22nd October. "As he had not fully recovered yet, the Emperor wished to be both physician and nurse to him. Azam Shah was lodged in a tent (specially) set up for him close to the Hall of Private Audience. . . . . The Emperor daily visited the prince and partook of the sick-diet with him and Zinat-unnisa Begam. And that was the only food which these two took till the prince recovered. . . . . On 23rd December, Muhammad Azam (on recovery) came to the Private Audience Chamber, sat down before the Emperor, and thus filled him with gladness." [*M.A.* 361—362.] After he had fully regained his health, there was much feasting and alms-giving. His chief officers spent much out of their own pockets in celebrating their beloved master's escape from death. His Begam sent Rs. 60,000 as a present to Najaf and Karbala. One lakh and twenty thousand Rupees were distributed to the poor of Mecca, Medina and other holy places. The imperial physician was given a purse of 2,000 gold pieces and a promotion of one thousand in rank, besides many presents.

This illness endeared him still more to his father. For over two years afterwards Azam was kept at Court.

In 1687 Muazzam (or Shah Alam), the eldest surviving son of Aurangzib, had been thrown into prison for secret negotiations with the enemy at the siege of Golkonda. The disgrace of this prince had been Muhammad Azam's opportunity, and he had been confidently looking forward to being publicly declared heir to the throne. But in 1694, Aurangzib decided to release Shah Alam from prison and appoint him again to a provincial viceroyalty and the command of an army. This was a set back to Azam's ambitious hopes, and he was at no pains to conceal his anger and disappointment at the elevation of his rival. It was the popular belief in the camp, and was probably also the apprehension of the Emperor, that Azam in his despair of getting the succession would either make a sudden attack upon his elder brother or even rise in rebellion against his father.

In this connection Khafi Khan tells the following characteristic story (ii. 407—410):—"Wild rumours were spread by idle talkers through the imperial camp that Prince Azam Shah wanted to attack his father and proclaim his own independence, while babblers in the prince's camp expressed the belief that the Emperor would arrest Azam by surprise. But Aurangzib wrote to Azam inviting him to meet him on a hunting trip with only an escort of 400 or 500 troopers and his two sons. He ordered a small hunting tent to be pitched outside on a low ground where his army would be out of sight; at the same time the provosts of the army were directed not to let the common people and sight-seers assemble there. On reaching this tent, the Emperor again sent to Azam to say that the place of encampment was too small, and therefore he should not bring more than 300 troopers with him. As soon as the prince had started with this escort, a fresh order reached him to bring only 200 men ; then, when he had advanced a few steps another message brought by a slave reduced the prince's escort to a hundred. Orders of this nature came in rapid succession, till at last when the prince arrived near the tent, the slave Jamal brought the Emperor's message, "The game that has been driven up for being shot might take fright, as the crowd is too large and the field too narrow. Don't bring with yourself more than three equeries, but send the rest away."

"When Azam Shah, with his sons, Wala Jah and Ala Tabar, arrived near the Emperor, and the last mentioned had a [loaded] musket with lighted match in his hand, the marshals so managed the thing that only two equeries could enter the place, so that there was no equery to hold the horse of Ala Tabar. In these circumstances the colour left the face of Azam Shah, and he felt himself about to perish in the snare of calamity, and then Mukhtar Khan conveyed to him the order that the three should come leaving their arms outside. This alarmed the prince still more. Mukhtar Khan tried to reassure him and led him in. At the interview, Azam, according to etiquette, walked round the Emperor twice, and presented *nazar* and *nisar* (propitiatory alms) to him. Aurangzib in extreme love clapsed him tightly in his embrace, handed his own musket to the prince, and asked him to fire it at the game. Then he brought him to the prayer-room [of the tent] ordered him to sit down, and professing to feel hot and uncomfortable asked how the prince was feeling.

"As it was rumoured that the prince had put on armour of mail under his vest, the Emperor asked for a cup of *argaja* (scent), and on the pretext of giving him ease and cooling his body, ordered him to take off his coat, and rubbed the essence on his body! Next, he unsheathed his sword, which he had laid down before his throne, praised it saying that it had come to him from Babar's time, and handed it to prince Azam. The prince's hand began to shake! After due courtesy, he examined the sword and wished to return it to his father; but the Emperor graciously presented it to him, and addressed him a few words full of preaching and advice, hinting that he had set the prince free after getting him into his claws, and that as the prince's family had heard of the interview and were sunk into the greatest anxiety and despair for his safety, he ought to depart soon. Then he sent Azam away with a robe of honour and jewels. It is said that so long as the news of the prince getting (his father's) leave to return did not reach them, Jani Begam [Jahanzeb Banu] his favourite wife, and other Begams and servants of his harem, being filled with utter despair, were wailing and lamenting, and when they heard of his liberation from such a danger the colour returned to their faces. A story runs that whenever any letter written by the Emperor reached Azam, of which the purport had not been previously notified to him by his Court-agent, the prince from the time of riding out to welcome the *farman* on the way to that of reading its contents used to so tremble at heart that the natural colour left his cheeks."*

Shah Alam became fully free in May 1695. But his restoration to full rank and power could not be effected without some sort of conflict with his rival, which, however, was cut short by Aurangzib's imperious authority and force of character. We narrate the incident in the words of the official historian, Mustad Khan.

"On the day of *Id-ul-fitr* (5th May, 1695) the Emperor was to go with all his sons to pray in the grand mosque at Bijapur, where he was then staying. As the eldest son always sits on the right hand of His Majesty, and during Shah Alam's captivity his younger brother Azam had been given this seat of honour, the eldest prince now asked, 'What is your Majesty's order about my rightful position on the day of *Id*?' Aurangzib replied, 'Go to the Idgah before my cortege and you will sit on my right hand.' He did so. When the imperial party reached the steps of the mosque, Shah Alam advanced, met the Emperor, and kissed his toes. His Majesty, after shaking hands with him, took his left hand in his own right, and entered the mosque. Thus the eldest prince was placed on the

* I find it difficult to date this incident. According to Khafi Khan it happened while Azam was by order marching from Bankapur towards Wagingera, passing the imperial camp on his way. That could not have been in 1694 or 1695. Manucci's story, ii. 467, refers to another event.

right of the Emperor. Azam, who was walking behind, touched the sleeve of his elder brother, as a sign to him to move away and make room for him on the Emperor's right. It caught His Majesty's eyes. With his right hand he grasped the skirt of Azam and dragged him away to his left. . . . . When the prayer was over, and the *khatib* ascended the pulpit [to proclaim the Emperor's titles] Aurangzib rose from his seat, holding the hand of Azam, and went out by the second gate, making a signal to Shah Alam to issue with his sons through the third gate."

[*M.A.* 372 ; *Storia* ii. 318-319.]

This was done to avert an armed collision between the two princes or their retainers. Manucci (ii. 465) mentions how in 1680 Azam had made a public scene at Ajmir by trying to take precedence of his brother by force: "Shah Alam was going to audience. Close to a bridge he saw the train of Azam pushing in great haste in the hope of passing over first, and fully resolved on resistance if they met any one. Shah Alam, from prudence or timidity, ... ordered his people to halt and yield free passage to his brother, Azam. The latter, taking no notice of him, with much haughtiness and making his horse curvet, passed the first without paying any attention or civility to his elder brother. . . . . For this reason, when the king sends one prince to any province to supersede another, one goes by one route and the other issues forth by another, escorted by Court mace-bearers with gold maces. Great care is taken that they do not encounter each other, in order to avoid any mishap or any fresh outbreak."

Two days after sending away Shah Alam to Northern India, the Emperor broke up his camp outside Bijapur, and soon afterwards (21st May 1695) reached Brahmapuri on the Bhima, where he was to live for the next four years and which his pious zeal renamed *Islampuri*. Muhammad Azam accompanied him. Aurangzib was so strict in enforcing regulations that the circuit of Azam's camp was reduced by his command to the area of Aurangzib's own before his accession to the throne [*M.A.* 373.]

Early in 1696, after the disasters to Qasim Khan and Himmat Khan at the hands of the Marathas in the Chittaldurg district, while Bidar Bakht was sent to restore imperial prestige there, Azam was moved back to Pedgaon [Bahadurgarh] to guard the Mughal rear. [*Ibid.* 380.]

At last after more than four years' stay at Islampuri Aurangzib set out in person (October 1699) to capture the great forts of Maharashtra. At his summons Azam left Pedgaon, joined him at Miraj (10th November), and accompanied him during the sieges of Satara and Parli, which fell in April and June 1700 respectively. The qiladar of Satara made his submission through the mediation of the prince, and therefore the conquered fort was newly named after him *Azam-tara*. [*M.A.* 421.] Parli, too, capitulated through him.

The imperial army began its return march from Parli, on 21st June, amidst indescribable hardships. The rivers and *nalas* were in high flood; the incessant rain turned the roads into muddy bogs; all transport animals had perished, and as the Court historian humorously describes it, "the gypsies of the army had to load their household goods on the backs of their fowls." It took them three days' marching to cover ten miles. In this way they reached Bhushangarh, some 70 miles from Parli, in 35 days. From this place the Emperor sent Azam with his contingent to Khandesh and Malwa to give rest to his war-worn soldiers and refresh their exhausted mounts. [*Ibid.* 429.]

When encamped at Dhar (in Malwa) the prince received an order (July 1701) to go to Gujrat as its governor, under whom the lately annexed State of Marwar also had been placed some years ago. Before giving him this post, Aurangzib correctly hits off his son's character in a letter to his wazir, "Shujaet Khan (the late governor of Gujrat) is dead. A *subahdar* should be selected for that province. Prince Alijah (*i.e.* Azam), desires the post. If he does not play the rôle of an Emperor's son he can do the work better than others. It may be given to him."*

Azam arrived at Ahmadabad, the seat of his government, on 14th November, 1701, and lived there for nearly five years. Large numbers of letters written to him by

---

* *Ruqat* 118. The same estimate of Azam's character is made by Aurangzib in another letter.—"Muhammad Azam Shah has done better work than others. If he does not play the Padishah-zada, good and suitable performance of tasks will come out of his hands . . . . Send him gold-embroidered robes, a khilat, a sword, a horse and a farman . . . . and summon him to my presence. Soothing his wise mind is really doing my own work". [I-O-L. MS. 3301, f. 33 b.]

Aurangzib during this period have been preserved and also the daily newsletters of the prince's court for two years. From these we learn only administrative details, and they have been woven, with some other pieces of information, into one chapter of Ali Muhammad Khan's Persian history of Gujrat entitled the *Mirat-i-Ahmadi* (i. 346-357). In April 1703 the province of Ajmir was added to the prince's charge [*M.A.* 473].

The viceroy of Gujrat held an important and very difficult office; he had to watch the frontier carefully for roving Maratha bands, who made frequent dashes into that province through the broken country of Jhabua and the gap in the Western Ghats near Nandurbar. The eternal struggle with these elusive freebooters seems to have worn him out, as the following incident shows:—

The Emperor learnt from the newsletter of the province of Gujrat that Janaji Dalvi, a Maratha general, had robbed some traders on the road to Surat, and that on the matter being reported to the prince he had remarked, "It has taken place within the limits of the faujdari of Amanat Khan, collector of Surat; it does not concern me." Aurangzib wrote across the sheet in anger, "Reduce Azam's rank by 5,000 and take from him the value of what the traders have lost......Bravo for your princeship, that you consider yourself lower than Amanat Khan! In my lifetime you have a claim to inherit my empire, why then do you not make Amanat Khan a sharer of your heritage?" [*Anecdotes*, §21.]

Early in 1705 a great sorrow fell on Azam and darkened the remainder of his life. His beloved wife

Jahanzeb Banu Begam (popularly called Jani Begam), a daughter of Dara Shukoh and the nursling of the saintly Jahanara, died of an abscess in the right breast. The French doctor, Mons. Martin, had proposed that the patient should be examined by one of his female relatives then living in Delhi, (evidently an Indo-Portuguese Christian woman) who was skilled in surgery (*haziqa*), so that he might prescribe medicines according to her report. But the Begam refused to be examined by a woman who drank wine, lest her body should be defiled by her touch! The disease lingered on for two years and then she died in great pain. Two lakhs of Rupees were spent in furnishing the corpse, distributing alms, and despatching the coffin to Delhi for burial there in the cemetery of the saint Qutb-uddin Bakhtiari. Her princely husband's mourning for her is only paralleled in Mughal history by that of Shah Jahan for his Mumtaz Mahal or of Dara for his Nadira Banu (the mother of this lady). Azam Shah was heartbroken at being left lonely of his life-long companion. He was now 52, and had only two years more to live. He gave up hearing music and attending dances, though he had been very fond of them from his youth upwards. His wife's property reverted to him, but he would not touch it; he gave away her jewels to their son Bidar Bakht and the other effects to their daughter Najib-unnisa. [*M.A.* 494, 495].

The Emperor had by this time grown very old and his death might happen any day. Azam, therefore, begged to be allowed to come to his presence, alleging that the climate of Gujrat did not agree with him, and that

6

a fever had made him "so weak that he could not utter words." Aurangzib was too suspicious of his sons and afraid lest they should imitate his conduct to his own father in Shah Jahan's old age. He wrote back to Azam, "I, too, had begged for the same thing from my father during his illness (on the eve of the war of succession), and he had replied to me that the wind of every place is congenial to men except the wind of evil passions!" [K.K. ii. 541 ; *Anecdotes*, §24].

But Azam continued pressing his request, and at last the old man yielded. Leaving Gujrat (25th November 1705) in charge of one of his servants, pending the arrival of the next subahdar Ibrahim Khan from Kashmir, the prince started for his father's camp at Ahmadnagar, where he arrived on 25th March 1706, and continued to live with him till the February of next year. [*M.A.* 512, *Mirat* i. 357.]

When the unmistakable approach of death warned Aurangzib that he must send his two sons far away from his bedside, if he wished to avert a bloody civil war between them immediately after his death or even before he closed his eyes, he issued his orders and on 5th February 1707 Kam Bakhsh was sent off to Bijapur, his viceroyalty, and on the 11th Azam was despatched to Malwa.

The Emperor, an old man of ninety, was now left alone on his deathbed. He wrote the following pathetic letter to Azam.

"Peace be on you!

"Old age has arrived and weakness has grown strong, strength has left my limbs. I came alone and am going away a stranger. I know not who I am and what I have been doing. The days that have been spent except in austerities have left only regret behind them. I have not at all done any (true) government of the realm or cherishing of the peasantry.

"Life, so valuable, has gone away for nothing. The Master has been in my house, but my darkened eyes do not see His splendour. Life lasts not ; no trace is left of the days that are no more ; and of the future there is no hope.

"My fever has departed, leaving only the skin and husks behind it. My son Kam Bakhsh, though gone to Bijapur, is near me. And you are nearer even than he. Dear Shah Alam is farthest of all. Grandson Muhammad Azim has, by order of the Great God, arrived near Hindustan (from Bengal).

All the soldiers are feeling helpless, bewildered, and perturbed like me, who having chosen to leave my Master, am now in a state of trepidation. Unsteady like quicksilver, they realise not that we have our Lord Father (ever with us). I brought nothing with me (into the world), and am carrying away with me the fruits of my sins. I know not what punishment will fall on me. Though I have strong hopes of His grace and kindness, yet in view of my acts anxiety does not leave me. When I am parting from my ownself, who else would remain to me? (Verse)

Whatever the wind may be
I am launching my boat on the water.

"Though the Lord Cherisher will preserve His slaves, yet from the point of view of the outer world, it is also the duty of my sons to see that God's creatures and Muslims may not be unjustly slain.

"Convey to my grandson Bahadur (*i.e.*, Bidar Bakht) my parting blessing. At the time of going away I do not see him; the desire of meeting remains (unsatisfied). Though the Begam is, as can be seen, afflicted with grief, yet God is the master of hearts. Shortness of sight bears no other fruit than disappointment.

"Farewell! farewell! farewell!"*

Azam had left Ahmadnagar on 11th February, but knowing that his father's death was a matter of a few days only, he marched very slowly halting on alternate days, and had gone only 40 miles when, on 21st February 1707, he received news of Aurangzib's death the day before. He immediately rode back to Ahmadnagar and arrived there in the night of the 22nd.

How Prince Muhammad Azam buried his father, and then crowned himself Emperor and set out for Northern India to seize Agra and Delhi and fight his elder brother Bahadur Shah, and how he fell (8th June 1707) with his sons in the battle of Jajau (some 16 miles south-west of Agra) have been fully described in Irvine's *Later Mughals*, Vol. I, chapter 1.

In July 1683 an incident happened in which Azam

---

* Translated by me from Br. Museum Addl 26240. The version given in the lithographed bazar edition of the *Ruqat* has been rejected.

proved by his cool courage that he was a true son of Aurangzib, who had faced a furious elephant without flinching when he was a lad of fifteen only. Azam was coming by command from the bank of the Nira river to the Emperor's Court at Aurangabad. In the evening when he was approaching the city on horseback, an elephant of Fath Jang Khan turned wild, charged the troops, and came upon the prince himself. Azam shot an arrow at it, but it came rushing on. As his horse began to shy, he dismounted, faced the elephant on foot, and slashed at its trunk, with his sword. His retinue, who had scattered at the first alarm, now rallied, came to the spot, and put the beast to death. [*M.A.* 230.] A hereditary officer named Mir Baddhu* had shown the greatest courage in turning the elephant back from the prince, but he declined the robe of honour offered to him by the Emperor, saying "I have merely done the duty of a *khānazād* (hereditary slave). Why should I accept wages for it?" [*Ruqat-i-Alamgiri*, No. 24 ; Ishwardas, 84*b*.]

The collection named *Ahkam-i-Alamgiri,* ascribed to Hamid-ud-din Khan Bahadur, gives eight very interesting anecdotes, characteristic of both father and son, in which Azam figures. (Nos. 17-24 of my translation, *Anecdotes of Aurangzib*).

The *Ruqat-i-Alamgiri* contains 64 letters (Nos. 8-71) written by order of Aurangzib to Azam and 11 letters

---

* It appears from the context that Mir Baddhu was Azam's foster-brother. If his mother's name was Zahida Banu, then she must have been Azam's wet-nurse.

(Nos. 76-86) addressed by the Emperor to Bidar Bakht. There are important references to Azam in several other letters in this volume and also in the extremely rare collection, *Kalimat-i-Aurangzib*, of which the only complete manuscript is in Rampur. From the following letters of Aurangzib we get a vivid idea of his attitude towards his sons.

To Asad Khan (the wazir).—"Convey Kam Bakhsh, ignorant of affairs, to the house of Muhammad Azam Shah and make him beg his brother's pardon so as to reconcile the two." [*Ruqat* No. 110.]

To Hamid-ud-din Khan.—"Some days ago, *Shah-i-Alijah* (*i.e.* Azam) told me that three men are his deadly enemies, namely, Hamid-ud-din Khan, Amir Khan and Munim Khan. I answered, 'Amir Khan has a good nature and is no man's enemy. Nor probably is Khan Hamid. As for Munim Khan, his character is unknown to this oppressed fool. The Lord God has Himself arranged for both [the first two] by granting them life. Why are you negligent about your *own* condition? Alas! alas! ......' " [Br. Mus. Addl. 26240, p. 101-102.]

To Asad Khan.—"From the letter of a friend I learn that Muhammad Azam has posted his own servants on the royal highway to convey news by relays of horses (*dak chauki.*) What does it mean when newsletters [from my Court] are reaching him [regularly]? It is surprising that he has not reported this action to me. Probably his brain did not come to his aid ...... Write to him to remove this private innovation which he has set up on the roads, or else I shall do so." [*Ruqat* No. 96.]

But, on the whole, Aurangzib cherished the greatest affection and felt the least contempt for Azam among all his sons. It is a pleasant surprise to find Aurangzib, who has been well called "the weary Titan" and "the sour old Puritan", relaxing in a letter to Azam and even composing a set of doggerel verses in Persian to describe to him the sorry condition of the imperialists at the siege of Satara. We give the first of these below.

"To my son Alijah.— ... Fort Satara has been renamed *Azam tara*. Play the music of rejoicing and recall to your memory the words of your childhood, namely *Babaji dhun dhun*!" [*Ruqat*, No. 43.]

VI

MUHAMMAD AKBAR:

THE NEMESIS OF AURANGZIB.

"............But in these cases
We still have judgment here: that we but teach
Bloody instructions, which being taught return
To plague th' inventor: this even-handed justice
Commends th' ingredients of our poison'd chalice
To our own lips."—*Macbeth.*

We all know that the Emperor Aurangzib gained the throne by deposing his father and murdering his brothers. But it is not so well-known that an exactly similar fate threatened him in 1681, when his fourth son Muhammad Akbar made an attempt to seize his throne. When in June 1658 Aurangzib imprisoned his father in Agra fort, Shah Jahan wrote to him, "You have treated your loving father in this way. May not your sons too treat you in the same manner?" To this warning Aurangzib had replied with the confident self-righteousness of the Pharisee, "Well, nothing happens without God's will...... Every one gets from God a return according to his intentions; and as my motives are good, I believe that I shall never meet with anything but good (from my sons.)" But Shah Jahan proved a true prophet; the Nemesis of Aurangzib came in the person of Muhammad Akbar.

This prince was born at Aurangabad on 11th September 1657. As his mother Dilras Bānu Begam of the Persian royal blood died within a month of his birth, he was regarded by all his family with that peculiar tenderness which such young orphans always excite in Indian homes. As his father wrote to him long afterwards, "God be my witness that I have loved you more than my other sons." His sister Zebunnisa, 17 years his senior, doted on him like a mother and controlled his household even after he had married and reared a family. After serving for short terms as governor of Malwa and Multan, Akbar was given a very important command in the Rajput war that broke out in 1679.

On 10th December, 1678, Maharajah Jaswant Singh of Jodhpur died in the imperial service at Jamrud in Afghanistan. The Emperor immediately seized Jodhpur and sent an army into Marwar to bring it under his direct rule. The deceased Maharajah's property in the fort of Siwana was ordered to be confiscated. His widowed queens delivered two sons on reaching Lahor in February, 1679, and then proceeded to Delhi intending to return to Jodhpur. Aurangzib sold the kingdom of Marwar to Jaswant's nephew Indra Singh (26 May 1679), destroyed the temples of Jodhpur, and ordered the cartloads of idols brought from the city to be flung down in the cavalry square of the imperial Court and under the steps of the Jama Masjid to be trodden on by the Muslims. From 2nd April the *jaziya* or poll-tax was reimposed on the non-Muslims in order, as the official history of the reign asserts, "to spread the law of Islam and to overthrow the practices of the infidels." (*Masir-i-Alamgiri*, 171—177.)

At Delhi the leading Rāthor adherents of Jaswant,—Durgadas, Ranchhordas, and Raghunath Bhatti,—continued to urge the Emperor to allow Jaswant's surviving infant, Ajit Singh,—the other having died in the meantime,—to go home and declare him as the heir of Marwar. But Aurangzib (15th July) ordered the baby prince to be seized and confined in the prison of Nurgarh. The Rāthor escort offered a most heroic resistance to the arrest, and their leaders, by successively sacrificing themselves and their devoted followers in rearguard actions, carried Ajit Singh away in safety to Jodhpur (23rd July), after maintaining a running fight with the Mughal army for some days. One of the Rānis was killed to save her from capture.

The Rāthor ministers immediately got possession of Jodhpur. The Mughal *faujdar* of that place and the *faineant* Rājah Indra Singh were dismissed by the Emperor for incompetence. Mughal armies now marched into Rajputana to wrest Jodhpur from the Rāthors. The Emperor himself went to Ajmir (25th September) to be near the seat of war. Prince Akbar accompanied him, and moved in advance with the vanguard. Maharana Raj Singh of Udaipur having taken up the cause of the orphan heir of Jodhpur, the imperial army started from Ajmir (30th November) to punish him. Prince Akbar entered Udaipur (in January, 1680), after its evacuation by the Maharana. Mewar was ravaged by the Mughals and 176 temples were destroyed at Udaipur and its environs, besides 63 others in Chitor (*Masir-i-Alamgiri*, 183-188). The war dragged on for some time. In this war, Prince Akbar commanded the Mughal vanguard, and at first gained some victories through his able lieutenants Tahawwur Khan and Sayyid Hasan Ali Khan. But when posted in the Chitor district, he suffered successively heavy losses by surprise attacks on the part of Maharana Raj Singh.* The Emperor in anger transferred him to Marwar (26th June, 1680), where he fought languidly against the Rajputs for some time longer, but in the end formed a treasonable plot with the enemy to depose his father and crown himself!

The Emperor had been staying at Ajmir, the bulk of his army being detached under Akbar. On 7th January, 1681, he received the startling news that Prince Akbar had rebelled "at the instigation of the Rāthors and some traitors among the imperial servants," issued a manifesto signed by four mullas deposing Aurangzib for having violated the laws of Islam, and proclaimed himself Emperor, and was planning to attack his father who was

---

* For these defeats Akbar apologised to the Emperor (*c.* 16 June) thus: "For shortage of words and sense my tongue cannot express even a particle of the shame that has visited this beginner in the school of practical work and the pain that oppresses the heart of this learner of the alphabet of understanding affairs, in consequence of the astonishing movements and activity of the infidels. Verily, I have erred through human frailty and my inexperience, for which I crave pardon." [*Abad-i-Ālamgiri*, f. 270*b*.]

slenderly guarded. But loyal officers made forced marches to join the Emperor, who boldly issued from Ajmir and reached Dorāhah (10 miles southwards) on the 15th. Akbar too arrived within three miles of the place and encamped for the night. The battle was fixed for the next morning. But at night Tahawwur Khan (surnamed Padishah Quli Khan), the chief adviser of Akbar, came to the Emperor's Court at the invitation of his father-in-law, a loyal officer. As he declined to take off his arms before entering the Emperor's tent, there was an altercation with the courtiers; then he turned to go back, but was beaten to death by the imperial guards. Aurangzib also sent a false letter to Akbar and contrived that it should fall into the hands of the Rajputs. In it he praised the prince for his success in pretending to rise in rebellion in order to deceive the Rajputs and bring them easily within the clutches of the imperial army!

The Rajput leaders on intercepting this letter went to Akbar for an explanation, but could not see him as he was then sleeping. The journey of Padishah Quli Khan to the imperial camp doubled their suspicion of a trap having been laid against them; the vast Rajput army melted away during the night and Aurangzib was saved! Next morning (16th January) Akbar woke to find himself utterly deserted, and he fled from his camp, leaving his family and children behind. Durgadas returned to him when the truth became known, two days later. The Emperor's severest chastisement fell upon the rebel's partisans. Three mullas who had given Akbar a *fatwa* in favour of deposing Aurangzib were caught and punished thus: they were taken barefooted to the top of Bithli hill and dragged down its side, led to the qazi's house and given some stripes with a lash, then taken up to the top of the hill barefooted and forced to run down to the base again. This was to be repeated throughout the day; at sunset they were to be chained and thrown into prison.

Later, a newsletter from the Deccan brought the report that Akbar had effected his escape there by disguising himself as a Rajput,—shaving his beard off, growing moustaches, and hanging pearls from his ears *à la Rajput*. "On hearing this the Emperor grew angry, put his beard into his mouth, and began to chew it"! He censured all the imperial officers in the Deccan for failing to stop Akbar. [Jaipur Records, 3.] In all official papers the prince was ordered to be designated as *Akbar-i-ābtar* (the Worst) and *Bāghi* (the Rebel.).

After passing some months in Marwar and Mewar,* incessantly hunted by the imperial forces, Akbar at last fled to the Deccan under the escort of the faithful Durgadas, crossing the Narmada on 9th May, 1681, and passing by way of Burhanpur, Talnair and Baglana into Shambhuji's territory (1 June). A very amusing correspondence was now carried on between father and son, Aurangzib professing the greatest love and forgiveness for Akbar and that prince taunting the Emperor in scathing terms and doggerel verses for his administrative failure and claiming that in rebelling against his father he was

* The Rajput war and the wanderings of Akbar have been described in detail in my *History of Aurangzib*, Vol. III.

only following a course sanctified by the example of Aurangzib himself! I translate it here.

Accounts vary as to the treatment of Akbar by Shambhuji. Khafi Khan says that he was at first well received and lodged in a place six miles [25 miles] from Raigarh, but that afterwards he was treated with scant courtesy and allowed too small a pension for the support of his followers. Bhimsen, on the other hand, says that Shambhu gave the refugee a royal welcome and a liberal allowance. But the fact is clear from the prince's letters that Akbar tried to play the Padishah in his exile, while Shambhu stood on his own dignity and could never forget that the self-styled Emperor of Delhi was really a beggar living on his bounty. Besides, Akbar was ever haunted by the fear that the Maratha Court would make terms with the imperial Government by delivering him up to his father's vengeance. At last, in search of a securer haven, Akbar left Shambhu, went to the Portuguese possessions on the Bombay coast and thence took ship for Persia in January 1687. His life and correspondence when in Shambhuji's kingdom have been fully treated in my *History of Aurangzib*, vol. IV, and essays in Maratha history.

I.—Aurangzib to his son Muhammad Akbar.*

Muhammad Akbar, my son! close to my heart, a piece of my liver [as it were], dear as my life—be assured of and exalted with my sincere kindness, and know:—

* The following letters have been translated from Persian Ms. No. 71 of the Royal Asiatic Society's Library, (London.) The

God be my witness, that I held you dearer and more beloved than all my other sons. But you, through your own ill-luck, were tempted by the deception and stratagem of the Rajputs, those Satans in a human shape, to lose your portion of the wealth of Paradise and to become a wanderer in the hill and wilderness of Misfortune. What remedy can I contrive and what help can I give? My heart became plunged into extreme sorrow and grief when I heard of your present miserable condition of anxiety, perplexity, ruin and wretchedness. Nay more, life itself tasted bitter to me; what need I say of other things? Alas! a thousand times alas! leaving out of your sight your [legitimate] pride of rank and majesty as a prince and Emperor's son, you in your simplicity took no pity on your own [extreme] youth; you showed no regard for your wives and children, but in the most wretched condition threw [them] into the captivity of those beast-looking beast-hearted wicked Rajputs! And you are roaming in all directions like a polo ball, now rising, now falling, now fleeing!

As the Universal Father has planted in all fathers' bosoms affection for their sons, I do not, in spite of the heavy sins you have committed against me, wish that you should meet with the due punishment of your deeds:—(*Verses*)

---

first two of them also occur, with many variants of reading, in the Bengal Asiatic Society's Ms. F. 56, the lithographed *Zahir-ul-insha*, and a Persian Ms. belonging to me.

Even though the son may be a heap of ashes
His father and mother regard him as collyrium for their eyes!

Let what is past, be past! Now if you are so guided by Fortune as to repent of your improper deeds, you may wait on me at any place that you like; the pen of forgiveness will be drawn across the pages of your book of errors and offences; and such favours and grace will be shown to you as you have not conceived in your mind; and all your troubles and hardships will be compensated for. Although the granting of my favours does not depend upon your presenting yourself before me, yet, as the cup of your disgrace has fallen from above, it is proper that you should come to my presence even once to remove the shame of evil repute from yourself. Jaswant, the chief of Rajputs, assisted and joined Dara Shukoh, [but that prince] met with nothing save humiliation and reverses in consequence. Know for certain [that the same will be your fate, too.] Providence befriend you! God make it your lot to follow the right path.

II. Muhammad Akbar to the Emperor Aurangzib.

The petition of the humblest of sons, Muhammad Akbar, who performs all the necessary ceremonies of adoration and devotion, submission and obedience, and like an atom lays the following before your Majesty,—the centre of adoration and the holiest shrine of this world and the next:—

The royal letter which, in a spirit of graciousness to slaves, had been addresed to this the humblest of sons, arrived at the happiest of times and the best of places. I laid that auspicious celestial disc on the crown of my head, and rubbed its white portion into my eyes like light and its black portion like collyrium, and illuminated my heart and eyes by reading its gracious contents. I submit a short commentary on all matters which have flowed from your pen, so full of advice and graciousness,—which [commentary], as Truth is the essence of a matter, will not be far [from appropriate] in proportion as it approaches Justice.

Your Majesty has written with your gem-showering pen, "I have loved this son *above* all my other sons, but he through his own ill-luck has lost his share of [my] great wealth and thrown himself into the tempest of thoughtlessness." Hail, Lord of the inner and outer worlds! Just as it is the duty of a son to seek the satisfaction of his father and devote himself to his father's service, so, too, it is an obligation and duty on the part of the father to bring up *all* his sons and attend to their interests, material and moral, and their rights. God be praised, that I have not hitherto failed in any way in rendering all the devotion of a son. How can I narrate in detail all the favours and graces of your Majesty, of which I cannot write about even one in a thousand or a few out of many? The care and protection of the younger son is everywhere and always the paramount aim of [all] great fathers. But your Majesty, contrary to the practice of the world, has shown small regard for all your younger sons and honoured your eldest son with the title of Shah [Alam], and appointed him as your heir. In what [code] of justice and equity can we enter this act? All sons have equal claims to the property of their father. Under what rule of the Holy Law and Faith can one [son] be exalted and the others thrown down Although the True Emperor is another being, in whose administration "when" and "why" have no jurisdiction, and the raising or overthrowing [of kings] belongs to Him of luminous splendour,—yet, [how does such partiality consist with] your Majesty's devotion to the Canon Law, love of the righteous path, spiritual insight, and regard for truth, which are known and manifest to the world and its inmates, [as is proved by Shah Jahan's verses on your Majesty in youth]: (*Verse*)

> Whom will he wish for as a friend,
> and to whom will his heart incline?

Verily, the guide and teacher of this path [of rebellion against a reigning father] is your Majesty; others are merely following your footsteps. How can the path which your Majesty himself chose to follow be called "the path of ill-luck?" (*Verses*)

> My father bartered away the garden of Eden for
> two grains of wheat;
> I shall be an unworthy son if I do not sell it for a
> grain of barley!

Hail, centre of the worlds, spiritual and temporal! Men draw hardship and labour on themselves. Former emperors like Akbar, Jahangir and Shah Jahan [deliberately] raised troubles, and in the end attained to their hearts' desires. The volumes of history prove that so long as a king [like Alexander the Great] does not penetrate to the wilderness of gloom (*zulmat*) he cannot taste the water of eternal life. No rose without a thorn, and no buried treasure without [its guardian] snake. (*Verses*)

That man alone can tightly clasp the bride of
Fortune in his arms,
Who can plant kisses on the lip of the keen-edged
sword.

Since ease has been ordained as the result of every fatigue, I firmly hope that, through the grace of the Doer of All Works,—the Cherisher of His slaves,—my heart's desire will soon manifest itself in the happiest manner and all my anxieties and exertions will be converted into rejoicing.

Your Majesty has written, "Jaswant was the chief of the Rajputs ; what sort of assistance and support he rendered to Dara Shukoh is known to the world. Hence the words of this false race do not deserve trust." Your Majesty has spoken very well indeed, but has not reached the marrow of the matter. In fact Dara Shukoh bore hatred and antipathy to this race, and what he suffered was the consequence of it. If he had agreed with them from the outset, his affairs would not have come to such a pass. Former emperors like Akbar had contracted alliance and kinship with this race and conquered the realm of Hindustan with *their* help. This is the race with whose aid and support Mahabat Khan made the Emperor Jahangir his captive and meted out due punishment to the tricksters and deceivers. This is the race which, when your Majesty was adorning the throne at Delhi, and the Rajputs [there] did not number more than three hundred men, performed heroic deeds, whose narrative is manifest to the age; such heroism and victory [were theirs] as the commanders of the age have not heard of. Jaswant it was who in the midst of the battle with Shuja displayed unpardonable insolence and violence to your Majesty; and yet your Majesty knowingly and deliberately overlooked his act. The same Jaswant it was whom your Majesty won over with many charms and soft speeches and detached from the side of Dara Shukoh, so that victory fell to your side. Blessings be on this race's fidelity to salt, who, without hesitation in giving up their lives for their master's sons, have done such deeds of heroism that for three years the Emperor of India, his mighty sons, famous ministers and high grandees have been moving in distraction [against them], though this is only the beginning of the contest.

And why should it not be so, seeing that in your Majesty's reign the ministers have no power, the nobles enjoy no trust, the soldiers are wretchedly poor, the writers are without employment, the traders are without means, the peasantry are down-trodden? So, too, the kingdom of the Deccan—which is a spacious country and a paradise on earth,—has become desolate and ruined like a hill or desert; and the city of Burhanpur,—a mole of beauty on the cheek of the earth,—has become ruined and plundered; the city of Aurangabad, glorified by connection with your Majesty's name, is perturbed like quicksilver at the shock and injury given by the enemy's armies. On the Hindu tribes two calamities have descended, (first) the exaction of the *jaziya* in the towns and (second) the oppression of the enemy in the country. When such sufferings have come down upon the heads of the people from all sides, why should they not fail to pray for or thank their ruler? Men of high extraction and pure breed belonging to ancient families, have disappeared, and the offices and departments of your Majesty's government and the function of counselling on the affairs of the State, are in the hands of mechanics, low people and rascals,—like weavers, soap-vendors and tailors. These men, carrying the broad cloaks of fraud under their arms, and the snare of fraud and trickery (to wit, the rosary) in their hands, roll on their tongues certain traditions and religious maxims. Your Majesty trusts these confidants, counsellors and companions as if they were Gabriel and Michael, and places yourself helplessly under their control. And these men showing wheat [as sample] but delivering barley,—by such pretexts make grass appear as a hill and a hill as grass [to you.] (*Verses*)

In the reign of King Alamgir, the Ghāzi,
Soap-vendors have become Sadar and Qāzi!
Weavers and jolahas are bragging
That at this banquet the king is their comrade!
Low people have gained so much power,
That cultured men have to seek shelter at their doors!
Such rank has been acquired by fools
As even scholars can never attain to!
God save us from this calamitous age,
In which the ass kicks at the Arab steed!

The supreme magistrate is [vainly] treading
on the wind,
While justice has become [as rare] as the
phœnix itself!

The clerks and officers of State have taken to the practice of traders, and are buying posts with gold and selling them for shameful considerations. Every one who eats salt destroys the salt-cellar. The day seemed near when the edifice of the State would be cracked.

When I beheld this to be the state of affairs [in the realm] and saw no possibility of your Majesty's character being reformed, kingly spirit urged me to cleanse the realm of Hindustan of the brambles and weeds (*viz.*, oppressors and lawless men), to promote men of learning and culture, and to destroy the foundations of tyranny and meanness,—so that mankind might, in easy circumstances and peaceful minds, engage in their respective professions, and good name,—which is synonymous with 'next life' and 'eternal existence'—might remain [for me] in the pages of [the history of] the age. How happy would it be if Providence so befriends [your Majesty] that leaving this work in the hands of the humblest of your sons, your Majesty seeks the blessedness of going on a pilgrimage to the Holy Cities [Mecca and Medina], and thereby induces the whole world to utter praises and prayers for you!

Hitherto your Majesty has spent all your life in the quest of the things of this world—which are even more false than dreams, and even less constant than shadows. Now is the proper time for you to lay in provisions for the next life, in order to atone for your former deeds, done out of greed for this transitory world against your august father and noble brothers in the days of your youth. (*Verses*)

O! thou art past eighty years and art still asleep!
Thou wilt not get more than these few days.

As for the lecture your Majesty has read to me in your letter, I am ashamed of your presumption [in writing in that strain.] (*Verses*)

What good did you do to your father,
That you expect all these [services] from your son?
O thou that art teaching wisdom to mankind,
Administer to thy ownself what thou art preaching to others!
Thou art not curing thyself,
Then, for once, give up counselling others!

Concerning what your Majesty has written to me to go to your presence, although it is the highest blessing to enter your presence, yet by reason of my youth and my apprehension of your Majesty's vengeance—who has behaved so notoriously towards your father and brothers—my heart is naturally full of suspicion of such undeserved punishment. If, however, your Majesty goes to Ajmir with a small body of attendants, all these fears will be removed from my heart; it will gain confidence, and I shall secure the honour of waiting on you. Thereafter, with perfect composure of mind I shall carry out all your commands.

[NOTES. *My father bartered away, etc.*—In Muslim

theology Adam is said to have been expelled from Paradise for breaking God's command by eating two grains of wheat (*i.e.*, the fruit of the forbidden tree) at the instigation of Satan.

Wilderness of gloom.—There is a Muslim tradition that Alexander the Great penetrated through the Egyptian desert to a terrible dark region where the *elixir vitae* was preserved. He tasted it as the reward of his daring and hardiness. The poet Sadi uses the story in his *Gulistan.*

Your Majesty at Delhi.—The allusion is to the desperate battles by which Durgadas and other Rathors carried off Jaswant's infant son Ajit Singh from Delhi when Aurangzib tried to imprison him. See my *History of Aurangzib*, iii. Ch. 36.

The battle with Shuja—The battle of Khajwa, 5th January, 1659, on the eve of which Jaswant treacherously plundered Aurangzib's camp and then fled to Jodhpur. See my *History of Aurangzib*, ii. Ch. 19.

For three years the Emperor of Hindustan, etc.—The allusion is to the war which broke out in Rajputana early in 1679, when Aurangzib tried to annex Marwar on the death of Jaswant Singh. Mewar was speedily involved in it, and though the new Maharana Jai Singh made peace on 14th June, 1681, the quarrel with Marwar continued without cessation for 30 years, and ended only with the formal recognition of Ajit Singh by Aurangzib's successor in August, 1709.

The spirited defence of the Rajput character for fidelity and of Jaswant's memory against Aurangzib's aspersions, shows that this letter was inspired by Durgadas. The stinging satire on Aurangzib contained in the second half of the letter could never have been forgiven by that Emperor.]

III. Aurangzib to Prince Akbar.

Alas for this son's lack of wisdom and sense, who has stepped aside from the path of obedience and devotion,—which befits the relation of a son to a father,—displayed crookedness of action and evil disposition, and, with the aim of gaining the crown and the throne, has uplifted the sword in his hand against his own father! In the race of the Emperors of India which son ever fought against his father? You have advanced most presumptuously. If your heart's desire is to play your sword and conquer kingdoms, what can be better? With faithful nobles and devoted followers go to Persia, whose king Shah Abbas [the Second] has fought battles with thy father and broken his coin of Qandahar. You ought to destroy *his* cities, for such is the duty of a true son. Why engage in battle with your own father in the hope of sitting on the throne? The key to the locks of endless victories lies in the hands of the Divine Treasurer, and kingship is His holy gift. What better than this? You, my son, ought to turn the reins of your enterprise from that side with all the circumstances of humility and defeat, and put the ring of servitude and obedience in the ear of your life, and come like a point to the centre of [my] celestial power, and rub the forehead of gratitude on the dust of my imperial threshhold. Then, probably, will my grace be your lot. Know that my wish is urgent in this matter ; delay not in acting up to my command.

[NOTES. *Qandahar.*—After Shah Abbas II had captured the fort of Qandahar from its Mughal garrison, Aurangzib besieged it twice without success.

Ring in the ear.—Slaves in Islamic countries (as also among the ancient Teutons) were distinguished by putting rings in their ears.]

IV. MUHAMMAD AKBAR TO SHAMBHUJI.

Shambhuji, the chief of great Rajahs, etc.! hope for my boundless favours and know that,—

From the beginning of his reign it was the intention of Alamgir to utterly ruin all the Hindus alike. On the death of Maharajah Jaswant Singh this intention became revealed. His war with the Rana [Raj Singh, of Udaipur] was also the outcome of this design.

As all men are the creation of God, and He is the protector of them all, it is not proper for us as Emperors of India to try to uproot the race of landowners, for whom is India. As the Emperor Alamgir carried matters beyond their limit, I became convinced that if these men were overthrown then Hindustan would not remain in the hands of our family. Therefore, with a view to saving my heritage and also taking pity on this race [Rajput Rajahs] who have been loyal to us from olden times,—I decided, at the request of Rana Rāj Singh and Durgādās Rāthor, to ride to Ajmir and fight a battle for the throne, so that the intention of God might become known. In this state of things, as the Rana happened to die, this business was delayed for some days. One month afterwards, Rana Jai Singh submitted the same prayer as that of his father [to me,] through Padishah Quli Khan,—who had gone to Jhilwara in order to plunder his dominions,—saying, "If you wish that the honour of Hindustan should remain [inviolate,] then we all, laying our hands on the skirt of your robes, hope for our deliverance and prosperity from your Majesty.".

At the request of these two great clans, I set out to take possession of my heritage. When I arrived within two miles of the encampment of Alamgir,—the battle having been fixed for the next morning,—three hours after sunset Death dragged the coward Padishah Quli Khan bound [with ropes, as it were, to the Court of] Alamgir, who slew him immediately on his arrival. Although the going away of any one was not really subversive of my undertaking, yet, as Padishah Quli Khan had been the intermediary in bringing over to my side the Sisodias and Rathors, both these clans were seized with a groundless suspicion that the whole affair was a stratagem [of Alamgir]. So they decamped towards their homes, without informing me. At their departure my soldiers lost heart and fled away, so that no battle was fought.

At this I took a small portion of the people of my harem with me and went towards Mārwār. The night after the next day Durgadas Rathor saw me with all his troops, and decided to accompany me. I made two or three trips and circuits in the kingdom of Mārwār. As Muazzam,—who had been appointed to pursue me,—

could not overtake [me] in these rambles, he divided his troops and stationed them in different places of the kingdom of Marwar as outposts. Therefore, I passed [into the dominion of] Rānā Jai Singh, and he, after offering to me horses and other presents, begged me to remain in his kingdom. But as his country was close to the seat of the Emperor, I did not consider it prudent to stay there. Therefore, calling to my mind your bravery and high spirit, I decided to march [to your country.] So, helped by the favour of the gracious Accomplisher of Tasks, on the 1st Jamadi-ul-āwwal, year 1092 A. H. (=9th May, 1681), I safely forded the river Narmada at Maheshwar. · Durgadas Rathor is with me. Keep your mind composed about me and cherish the hope that, God willing, when I have gained the throne, the name will be mine and the State will be yours. Fully realising the fact of Alamgir's enmity to yourself and to me, set your heart on this that we may so act as to promote our business. (*Verses*)

As the world does not stay in the same condition,
It is better to have a good name, which endures as a memorial.

This is what one expects from a man and a hero. What more need I say than that 'A hint is enough for the wise?' Written on 3rd Jamadi-ul-āwwal, year 1092, (=11th May, 1681).

NOTES.—Maharana *Jai Singh* was the son and successor of Raj Singh. *Jilwar,* the Jilwarra pass leading into Mewar from the west. Akbar forded the Narmada "at one of the crossing places appertaining to the ferry of Akbarpur, at a distance of 16 miles, close to the frontier of Rajah Mohan Singh," according to Khafi

Khan (ii. 276). Akbarpur is south of Mandu. Maheshwar, a noted place 8 miles east of Akbarpur.

AKBAR AN EXILE IN PERSIA.

Khafi Khan, who was a Shia and kept touch with Persia through his kinsmen in the port of Surat, gives the following account of Akbar's adventures in that country :—

Prince Akbar decided to go to Persia by any means he could. Fitting out two small ships with provisions for forty days, he prepared to sail away. Siddi Yaqut (the Mughal admiral in the Bombay seas) at first tried to get some war-vessels ready for barring the prince's path so that the Emperor might not suspect him ; but in the end he winked at it and Akbar left India with Ziauddin Muhammad, an old servant of Shuja, and some forty or fifty followers. On the way a great tempest overtook and separated the ships. Akbar was driven by stress of weather to an island under the Imām of Masqat. The local people seized the prince and carried him to the Imām, who was a vassal of the king of Persia. This Imām, while outwardly playing the part of an obliging host to the prince, kept him under surveillance and sent a fast courier to Aurangzib offering to hand Akbar over to him for two lakhs of Rupees in cash and a charter remitting the ten per cent. duty on all goods exported from Masqat to Surat. Aurangzib agreed . . . and appointed Hāji Fāzil, a ship captain, to go to Masqat and bring Akbar away.

Meantime, the Persian king, having heard of it,

repeatedly wrote threatening letters to the Imām, ordering him to send the Mughal prince to him quickly as a royal guest, otherwise a Persian army would be despatched to his country.

I here write (Khafi Khan continues) what I have heard from Muhammad Hāshim Tabrezi, the paymaster and news-writer of Burhanpur and sister's son to Md. Ibrahim, the grand *mustaufi* of Irān and care-taker of Akbar while he was a guest of the Shāh. When Akbar arrived [from Masqat] at a port of Persia, Shah Sulaimān sent Md. Ibrahim to look after him, with a clever painter who was ordered to take the prince's portrait secretly and send it to the Shah at Isfahān [in order to prove his identity.] Akbar arrived within six miles of Isfahān and alighted in the royal garden. Shah Sulaimān went there to welcome him.* Akbar advanced to the gate of the park and met the Shāh, presenting him with five diamonds and rubies of high price and saying, "It is not the custom with the great men of Irān to offer presents when visiting the great; but in Hindustan it is considered

* Kæmpfer in his *Amænitates Exoticæ* writes, "Akbar arrived in that part of Arabia bordering on Persia (*i.e.*, Masqat) in the beginning of the year 1687; and the governor of Lar had like to have lost his head for neglecting to give early intelligence to the king [of Persia] of Akbar's arrival. Akbar arrived at Isfahan on 24th January 1688." [Orme's *Frag.* 292.] *Jedhe Shakavali* mentions that Akbar went to Iran by ship in Feb. 1687. Orme's statement that Akbar arrived at Masqat in Nov. 1686 is probably wrong by some months (*Ibid.* 149), being based upon the report of Dobson of Calicut to Madras factory.

impolite to visit a patron empty-handed." The Shāh with extreme kindness addressed words of welcome to him, recited a verse of Hāfiz in thanksgiving at the arrival of a guest, and graciously taking up the jewels presented placed them in his turban. Muhammad Akbar replied with another verse of Hāfiz. After dinner the two set out on horseback for the capital, talking together on the way. On arrival at Isfahan, Akbar was dismissed with all honour to the guest-house appointed for him. Here the Shāh visited him the next day, spoke soothing words, and took him with himself to see his palace. Feasts and entertainments were daily held for Akbar . . .

Afterwards Muhammad Akbar pressed the Shāh to give him (armed) help in going to India, but the latter replied, "Live here as my cherished guest during your father's lifetime. After that, when it will be a struggle between you and your brothers, I shall do all I can to assist you." [K.K. ii. 285—289 ; also *Mirat-i-Ahmadi*, i. 316.]

Akbar had therefore to repress his ambition perforce and live on the Persian king's bounty, sighing for the speedy death of his father. But the cordial welcome which the Shāh had given him created the wildest rumours in the Indian bazars. In April 1688 M. Chardin recorded the popular gossip in Golkonda that "the king of Persia marches in person with a great army after Sultan Akbar, to give him help, in case the 60,000 horsemen he [Akbar] has already be not sufficient, and has sworn upon his beard that he will set him upon the Hindustan throne." [*Fort St. George Diary.*]

Years passed in this way, Shāh Husain succeeded Sulaimān on the throne of Persia (1694) and showed the same honour and liberality to the Indian exile as his father had done. But hope deferred made Akbar's heart sick. One day, alleging that he had received a letter from the wazir Asad Khan reporting his father's death, he besought the Persian king to give him the promised troops and money for the invasion of India. The Shāh waited for the reports of his spies at Tatta and other Indian ports. When shortly afterwards Akbar's information was proved groundless, he was put to shame and his host's attitude towards him became less cordial and respectful.

At last Akbar could not bear such a life any longer. Alleging that the climate of Persia did not agree with him, he pressed the Shāh again and again till he secured his consent to go to the district of Garmsir in Khurāsān, close to the western frontier of Mughal India, which then included Afghanistan, and there he waited for the war of succession with his brothers after Aurangzib's death, when the Persian governor of the province would help him with 10,000 cavalry, as ordered by the king. [K.K. ii. 289-290 ; 450-451.]

His departure from Isfahān is thus described in the letters of the English traders of that town:—"The 23rd March, 1696, Akbar departed this city, notwithstanding all the persuasions the king of Persia and his noblemen could use ; they gave him great promises of providing him an army if he would stay but one year longer. But he told the king that he had been long enough and they had not done anything for him ; and could he get but 100 men, besides his servants, he would depart, which accordingly he did." [Orme MSS 119, Isfahan to Bombay, 27 March.]

Some Armenians arrived from Persia reported at Surat that in Isfahan they saw the king put a crown on Akbar's head, valued at 24,000 *tomans,* and gird him with a scimitar . . . and that he ordered [for] him 15,000 soldiers, but he [Akbar] waived it and desired 1,200 officers only, to head the people he expected to flock to him on his approach to India. [*Ibid,* Surat to Bombay, 6 Nov. 1696.]

Akbar took up his residence at Farah in the Persian province of Qandahār and 210 miles west of that fort. As the frontier of Mughal Afghanistan was only 184 miles north of Qandahār, this move caused the greatest alarm to Aurangzib and his governor of Kabul (Amir Khan.) Prince Shah Alam, under the Emperor's orders, started from Agra (on 13 July, 1696) to take post at Multan and bar Akbar's path through the southern section of our north-western. frontier (*M.A.* 382). In September next, rumours reached Surat that Akbar with the Persian governor of Qandahār had taken the field and captured Ghazni and another important fort from the Mughals. This, we know, was not true. Report swelled the number of Akbar's auxiliaries to 40,000 Qizilbashes supplied, or at least promised, by the Shāh of Persia. [Orme MSS 119, Surat to Bombay, 5 and 25 Sep. 1696.]

Akbar's close approach and hostile intentions immediately threw the western frontier of India into unrest. Lawless Baluches began to raise their heads in the hope of profiting by the disturbance and the Government's anxieties. The chieftain of the Dongar tribe in Sindh rose in arms and it took four years to subdue him. In December a report was received at Court that near Bhakkar a party of Akbar's men had fought some troops of Muizz-ud-din (the son of Shah Alam); but they were evidently local rebels and not a detachment from Akbar's army. [Orme MSS. 119, Surat to Bombay, 22nd Dec., 1696.] As Akbar was reported to have come near Multan, the Emperor ordered the zamindars of that province to sign undertakings that if he entered their territory they would arrest or slay him regardless of his being the Emperor's son. [*Mirat-i-Ahmadi*, i. 336.]

But the truth of the matter was that Akbar's men and money were quite insufficient for an invasion of India, and he did not venture to penetrate to southern Panjab or Sindh. From an English letter written at Isfahan on 29th March 1697 we learn that he was still near Qandahar and "from thence he has demanded the Persian Shāh's promised assistance. But the latter only intends to send an ambassador to Aurangzib to pardon Akbar and give him a provincial governorship." [Orme MSS. 119.] In fact, the Shah's idea never matured, though his envoy Taqi paid a visit to India and was presented to the Emperor, about Oct. 1699. [*M.A.* 406.]

The Mughal position on the north-western frontier changed greatly for the worse on 28th April 1698 when Amir Khan, the exceptionally able and successful governor of Afghanistan, died and was succeeded by the easy-going pleasure-seeker, Prince Shah Alam. But even then Akbar was unable to force a trial of arms on. On the contrary, a petition alleged to be from Akbar reached the Emperor in April 1699, begging his forgiveness. Durgadas was the intermediary in this affair. By order of the Emperor he started from Merta for the Qandahar frontier with a gracious *farman* and a robe of honour, tents, dresses &c. and Rs. 50,000 in cash for Akbar, to conduct him back to his father's presence with suitable pomp. The Emperor, afterwards learning that the proposal was insincere, recalled this letter and the mission. [*Mirat-i-Ahmadi*, i. 344 ; *Akhbarat*, 7th May 1699.]

A few months later (21st October 1699), Siddi Hasan and another servant of Akbar arrived from Qandahar in the Emperor's camp in the Deccan with a genuine letter from Akbar asking for pardon and sending some caskets of *attar* as a present. They were sent back with a robe of honour and an imperial letter for the prince, in which he was told that so long as he remained outside the frontiers of India he could not be pardoned, but that immediately after his crossing the Mughal frontier a gracious order would be issued, appointing him *subahdar* of Bengal and conferring many favours on him. [*M.A.* 412 ; *Akhbarat*, 21 Oct. 1699.]

But Akbar still hesitated to trust his father, and nothing came of these parleys. The exiled prince continued his secret intrigues with certain nobles in India and his armed watch on the north-western frontier. In 1701, Prince Muizz-ud-din intercepted a letter from Akbar and another from Akbar's diwan addressed to Kshemkarn, the brother of Durgadas. These were sent to the Emperor, who immediately dismissed Kshemkarn from his *mansab*, and issued a secret order for the arrest of Durgadas and, if necessary, for slaying him. [Inayet-ullah's *Ahkam, 4b, K.T.* 122]. On 4th June 1701, four agents of Akbar (Nazar Ali Khan, Md. Bāqar and two others) were sent by the Emperor to Shujaet Khan, the governor of Gujrat. [*Akhbarat.*] They had brought a casket of letters from the prince.

By this time Aurangzib was an old man well over 80 years of age and his death might be expected any day. Reports of his increasing difficulties with the Marathas and his military failure in the Deccan and of the growing anarchy in Northern India as well, began to reach Akbar in Qandahar, and his intrigues and active preparations were quickened thereby. Aurangzib had, therefore, to write to Shah Alam, now governor of Afghanistan, letter after letter urging him to be more active and vigilant against his rival. In one of these letters he says, "I learn that Akbar has raised his head in tumult in that country and proclaimed himself my heir. Order Shah Alam to be watchful, or else he will never succeed me on the throne." In another he tells his wazir, "From a news-letter sent by Faramurz Beg Sistani of Farah, who from Shah Jahan's time to this age has been noted for his wisdom and carefulness, I learn that the Irani, (deceptive like) the *ghoul* or demon of the wilderness, has instigated Akbar to raid and devastate places on the frontier in Shah Alam's charge, and yet Shah Alam is negligent in this matter!" And, again, he writes to the same wazir, "Akbar inspite of his long [and fruitless] wanderings is working hard to gather together material resources and to equip himself for action. . . . As my paternal love is still flowing, I may forgive him for his offences."

When Munim Khan, the agent of Shah Alam, was appointed diwān of Kabul and sent to join his master there, Aurangzib called him to an interview, on 10th November 1703, wishing, as he writes to his wazir, "that I may speak to him about the evil ambition of Akbar, who in hopes of the Persian [king],—that corpse-eating demon,—has taken up his abode at Farah near Qandahar, and at the hint of the governor of that place does not move to any other side, but is waiting for the inevitable event (my death.) *Verses*

> My mind cannot forget the words of that cup-maker
> Who said to a fragile cup that he had made:
> 'I know not whether the stone thrown from the sphere of Fate
> Will break you or me first.'

There is no remedy for it except to leave one of my sons with a large army in Kabul and Muizz-ud-din Bahadur with powerful resources in Multan till the decision of the case,—or in other words, the passing away of this perishable creature [Aurangzib], and then making peace by agreeing to a partition of the empire (among my sons.)

By way of advice I say, that many famous men of ambition have lost their fortune and fallen into misery by kindling the flames of slaughter and consigned their lives to bitterness. One of these was Dara Shukoh, who would not have seen the evil days he did if he had listened to Shah Jahan's advice."

Akbar's life was, in truth, destined to end in exile and disappointment. He did not outlive his father. In November 1704, Aurangzib learnt from a correspondent on the Persian frontier that his rebel son had at last died. The Emperor, as his official history tells us, consoled his heart by reciting the *tarjia* verses of the *Quran,* and remarked "The great disturber of India has subsided." Mourning robes were presented to Akbar's sons and daughters, all of whom were now in the Emperor's hands. [*M.A.* 483.]

VII

AURANGZIB'S FAVOURITE SON.

Kām Bakhsh, the youngest son of Aurangzib, was the spoilt child of his father's old age. At the time of his birth (24 Feb., 1667), Aurangzib was nearly 50 years old and doted on his young wife Udaipuri Mahal, this prince's mother, who had once been a beauty of Dara's harem and who was henceforth to be Aurangzib's sole companion and comforter till his death. The Emperor's infatuation for this lady kept him back from subjecting her son to discipline in the school-room or to practical training in warfare. His education was neglected. It is true that learned tutors were appointed for Kām Bakhsh, but he learnt little and was never made to learn anything by taking pains, as his mother saw to it that his negligence*

---

* Ishwardās, 133*b*, tells a story about this :—

The prince did not apply his heart to the acquisition of knowledge. One day his tutor Siādat Khan came to the palace school-room and sent to call the prince. But Kām Bakhsh did not come. The Khan waited for 2 or 3 hours, after which he reported the matter to the Emperor. On being asked the reason of his neglect, Kām Bakhsh replied, "I have devoted all my time till now to the acquisition of knowledge, and I have learnt what was in my lot to learn. How can I spend all my life for years to come in the school-room?" As this speech savoured of love of ease, the Emperor was enraged, and calling the prince before him remarked, "A man without knowledge is like a beast. A prince, in particular, should have a refined mind." So, he ordered went unpunished, and even uncensured. We are told that he was taught to repeat the *Qurān* from memory at the age of ten, but his intellect was not cultivated. Udaipuri's giddy and voluptuous character and low brain-power were reflected in her son, who throughout life displayed a capriciousness, levity and headstrong passions that bordered on insanity.

It was Kām Bakhsh's proud boast that he had a better right to the throne of Delhi than any of the other sons of Aurangzib, as he was born of a reigning Emperor, while his brothers had been born when their father was a mere prince. His half-brothers, on the other hand, despised him as the son of a dancing-girl and bearing the stigma of his origin from a bondswoman.

It was the practice of the Mughal Emperors to send their sons away from home at the age of 16 or 17 in independent command of a field army, but under the control of some trusted old noble of the highest rank, who acted as their guardian and minister (*ātāliq*). But this education in the school of action was denied to Kām Bakhsh by his doting parents till he was past 24 years. He was married as early as the age of fourteen and more than once, and he became a father when only 17 years and 3 months old. By being constantly kept with his father and employed only in Court ceremonies and social functions,—such as

---

that Kām Bakhsh should not be allowed to come out of his house, not even to join in the public prayer on Fridays. After a month and a half the Emperor pardoned him with a warning not to be slack in acquiring the arts.

welcoming some distinguished visitor on the way, or condoling with bereaved nobles, on behalf of the Emperor,—he grew up a carpet knight. In what was intended to be his first and very much belated "baptism of fire," namely, his participation in the siege of Jinji, he proved worse than a failure, and his foolish plans and acts could be checked only by placing him under arrest.

This fort, situated in the north side of the South Arcot district of the Madras Presidency, was then the refuge of Rājarām, the fugitive king of the Marāthas. It had been besieged by the Mughal general Zulfiqār Khān as early as September 1690 ; but his position was made so difficult by the enemy bands roving outside that the Emperor had to send heavy reinforcements under his *wazir* Asad Khan and Prince Kām Bakhsh, who arrived there on 16th December 1691.

Here the prince, chafing under the control of the *wazir*, was so ill-advised as to open a secret correspondence with Rājarām. The Marāthas flattered his humour and mischievously instigated him in new evil projects. A year later, vast Marātha forces, raised in Western India, reached Jinji under Dhana Jādav and Sāntā Ghorparé. The grain supply of the Mughal camp was cut off, and for some weeks communication with the Emperor and the Mughal base ceased altogether. Alarming rumours arose immediately, which the Marāthas spread and exaggerated. It was said that Aurangzib was dead and that Shāh Alam had succeeded to the throne. Kām Bakhsh considered himself in a most perilous position: Asad Khan and Zulfiqār were his enemies and might seize and deliver him up to his brother and rival. His only hope of safety now, so his servants told him, lay in his making terms with Rājarām and escaping into Jinji fort with his family on a dark night. And he made his retinue ready for taking such a step.

But his secret was betrayed by these two generals' spies in his camp. Asad and Zulfiqār consulted the leading officers of the imperial army, and they urged that the prince should be placed under strict guard and the entire army withdrawn from the siege-lines and concentrated in a safer position in the rear.

Zulfiqār Khān effected his withdrawal from the front after hard fighting, losing 400 troopers killed and many others wounded. At the close of the day he reached Asad Khan's quarters in the rear, adjoining Kām Bakhsh's camp.

Here the prince had been exulting as danger thickened round Zulfiqār and Asad. He had even plotted with his silly courtiers to arrest these two generals at their next visit to him and then grasp the supreme power. But this plot, like all others, had leaked out. Zulfiqār Khan, worn out with his all-day fighting and anxieties, reached his father's side at night, learnt of the new plot, and then the two leaders quickly decided that the safety of the entire army and the preservation of the Emperor's prestige alike demanded that the prince should be deprived of the power of creating mischief. They immediately rode to Kām Bakhsh's quarters, unceremoniously entered within the outer canvas-wall (*jāli*) seated on their elephants, and knocked down the screens of his audience hall. The other nobles stood by as idle spectators, leaving the odium of arresting their master's son to rest solely on these two leaders. The servants of the prince foolishly discharged some bullets and arrows and raised a vain uproar and tumult. But Asad Khan's force was overwhelming and his movements quick. Kām Bakhsh lost heart, and in utter distraction came out of his harem by the main gate. He had advanced only a few steps when the Khān's musketeers (*bahelias*) seized both his arms and dragged him with unshod feet to Asad. Rao Dalpat, seeing it, promptly drove his elephant forward, and with great agility lifted the prince up on his *haudā*, sat behind him as his keeper, and brought him to Asad Khan.*

The *wazir* was in a towering rage. He severely rebuked the prince, calling him a dancing-girl's son, unworthy to rule over men or to command in war. Then he continued, "The rumours you have heard are false. The Emperor is alive. What is this that you have done? You have disgraced yourself, and covered my gray hairs with shame." The prisoner was taken to Asad Khan's own tent and treated with every courtesy consistent with his safe custody. The grand *wazir* saluted him and served his dishes with his own hands. (*Dil.* 108*a.*)

When day broke, Zulfiqār called together all the officers of the army, great and small, explained his late action, reassured them, and bound them to his side by a lavish distribution of money and presents. Thus the

---

* *Dil.* 108*a.* *M. A.* 358. *Storia,* ii, 316. Khafi, ii. 420, is useless.

imperial army was saved by establishing unity of control (*c.* 28th Dec. 1692.)

Then the Mughal force, finding its position before Jinji extremely unsafe, withdrew to Wandiwāsh, 24 miles north-east of it (23rd January, 1693). Here the generals waited for the Emperor's orders about Kām Bakhsh. The officers of the Karnātak army, especially Asad and Zulfiqār, lay quaking in mortal anxiety as to how the Emperor would regard the arrest of his favourite son. The wildest rumours circulated as to his wrath towards his generals. A story even ran through the Wandiwāsh camp that Asad Khan, on being sentenced to disgrace by the Emperor, has poisoned himself (July).

Aurangzib at first ordered the prince to be brought to his presence in charge of Asad Khan, and fresh equipment and furniture to be given to him on his way, to replace what had been abandoned or looted at Jinji. Kām Bakhsh arrived at his father's camp at Galgalā (on the Krishnā) on the 14th of June, and was presented to the Emperor in the harem through the mediation of his sister Zinat-unnisā. Here the spoilt youth tried to justify his late conduct by charging Zulfiqār Khan with treachery and the collusive prolongation of the siege for enriching himself. (*M.A.* 359 ; *Dil.* 112*a.*)

But Aurangzib was too wise a man to believe in Kām Bakhsh's counter-charges against his faithful generals.

The memory of the prince's misdeeds was swept away by the flood of Udaipuri's tears, though the Emperor was greatly annoyed at this unexpected result of his attempt to give his favourite son an experience of war. His grief is graphically described in Hamid-ud-din's *Anecdotes of Aurangzib* (§ 25 of my translation).

After the signal failure of this his first expedition, Kām Bakhsh was always kept in his father's Court, and never sent to any distant province or expedition. True, the viceroyalty of Berār was conferred on him in 1687, and again in 1697, and that of Haidarābād and Bijāpur in 1701 and 1704, but he was allowed to govern them by deputy, without having to leave his father's side.

While continuing to lead this life of idle ease and safety, Kām Bakhsh brought himself again into trouble by another childish outburst of passion in 1698, when he was already thirty-one years old.

It was the night of 12th December. Khwājah Yaqut, the superintendent (*nāzir*) of Kām Bakhsh's household, was returning from the prince's quarters to his own rooms in Brahmapuri, when he was hit by an arrow in the darkness. Happily his arm, which was hanging down in front, received the blow, otherwise his stomach would have been cut open. The bleeding man immediately ran back to the Emperor's presence and complained of the attack. The prefect of the camp police made an investigation, and it came to light that Yaqut's honest and strict administration of his master's affairs had made enemies of some rogues among the prince's servants in whose unworthy society he delighted, particularly his foster-brother (*Kokah*), who had planned this ambush for getting rid of the *nāzir*. Four captains of the prince's contingent who were also suspected, were arrested without trouble. But the *Kokah* resisted. The Emperor then ordered the prince's *bakhshi* to bring the man to him. But on the way, the *Kokah* changed his mind at the instigation of some evil counsellors, and ran away from the palace gate. When this was reported, Aurangzib wrote to his son to expel the man from the camp. The prince dismissed the *Kokah* to his own *jāgirs*, with the present of 200 gold pieces, a tent and porters, embracing him at the time of parting, with tears in his eyes.

The news softened Aurangzib's heart; he could not bear to see Kām Bakhsh weeping. So, a third order was issued, requiring the prince to bring his Kokah to the Emperor and gain his pardon by his intercession! When the two reached the Court, the Emperor directed the prince to be ushered in and his foster-brother to be left behind in an anteroom. But Kām Bakhsh refused to part from his *Kokah* and tied him to his own waist with his scarf! The Emperor, on hearing of it, was annoyed, and sent minister after minister to reason with Kām Bakhsh, but the unlucky prince would not listen to good counsel. At last Hamid-ud-din Khan was sent to separate the *Kokah* from the prince and hand him over to the police. The prince drew his dagger menacing the officers. Hamid-ud-din tried to wrest it from his grasp and was wounded in the attempt. During this scuffle his attendants rushed in a crowd and dragged away the *Kokah* to prison with kicks, *lathi* blows and cuffs. Kām Bakhsh was confined in a small tent near the jewel-room, his rank was taken away, and all his property confiscated. His army was absorbed in the imperial forces. The

Emperor ascribed the prince's conduct to the effect of bad company. (*M.A.* 398-400 ; *Ruqāt* No. 126.)

But in less than six months Kām Bakhsh was pardoned and restored to his rank and property. From December 1699 he again began to attend his father's Court, sometimes escorting his sister Zinat-un-nisā from the base to the imperial camp, at others condoling with high nobles in bereavement. At the siege of Wagingera, the Berad capital, (now in the Shorāpur district of the Nizām's territory), he was placed in nominal command of one section of the lines of investment (1705). In this year he was to have gone to his viceroyalty of Haidarabad, but the Emperor lovingly put off his departure.

At last at the beginning of February 1707, Aurangzib fell ill at Ahmadnagar, and felt the approach of death. Of his three surviving sons, Muhammad Azam and Kām Bakhsh were with him. But the presence of these two rivals at the same place would lead to an armed conflict for the throne and bloodshed immediately after the old man had closed his eyes, or probably even before that event. So, Aurangzib hurriedly sent off Azam (13th Feb.) and Kām Bakhsh (9th Feb.) from his camp towards their respective viceroyalties of Mālwa and Haidarabad.

It broke Aurangzib's heart to part with the beloved son of his old age and to send him away from his own deathbed. (*Dil.* ii. 158*a.*) But it was the only means of saving that prince's life. In the last few days of his life the world-weary and aged Emperor wrote the following touching letter to Kām Bakhsh :—

"My son, (close to my heart like) my liver! Although,

in the days of my power, I gave advice for submission to the will of God and exerted myself beyond the limits of possibility, yet God having willed otherwise, none listened to me. Now that I am dying, it will do no good. I shall carry away with myself the fruits of all the punishments and sins I have done. What a marvel that I came (into the world) alone and am (now) departing with this (large) caravan. Wherever I cast my eyes, no caravan-leader save God comes into my view. Anxiety about my army and camp-followers has been the cause of (my) depression of mind and fear of final torment. Although God will undertake the protection of His people, yet it is also obligatory on Muslims and my sons. When I was full of strength, I could not at all protect them; and now I am unable to take care of myself! My limbs have ceased to move. The breath that subsides, there is no hope of its return. What else can I do in such a condition than to pray? Your mother Udaipuri (Begam) has attended me during my illness; she wishes to accompany me (to the next world). I consign thee and thy children to God. I am in trepidation. I bid you farewell . . . Worldly men are deceivers (literally, they show wheat as sample but deliver barley); do not do any work in reliance on their fidelity. Work ought to be done by means of hints and signs. Dārā Shukoh made unsound arrangements and hence he failed to reach his point. He increased the salaries of his retainers to more than what they were before, but at the time of need got less and less work out of them. Hence he was unhappy. Set your feet within the limits of your carpet.

"I have told you what I had to say, and now I take my leave. See to it that the peasantry and the people . . . . are not unjustly ruined, and that Musalmans may not be slain, lest punishment should descend on me." (India Office MS. 1344, *f.* 26 *a*)".*

A few days after writing this, Aurangzib breathed his last (20 Feb., 1707). A paper signed by him was found under his pillow, dividing his Empire among his sons and proposing to leave to Kām Bakhsh the two provinces of Bijāpur and Golkondā provided that he remained content with these. (*Ibid.*, *f.* 49 *b*). But he would not be content. He crowned himself after his father's death and issued coins in his own name as Emperor. His mad doings at Haidarabad during his brief reign are described in full detail in Irvine's *Later Mughals*, i. 50-62.

At last he provoked a contest with his eldest brother Bahādur Shāh I., and was mortally wounded in a battle fought 4 miles outside Haidarabad (2 January, 1709), and died in the course of the night. Thus, the disaster which his loving father had foreseen and done his utmost to ward off, at last befell him.

---

* I have not accepted the other version of this letter given in the lithographed bazar edition of *Ruqāt*, No. 73. Udaipuri died a natural death at Gwalior in June 1707.

VIII

THE ROMANCE OF A MUGHAL PRINCESS: ZEB-UN-NISA.

Zeb-un-nisa, or the "Ornament of Womankind," was the eldest child of Aurangzib and his Persian wife Dilras Banu Begam. Born at Daulatabad in the Deccan on 15th February, 1638, she was educated by a learned lady named Hafiza Mariam (the wife of Mirza Shukrullah of Kashmir, whose family originally came from Naishabur in Khurasan.)

She inherited her father's keenness of intellect and literary tastes, and completely mastered the Arabic and Persian languages. For her success in committing the whole *Quran* to memory she received from her delighted father a purse of 30,000 gold pieces. She could write the different kinds of Persian hand,—*nastaliq*, *naskh*, and *shikasta* with neatness and grace. Her library surpassed all other private collections of books, and she employed many scholars on liberal salaries to produce new works or copy old manuscripts for her. Aurangzib disliked poets as lying flatterers and their poetry as vain babblings; but his daughter's liberality compensated for the lack of Court patronage of literature in that reign, and most of the poets of the time were maintained by her. Supported by her bounty, Mulla Safiuddin Ardbeli lived in comfort in Kashmir and translated the gigantic Arabic *Tafsir-i-Kabir* (Great Commentary) into Persian and named it after his patroness, *Zeb-ut-tafasir*. Other theological tracts and books, written by her pensioners, bore her name. Zeb-un-nisa is said to have written Persian poetry under the pseudonym of *Makhfi* or the "Concealed One." But the extant *Diwan-i-Makhfi* cannot be her work.* The title of *Makhfi* was borne by several other poets, notably a wife of Akbar and Nur Jahan. (*M. A.* 538.)

Zeb-un-nisa is the heroine of some love-tales current in modern Indian literary circles. She was a gifted poetess and is alleged to have claimed an artist's independence of morality. Similar discreditable legends about Kalidas's life have long circulated among our old school of Sanskritists, but are rejected by sober historians (*Ind. Antiq.*, 1878, p. 115.) We shall to-day try to ascertain whether the traditions about the Princess Royal of Delhi had a stronger basis in fact than those about the laureate poet of the Court of Ujjayini.

No mention of Zeb-un-nisa's love-intrigue with Aqil Khan, or indeed with any person whatever, is made in any work of her father's reign or even for a century after his death. We can easily explain the silence of the Court historians and other official writers, who would naturally suppress every scandal about royalty. But perfect freedom of speech was enjoyed by the private

---

* The question has been fully discussed by Khan Sahib A. Muqtadir in the *O. P. L. Persian Catalogue*, Vol. III, pp. 250-1.

historians of the reign (especially the two Hindu authors, Bhimsen and Ishwardas), by Khafi Khan who wrote a quarter of a century after Aurangzib's death, and by the author of the biographical dictionary of the Mughal Peers (*Masir-ul-umara*), who lived a generation later still. The European travellers, Bernier and Manucci, wrote for the eyes of foreigners, and had nothing to fear from the wrath of Aurangzib or his posterity. Manucci, in particular, revelled in Court scandals, so much so that his history of the Mughals *(Storia do Mogor)* has been well called a *chronique scandaleuse*. Would he have passed over Zeb-un-nisa's failings, if he had heard of any, as such a topic would have made excellent "copy" for his book? The gossipy and outspoken Khafi Khan does not assail Zeb-un-nisa's character, though he openly proclaims the shames of Jahangir and Nur Jahan. The story of our heroine's love-intrigues is modern,—a growth of the 19th century and the creation of Urdu romancists, probably of Lucknow. The pretended Urdu life of Zeb-un-nisa that holds the field at present is the *Durr-i-Maktum* of Munshi Ahmaduddin, B.A., of Lahor, who quotes from an earlier work, *Haiyat-i-Zeb-un-nisa* by Munshi Muhammad-ud-din Khaliq.

This story, in its most developed form is conveniently summarized in English (evidently from Ahmaduddin's Urdu work) in Mrs. Westbrook's introduction to her *Diwan of Zeb-un-nisa* in the "Wisdom of the East Series" (1913). She writes:

"In the beginning of 1662 Aurangzib was taken ill, and, his physicians prescribing change of air, he took his family and court with him to Lahor. At that time Aqil Khan, the son of his *wazir*, was governor of that city. He was famous for his beauty and bravery, and was also a poet. He had heard of Zeb-un-nisa, and knew her verses, and was anxious to see her. On pretence of guarding the city, he used to ride round the walls of the palace, hoping to catch a glimpse of her. One day he was fortunate, he caught sight of her on the housetop at dawn, dressed in a robe of *gul-anar,* the colour of the flower of the pomegranate. He said, *A vision in red appears on the roof of the palace.* She heard and answered, completing the couplet, *Supplications nor force nor gold can win her.*

She liked Lahor as a residence, and was laying out a garden there: one day Aqil Khan heard that she had gone with her companions to see a marble pavilion which was being built in it. He disguised himself as a mason, and, carrying a hod, managed to pass the guards and enter. She was playing *chausar* with some of her girl friends, and he, passing near, said, *In my longing for thee I have become as the dust wandering round the earth.* She understood and answered immediately: *Even if thou hadst become as the wind, thou shouldst not touch a tress of my hair.* They met again and again, but some rumour reached the ears of Aurangzib, who was at Delhi, and he hastened back. He wished to hush up the matter by hurrying her into marriage at once. Zeb-un-nisa demanded freedom of choice, and asked that portraits of her suitors should be sent to her; and chose naturally that of Aqil Khan. Aurangzib sent for him; but a disappointed rival wrote to him: 'It is no child's play to be the lover of a daughter of a king. Aurangzib knows your doings; as soon as you come to Delhi, you will reap the fruit of your love.' Aqil Khan thought the Emperor planned revenge. So, alas for poor Zeb-un-nisa! at the critical moment her lover proved a coward; he declined the marriage, and wrote to the king resigning his service. Zeb-un-nisa was scornful and disappointed, and wrote: *'I hear that Aqil Khan has left off paying homage to me'* —or the words might also mean, *'has resigned service'—'on account of some foolishness.'* He answered also in verse, *'Why should a wise man do that which he knows he will regret?'* (*Aqil* also means, a wise man.)

But he came secretly to Delhi to see her again, perhaps regretting his fears. Again they met in her garden; the Emperor was told and came unexpectedly, and Zeb-un-nisa, taken unawares, could think of no hiding-place for her lover but a *deg,* or large cooking-vessel. The Emperor asked, 'What is in the *deg*?' and was answered, 'Only water to be heated.' 'Put it on the fire, then,' he ordered; and it was done. Zeb-un-nisa at that moment thought more of her reputation than of her lover, and came near the *deg* and whispered, 'Keep silence if you are my true lover, for the sake of my honour.' One of her verses says, *'What is the fate of a lover? It is to be crucified for the world's pleasure.'* One wonders if she thought of Aqil Khan's sacrifice of his life.* After this she was imprisoned in the fortress of Salimgarh." (Pp. 14-17).

Now, examining the above account in the light of known history we at once find that the story of the smuggled lover being done to death in a *deg* in the harem has been transferred to Zeb from her aunt Jahanara, of whom it is told by Manucci (*Storia,* i. 218) and Bernier (p. 13). The recorded facts of the life of Aqil Khan also contradict the story in every particular.

Mir Askari, afterwards surnamed Aqil Khan, was a native of Khwaf (in Persia)—and not the son of a Delhi *wazir.* He entered the service of Aurangzib in Shah Jahan's reign and attended the prince during his second viceroyalty of the Deccan (1652-1657) as his equerry

* This conjecture is incorrect. According to the conventions of Persian poetry the type of the perfect lover is the moth which consumes itself in the flame of a lamp without uttering a groan. Cf. Carlyle's 'Consume your own smoke'.

(*jilaudar*). He had already made his mark as a poet and adopted the pen-name of *Rāzi* from the saint Burhanuddin Raz-ullah whom he venerated. When Aurangzib started from the Deccan to contest the throne, he left his family behind in the fort of Daulatabad (6th February—December, 1658), and Aqil Khan acted as the governor of the city from 6th February and of the fort from August 1658 till near the end of 1659. Arriving at Delhi on 8th February 1660, he was, two months later, made *faujdar* of the land between the Ganges and the Jamuna (Mian Duab), but replaced by another officer in July, 1661. In the following November he temporarily retired from service on the ground of ill-health and was permitted to reside at Lahor on a pension of Rs. 750 a month. When in November 1663 Aurangzib was passing through Lahor with his family, on his return from Kashmir, Aqil Khan waited on him (2nd November) and was taken into the Emperor's train and appointed Superintendent of the Hall of Private Audience, a position of very close contact with the Emperor, (January, 1664). Evidently he continued to enjoy high favour, being promoted in October 1666 and given a royal present in May next. Later on he was made Postmaster-General (Darogha of Dak Chauki), but resigned in April 1669, and seems to have lived under a cloud for the next seven years, as we find no mention of him till October, 1676 when he was granted an allowance of Rs. 1,000 a month. In January, 1679 he was taken back into service as Second Paymaster. Being appointed *subahdar* of Delhi in October 1680, he held that office till his death in 1696.

Thus we find that the story of young Aqil Khan having been roasted to death in a cauldron by order of Aurangzib, is utterly false. No man below thirty could have been put in charge of a fort containing Aurangzib's wives and children on the eve of the war of succession, and, therefore, Aqil Khan must have been an old man at the time of his death in 1696.

So far was Aqil Khan from being cut off in the prime of youth through the vindictiveness of his mistress's father that he married, raised a family and died at the age of more than seventy surrounded by his grand-children. The *Letters of Mirza Bedil* (a favourite of Aqil Khan, when governor of Delhi towards the end of the 17th century,) mentions Qayyum Khan as this noble's son, and Shukrullah Khan and Shakir Khan as his sons-in-law.

And yet the Urdu biographer of Lahor has the audacity to say that Dr. Bernier witnessed the boiling of young Aqil Khan in a cauldron in the harem! Bernier's story refers to Jahanara's lover, and he took all his facts from Manucci.

From the life-sketch of Aqil Khan we find that he was at the same place with Zeb-un-nisa first at Daulatabad in 1658 (some ten months), then at Lahor in 1663 for a week only, thenceforth with the imperial Court at Delhi and Agra till his resignation in April 1669, again with the Court during the Rajput wars of 1679 and 1680, and finally at Delhi from January 1681 to 1696. It was only during the first and last of these periods that he could have been tempted to court the Princess by the absence of her august father.

The Khan's temporary retirement from service and residence at Lahor away from the Court (November, 1661 —October, 1663) could not have been due to imperial displeasure as he was given a large pension all the time. But his long removal from the capital and Emperor's entourage for ten years (1669—1679) during the first seven of which he was denied any imperial bounty, shows that he had for some reason, unknown to us, fallen under the Emperor's wrath.

Was it a punishment for making love to Zeb-un-nisa? A letter to her from her brother Prince Akbar, written in 1680, contains the statement, "As the Emperor has now ordered that no packet (*nalwo*) bearing the seal of Aqil should be admitted to the ladies' apartments of the palace, it is certain that papers will have to be now sent [by me?] after careful consideration."

Was this Aqil her alleged lover Aqil Khan Razi the poet? I think, not. There was at this time in Akbar's camp a Mulla named Muhammad Aqil, who afterwards signed a manifesto pronouncing canonical sentence of deposition on Aurangzib in favour of Akbar, for which the luckless theologian was imprisoned and severely bastinadoed when his patron's rebellion failed. Zeb being herself a Quranic scholar and a patron of new commentaries on the Muslim scripture, correspondence between her and a noted theologian like Mulla Muhammad Aqil would naturally pass unsuspected. The writer of the letter implies that his own confidential letters to his sister used to be sent under cover of Aqil's envelopes, which could reach her unchallenged, while packets bearing his own seal on the cover might have been intercepted by his enemies. This is quite clear from the concluding part of the letter: "The delay that has taken place in my writing to you is solely due to the fear lest my letters should fall into the hands of other people [lit., strangers, *i.e.*, enemies.]"

The theory that the Emperor stopped the poet and noble Aqil Khan's correspondence with his daughter on detecting an intrigue between them, is discredited by the fact that only a few months afterwards he was appointed to the highly responsible post of viceroy of Delhi, the very place where she was sent as a State-prisoner early next year.

Zeb-un-nisa was imprisoned by her father in January 1681, and the official history establishes beyond dispute the fact that it was in punishment of her complicity with Prince Akbar who had rebelled against the Emperor.

The letter from which we have quoted contains several passages showing how deeply engaged she was in her brother's interests. He says, "What belongs to you is as good as mine, and whatever I own is at your disposal," and, again, "The dismissal or appointment of the sons-in-law of Daulat and Sagar Mal is at your discretion. I have dismissed them at your bidding. I consider your orders in all affairs as sacred like the *Quran* and *Traditions* of the Prophet, and obedience to them as proper."

When Akbar's rebellion frizzled out and his abandoned camp near Ajmir was seized by the imperialists (16th January, 1681), "Zeb-un-nisa's correspondence with him was discovered, she was deprived of her pension of four lakhs of Rupees a year, her property was confiscated, and she was lodged in the fort of Salimgarh at Delhi." (*Masir-i-Alamgiri,* 204.) Here she lived till her death on 26th May, 1702. It would be sweet to imagine that during this captivity our

> High born maiden
> In her palace-tower,
> Soothed her love-laden
> Soul in secret hour
> With music sweet as love, which overflowed her bower,

and that she wrote at this time the pathetic laments which Mrs. Westbrook has translated on page 17:—

> So long these fetters cling to my feet!
> My friends have become enemies, my relations are strangers to me.
> What more have I to do with being anxious to keep my name undishonoured,
> When friends seek to disgrace me?
> Seek not relief from the prison of grief, O Makhfi; thy release is not politic.
> O Makhfi, no hope of release hast thou until the Day of Judgment come.

But history is silent on the point. On the other hand our ardour to weave a romance out of her captive life is chilled by the reflection that she was now an old maid of 43 and Aqil Khan was at least twelve years older and a grandfather.

Another legend makes her fall in love at first sight with Shivaji the Maratha hero on the occasion of his being presented to the Emperor at Agra on 12th May, 1666. Seventy years ago a novel was written by Bhudev Mukherji in Bengali describing how the lovers exchanged rings and parted. But it is a fiction and nothing more. Not to speak of the Persian histories of the time, no Marathi life of Shivaji mentions that a Mughal princess interested herself in the fate of the captive chieftain in her father's capital. None of them gives the smallest hint of the champion of Hindu revival having coquetted with a Muslim sweet-heart in the enemy's den. Zeb-un-nisa's æsthetic sense, too, would have saved her from throwing her heart away to a rugged and illiterate Deccani. The whole story is not only unhistoric, but improbable.

She was not released from captivity at Delhi during her life, but was otherwise well treated. Some six months after she had entered her palace-prison, the Emperor restored her monthly allowance of Rs. 30,000 though with a reduction of 10,000 (*Akh.* 15 Sep. 1681.) A few days later she was given the *Jahanara garden* in Agra, which had belonged to Princess Jahanara just deceased. (*Akh.* 19 Sep.)* The official history records her death thus:—"The Emperor learnt from the news-letter of Delhi that

* There seems to be a mistake in the *Akhbarat* here. The garden *named Jahanara* (and not *belonging to* Princess Jahanara) was laid out by Shah Jahan in Agra, whi'e Princess J's own garden was the *Tis Hazari* in Delhi.

the Princess Zeb-un-nisa had drawn on her face the veil of God's mercy and taken up her abode in the place of inexhaustible forgiveness, [26th May, 1702]. At the parting of his child, dear as his life, his heart was filled with grief and his eyes with tears. He could not control the weakness that overpowered him. [At last] he recovered self-possession [somehow], and ordered Saiyyid Amjad Khan, Shaikh Ataullah, and Hafiz Khan to give away alms [at her funeral] and build a place of repose for her, as had been decided beforehand, in the Garden of Thirty Thousand [outside Delhi] which was a bequest from Jahanara." (*M.A.*, 462.)

A short letter from Aurangzib to Zeb-un-nisa has been preserved in *Faiyyaz-ul-qawanin*, (p. 369) ; one half of it is in Arabic and it tells us nothing about her life. Similarly, some letters written to her by her brother Akbar in 1679-80 and given in *Adab-i-Alamgiri* throw no light on her biography. An Aligarh University manuscript contains some letters written by her secretary Mirza Khalil, thanking [? her] for presents of fruit, game, ice, and a pair of spectacles! In the 32nd year of Aurangzib's reign (1688-1689) Inayet-ullah, the son of her lady-tutor, was appointed steward (*Khan-i-saman*) of her household. (*M. U.*, ii. 828.)

She was buried in the "Garden of Thirty Thousand Trees" outside the Kabuli gate of Delhi ; but her tomb was demolished in making the Rajputana railway line. The current story of her having been buried at Nawakot in the Panjab is absolutely false.

IX

JAHANARA, THE INDIAN ANTIGONE.

The fall of the mighty, the misfortunes of those who had once stood on the crowning slope of rank and wealth, the sorrows that cloud the evening of a life once radiant with health and joy,—have been the apt themes of moralizing prophets and tragic poets. These purge our souls by exciting pity and terror; but they, at the same time, by one stroke sweep away the differences of birth and fame, riches and beauty, and reduce the greatest on earth to the level of the meanest among us. We then realize that the sons of Adam are equal brothers in this vale of tears.

But the instability of fortune is not the choric song heard in the last scene of every such tragedy in history. Enjoyment is not the supreme end of life, nor the highest test of human capacity.

—Life is not as idle ore,
But iron dug from central gloom,
And heated hot with burning fears,
And dipt in baths of hissing tears,
And battered with the shocks of doom
To shape and use.

Sorrow's crown of thorns has sometimes been transformed into a halo of celestial light by duty, by heroic endurance, by self-forgetting sacrifice. Then the victim of Fortune's frowns has triumphed over the worst that she could inflict, and has reached a higher pinnacle of glory than ever before—it may be in life, it may be as a departed name enshrined in the hearts of adoring posterity for all time to come.

II

One such blessed figure in our own land was Jahanara, the eldest child* of the Emperor Shah Jahan. When (in 1614) "this rose of her race first budded forth, the sun of Akbar was still crowning the azure," as a French poet has put it ; (which is true in the sense that the Indian sky was still radiant with the after-glow of Akbar's reign.) Early in the reign of her father, after the death of her mother (1631), she became the first lady in the land and the power behind the throne of the most magnificent of the Grand Mughals, and continued in that high position for twenty-seven years.

Up to the age of forty-four, her life was all happiness and glory, and nothing dimmed the splendour of her noontide. Independent sovereigns of other parts of India, vassal princes of the Mughal empire, members of the imperial family, and nobles of the realm,—all sought her kind intercession in their need, and they never sought it in vain. Her wealth was boundless, as fifty lakhs of Rupees, being one-half of the vast riches left behind by her mother, the glorious "Lady of the Taj," were given

* Not the eldest-born, as her sister Hur-un-nisa had been born a year before her, but she had died at the age of three and therefore did not count.

to her, in addition to her large annual stipend and the revenue of Surat, then the richest port of India. The presents which she received every year from kings and princes, nobles and humbler suppliants, were second in value only to the Emperor's.

And yet she used all this wealth and influence not to gratify insolent pride or love of enjoyment, but for the good of others. At the height of her glory she was known as a ministering angel,—relieving the distressed, healing discords in the royal family, cherishing orphans, and turning away the just anger of the Emperor from offenders by her gentleness.

She had known sorrow. Her loving mother,—mothers usually treat the eldest-born daughter more like a sister and friend than a child,— had died when she was only seventeen. Eleven years later she was most cruelly burnt by accident, and hovered between life and death for four months. She never married and never knew the joys of the highest fruition of woman's existence in motherhood.

At the height of earthly greatness her soul had turned to God and she had entered herself as a disciple (*murida*) of the religious order of the saint Mian Mir (of Lahor). She studied the life and teachings of an earlier saint, Shaikh Muin-ud-din Chishti, and wrote a short account of him in Persian (entitled *Munis-ul-arwah*) for the benefit of other seekers after spiritual light.

III

Within the royal family her mission was the blessed one of a peace-maker. Her brothers opened their hearts to her in their troubles. Dara (who was the nearest to her among them in age, being only one year younger) dearly loved her, and she shared his thoughts, aspirations and even spiritual communings as a Sufi or mystic ; and she treated Dara's wife as a sister and tenderly brought up their orphan daughters after the tragic death of the princely couple (1659), as if they had been her own. Even the cold calculating Aurangzib, who from an early age used to show an inborn aversion to Dara and Dara's friends,—unburdened his soul to her in his need, as the following letter will show:

AURANGZIB TO JAHANARA (1657).

"It is not unknown to you that ever since His Majesty conferred a *mansab* on me, I have performed, to the limit of possibility and my power, every task that he has laid on me. I know not what offence I have now committed that certain measures have been taken by him which are undeserved by a faithful servant like me and will cause my disgrace and show his distrust in me to men far and near. First, the fort of Asir had been originally conferred upon me and then on *Bhai* Murad Bakhsh, and finally on me again ; but now an order has arrived that I must not send my own *qiladar* there! . . .

What disfavour and distrust is being shown to me by His Majesty, as I after my twenty years of devoted and distinguished service to him in disregard of my life and property,—have not yet been judged equal to my nephew *Pathal* (*i.e.*, Sulaiman Shukoh) in gaining His Majesty's confidence!

Secondly, at this time, Dada Bhai Jiu (*i.e.*, Dara Shukoh),—whose characteristic friendliness to me is well-known to His Majesty,—has sent his own agent, named Mulla Shauki (?) to this place [*i.e.*, the Deccan] for the purpose of conveying to the ruler of Bijapur certain happy news and the acceptance of his prayers [by the Emperor] —which will make that ruler and others like him more turbulent. Dear sister, although I have never considered myself as worthy to be ranked among His Majesty's disciples and servants, and have claimed to be nothing more than his slave (*ghulam*), but have been content with any treatment he metes out to me,—yet, as I have spent my life in honour and respect and have governed this province as its supreme master . . . at His Majesty's free grant without any demand or petition from me,—disgrace and loss of authority will come down upon me as the natural consequence of this measure. I have fallen into a whirlpool of perplexity ; I cannot guess His Majesty's intentions with regard to me. . . . If his wish is that among all his servants I alone should spend my days in dishonour and finally be destroyed in an unworthy manner (*i.e.*, be murdered by my usurping eldest brother), then I have no help but to obey. But as it is hard to live and to die thus, . . . it is better that by order of His Majesty I should be released from the shame of continuing such an existence,—my life and head being always a ready sacrifice to His Majesty's pleasure—so that (certain) minds may rest at ease concerning me.

I had learnt this truth ten years before, and been convinced that my life was desired [by Dara.] I had therefore resigned my posts; but afterwards, solely in order to please my father, I had turned to this career (again). . . ."*

IV

The supreme trial came to Jahanarà in 1657. Her father fell seriously ill and then all his four sons took up arms to contest the throne even before the old Emperor had closed his eyes. The story of that tragedy has been unfolded in my *History of Aurangzib,* volumes 1 and 2, from contemporary records and often in the very words of the actors in the drama. It will be enough to say here, in outline, that Dara was the favourite and chosen heir of Shah Jahan; but Aurangzib was by far the ablest of the four brothers, and by a succession of victories made his way to Agra, where the aged Emperor was then in residence. Dara after a crushing defeat at Samugarh, some ten miles east of Agra, fled towards Delhi, and Aurangzib besieged his father in the fort of Agra, and by cutting off his water-supply forced him to capitulate unconditionally after three days of bloodless blockade.

Then Jahanara paid a visit to her victorious brothers (for Prince Murad Bakhsh was allied with Aurangzib) on 10th June 1658, in their camp in the Nur Manzil or Dhara

---

* There are 28 letters from Aurangzib to Jahanara in *Adab-i-Alamgiri*, 18 of which are formal and useless, and two very long and important. One of these two long letters has been translated in extracts above. Its date was not literally *ten years* after Aurangzib's resignation, which would give 1654, but 1657.

garden outside Agra city, and tried to effect a peaceful partition of the empire among the four. But her mission was as futile as the following letter which she had written to Aurangzib before the battle of Samugarh:

JAHANARA TO AURANGZIB (MAY 1658).

"It is the duty of the great Emperors—who are charged with the burden of keeping the empire safe, that they should not be the least remiss or idle in cherishing the people (who are all a trust from the Creator), but should guard them in every way. Praised be God, that His Majesty Shah Jahan is devoting all his time, both day and night,—after performing his religious duties,—to the regulation of the Church and the State; his constant endeavour is to promote the population and safety of the provinces and the happiness of his subjects. Up to now, always in accordance with the rules laid down in the Book and practices of the Best of Men (*i.e.* the Prophet Muhammad), he has made it his business to worship the Lord of Honours, and has not agreed to any conduct that is wrong or evil on the part of any man, especially on the part of his sons, who are adorned with all good qualities of conduct and character.

At this time, by reason of the occurrence of disturbances . . . characteristic of the present age . . . from the violence of turbulent men, disorder has taken place in the transaction of the business of the administration of the realm, far and near, and utter ruin has befallen the peasants and the weak. It is the aim of His Majesty to remedy the misdeeds of the wicked and to show mercy to the miserable and the oppressed.

It is very far removed from the rules of worshipping God and the manner and method of holding the true faith, to set your heart on becoming (at the advice of young people who possess neither the wisdom due to experience nor the sense to learn) the creator of disturbance and rebellion,—undertaking (by the performance of improper acts) the destruction of the life, property and family-honour of the soldiers and peasants who are all Musalmans of pure heart and true faith,—and (after shutting your eyes to what the time requires as most advisable) assembling troops and drawing up forces in battle order against your eldest brother, the heir to the Emperor Shah Jahan, which is externally and internally equivalent to the waging of war against your father.

It is proper that this valiant brother should bring himself close to the valley of true devotion and fair fidelity, promptly obey the imperial order from the bottom of his heart and with life, and not hesitate to manifest what devotion and fidelity require as his conduct. Consider it proper to avoid the wickedness of engaging in battle with your father and putting Muslims to death in the blessed month of Ramzan in which the *Quran* was revealed. Halt at whatever place you may have reached, and inform me of your heart's desires, so that I may report them to His Majesty and get all things done."*

* The text is very corrupt in the Persian MS. now before me and the translation is at places doubtful.

To this Aurangzib replied in a long letter addressed not to Jahanara but directly to Shah Jahan and justifying his own action by arguments which I have summarized in my *Aurangzib*, ch. 17, (vol. 2, p. 414).

V

At the final downfall of Shah Jahan, Jahanara might have imitated the conduct of her younger sister Raushanara and revelled in wealth, pleasure and freedom by coming over to Aurangzib's Court. But she chose the better part with Antigone and Cordelia. The story of her self-sacrifice for the sake of her afflicted father is told in a most dramatic fashion by the French poet Leconte de Lisle. Aurangzib cries out:

"See! I am Alamgir, the conquerer of the world.
I have conquered, I have punished, I have gathered in my arms
The sheaves of the goodly crop sown by Timur Khan,
And from the royal field burnt the tare unclean."
"—But what hast thou done with thy father, Aurang, son of Shah Jahan?"

To her indignant question Aurangzib replies,—

—"Jahanara! it was the will of God
That my brows should be branded under this band of flame.
Come, my guardian shadow shall watch thee, child,
And, whatever his fate, thy wish shall I grant.
My hands have respected my venerable father.

Fear no more. He shall live, honoured though captive be,
Pondering in his heart, of vain dreams chastened,
Over fragile human glory to swift end hastening."

Jahanara rejected this offer with scorn and said,

"Aurang! Load my arm with a part of his (*i.e.*, Shah Jahan's) chain;
That is my dearest prayer, my fairest dream!
In order that the aged [Shah] Jahan may pardon his executioner,
In order that I may abjure equally bitterness and hatred,
Bury us, living, in one and the same tomb."

Then, the French poet continues in enraptured verses,

Well, thou didst live ten years close to that sombre old man,
Jahanara! charming his sorrow and his calamity;
And when he laid himself down in his royal sepulchre.
Thy fair body was tarnished and became as a shadow,
And thy spirit took wing in a filial shriek.
Thus didst thou disappear, solitary star!
From this vast sky where nothing so pure has shone:
Thy very name,—thy name so sweet, was forgotten,
And God alone remembered, when thou didst quit the earth,
The angel whom He had sent to this world.

VI

Shah Jahan died in January 1666, after seven and a half years of captivity,—Jahanara nursing him to the end and, when all was over, arranging for his homely funeral, (as has been described fully in my *Aurangzib*, vol. 3). On the receipt of the news of his father's death, Aurangzib wrote this letter of condolence to his sister:

AURANGZIB TO JAHANARA (JANUARY 1666).

"The Creator of the Universe,—May His name be glorified!—give this gracious friend, in this great misfortune, perfect patience and thus bestow on her a great reward. What shall I write, and how can writing suffice, to express what passes in my sorrow-stricken mind at this inevitable occurrence? Has the pen the power to write one word about this heart-breaking pain? Where has the tongue strength enough to express this patience-robbing grief? Imagination of your sorrow and mourning throws my strengthless heart into greater weeping and agitation. But, against the divine dispensation and the will of Heaven, we have no remedy save helplessness and bowing the head down in submission. (Arabic prayer).

Know that, God willing, this ashamed creature will reach you soon, with all his pain of heart. It is certain that you are giving the needful consolation to the mourners for his late Majesty, especially [his widow] Akbarabadi Mahal.

Dear sister! the thing that will be useful to the late Emperor at this time is the conveying [to his soul] the religious merit of reciting the *Quran* and giving alms to beggars. Exert yourself to the utmost in this matter, and offer the merit of these acts as a present to the resplendent soul of his late Majesty. This sinner, too, is engaged in the same work; and he hopes that it would be accepted [by God]."

JAHANARA TO AURANGZIB (in reply to the above letter of condolence):

"May God ever keep the shadow of the favour of the Emperor Alamgir constant and enduring over the head of the universe! What power has the pen to describe this heart-piercing calamity and report even a fraction of the condition of this dark day? What capacity has the tongue to narrate to the mind the affliction that has come down [upon me]? What has befallen me in consequence of this event, would have dried up the ocean if it had struck it, and would have turned the day into a gloomy night if it had alighted on the day. It is true that wisdom tells us that in such calamities no remedy is possible save recourse to patience and self-control, and no help is conceivable except holding fast [to the reading of] the verses [of the Book] of God and the Traditions of the Prophet which have descended on earth for teaching resignation and peace of mind. But, the volume of my grief is more than the strength of my endurance.

At the time when I was sunk in the ocean of grief and mourning, with a heart full of sorrow and eyes covered with tears,—the rays of the Sun of this loving brother's grace shone forth; and at once it seemed as if the water of life had been thrown on the raging fire of my [grief]. Therefore, having withdrawn myself from prostration and uncontrolled grief, I gave my heart consolation from the [written] counsels of this august world-illuminating star of kingship and engaged myself in praying for the increase of your life and fortune. I am hoping that this life-destroying fire [of grief] would be quenched by the water of your visit and my dark night would be changed into the clearness of dawn.

You have written about the mourners for Shah Jahan, especially Akbarabadi Mahal. It is evident and clear that henceforth the full care of all those left behind by him* will depend upon your favour and attention. In these circumstances what can I write that is not obvious to you?"

This happened in 1666. The death of Shah Jahan freed Jahanara from her self-chosen captivity. She now came out of the fort and lived in the city in the former mansion of Ali Mardan Khan, honoured and consulted by Aurangzib and cherishing Dara's orphan daughters. Thus she lived on for 15 years more, and when she died, on 6th September, 1681, she desired to be buried in the low, roofless tomb uncovered by tombstone but with grass growing on its top, that she had built for herself under the shadow of the gorgeous sepulchre of the saint Nizam-ud-din Auliya, outside Shah Jahan's city of Delhi. There repose the mortal remains of the Indian Antigone. The epitaph runs thus:

Let no man cover my grave save with green grass, for this grass is the fittest mantle for the tomb of the lowly.

X

A MUSLIM HEROINE.

A WARDEN OF THE MARCHES.

A noble Persian family of Yezd into which two daughters of the Safavi kings of Persia had been married, took refuge in India early in the seventeenth century and rose to high distinction in the service of the Mughal Emperors. One grandson of the first immigrant was Paymaster under Shah Jahan, and another, named Khalilullah Khan, was a provincial governor and married a niece of the Empress Mumtaz Mahal. Their son Amir Khan was a noble of the first rank in the reign of Aurangzib and governed Afghanistan for 20 years with remarkable success and reputation.

He acquired his knowledge of mountaineers and hill-fighting by acting as the military commander of the Jammu hills and afterwards leading a punitive expedition against the Yusufzai Afghans of Shahbazgarhi (near Langarkot), whose villages he destroyed and whose cattle he drove away with great ability and firmness. Even when posted in Bihār as governor, he was not rid of the Afghans ; there was a colony of these turbulent men in that province at Shahjahanpur and Kant-golah, who rebelled and were defeated and captured by Amir Khan.

After these preparatory experiences came the great opportunity of his life ; in March, 1677, he was appointed *subahdar* (viceroy) of Afghanistan, and, arriving at Kabul on 8th June 1678, filled the post with undimmed brilliancy till the day of his death, 28th April, 1698.

Amir Khan's reputation for tact, administrative capacity and power of command was unequalled in his time, so that when in May 1683 Aurangzib proposed to return to Northern India leaving the Deccan in charge of Shah Alam, that prince declined the onerous task unless Amir Khan was given to him as his second in command. Amir Khan agreed to go to the Deccan if he was allowed to hold his Kabul viceroyalty by deputy while serving in the Deccan, a condition which was impossible. [Jaipur records, iii.]

His first meeting with his new subjects was not a happy one. An Afghan named Akmal Khan had set up as king of the hillmen and struck coins in his own name. The first expedition against the rebels near the Lamghanat ended in the rout of the imperial forces. The sword having failed, the new governor took to policy. He engaged himself in winning the hearts of the Afghans with such success that the chiefs of the clans "left their shy and unsocial manners and began to visit him without any suspicion."

His statesmanship bore such good fruit that "during his government of 20 years no disaster befell him, and no administrative failure or disorder took place. Robbery and oppression were kept down by his firmness and activity. Whatever he planned succeeded ; all his desires were fulfilled."

On 25th October 1681, Aurangzib received a despatch

from Amir Khan stating, "Six lakhs of Rupees are allotted by Government every year to be paid to the Afghans for guarding the roads. I have spent one and a half lakhs for this purpose, and saved the remainder to the State." After this governor's death Aurangzib wrote a letter describing Amir Khan's administrative methods, how he was a just ruler, possessed of practical skill and tact in dealing with all men; how he used to make savings in the budgeted expenditure of the province and keep the passes open to traffic; how he kept many of the hillmen usefully employed by enlisting them in the imperial army and profusely bribed the clans to keep the peace, paying them out of the imperial coffers, his private income and his illegal exactions. [*Kalimat-i-Tay*. 16*b*, 11*b*.]

The tribal chiefs became thoroughly obedient to him; every one of them looked up to him for advice in conducting his own affairs. Under his astute guidance they ceased to trouble the imperial Government and spent their energies in internecine quarrels! His cleverness made him triumph over every difficulty.

Once there was a great gathering of the Afghans under Akmal. There was hardly any tribe that did not join him. Every male fighter in the hills took provisions for a few days and attended the muster. The *subahdar's* army was too small to encounter a nation in arms. Amir Khan was alarmed. took counsel with a very clever subordinate, Abdullah Khan Kheshgi, and made him write feigned letters to the head of every tribe in the rebel camp, saying, "We had long been waiting for such a happy event as that the government of the country would pass to the Afghans. Thank God, our long deferred hope is at last being fulfilled. But we do not know the character of your new king. If he is worthy to rule, write, and we shall join you, as service under the Mughals is not to our liking."

The Afghan chieftains highly praised Akmal Khan in their replies. Then Abdullah Khan wrote again, "All this praise is good no doubt; but is your leader so eminently just as to treat his kinsmen and strangers with impartial equality? Try him by asking him to parcel out among the clans the land already conquered. Then you will find out whether he has any greed or reluctance to be impartial to all."

At this the tribesmen made the proposal to him. Akmal declined, saying, "How can a small territory be divided among so many men?"

All was now dissension in the Afghan camp. Many of the hillmen immediately returned home in anger. Akmal Khan had at last to make a division of land; but as he naturally showed greater consideration to his own clan and kinsmen, the quarrel broke out afresh. All the other chiefs left him in disgust, and wrote to dissuade Abdullah Khan from joining such a bad king! Surely the policy of *divide et impera* has never triumphed so well in Afghanistan.

Amir Khan was a bigoted Shia, for which reason the equally bigoted Sunni Aurangzib hated him at heart. But the Emperor concealed his ill-will during the governor's lifetime and kept him satisfied for his eminent services, as he frankly admits in one of his letters. It was only after Amir Khan's death that Aurangzib threw off the mask and ordered a strict escheat of his property from his sons. [*Ruqat*, No. 99 ; *K. T.* 26*b*.]

A WOMAN WHO RULED THE AFGHANS.

Amir Khan's wife, Sahibji (=Her Ladyship), was a daughter of Ali Mardan Khan, a highly gifted Persian, who rose to be the Premier Noble of the Court of Shah Jahan. She was a wonderfully clever and expert woman. In conducting the administration she was her husband's partner. His success in many a difficulty was due to her wise suggestions and business capacity. *She* was the real governor of Kabul.

One night the Emperor Aurangzib learnt from the report of Kabul the news of Amir Khan's death. Immediately summoning Arshad Khan (who had formerly acted as *diwan* of Afghanistan), he said in a tone of concern, "A great difficulty has cropped up. Amir Khan is dead. That province, which is ever ripe for a thousand disturbances and troubles, has now none to govern it. A disaster may happen before the arrival of his successor."

Arshad Khan boldly replied, "Amir Khan lives. Who calls him dead?"

The Emperor handed him the report from Kabul. The Khan read it and added, "Yes ; but then it is Sahibji who governed and controlled the province. So long as *she* lives your Majesty need not fear any disorder."

The Emperor at once wrote to the lady to guard the province till the arrival of her husband's successor in office, which, however, happened two years afterwards.* During this interval she was the sole governor of Afghanistan, as she had been in all but the name in her husband's lifetime.

Death overtook Amir Khan when he was out among the valleys. If the fact had got wind, the Afghans would have taken heart and massacred his leaderless escort in their narrow defiles. Sahibji with great presence of mind suppressed her grief, concealed his death, dressed a man like Amir Khan, made him sit in a *palki* with glass doors, and thus marched long distances. Every day she inspected the troops and received their salute. It was only after issuing safely from the hills that she went into mourning.

After her husband's death, all the Afghan chieftains sent their relatives to condole with her. She treated them with great respect and sent word to the headmen, "Take your customary dues. Do not rebel or rob, but remain obedient as before. Otherwise, I defy you to a fight.† If I defeat you, my name will remain famous to the end of time."

The headmen out of regard for fair play gave her new promises and assurances of their loyalty and did not break out in lawlessness.

---

* This story of the *Masir-ul-umara* is contradicted by the official records of Aurangzib's reign which tell us that Amir Khan's *son* was put in temporary charge of the Government of Kabul after his death, and that Prince Shah Alam assumed the subahdarship soon after that event.

† Lit., "Here is the ball and here the polo field," *i.e.*, a challenge to a contest.

Her courage and presence of mind had been as conspicuous in her youth. Years ago at Delhi she was passing by a lane in a *chaudol*. (sedan chair). The Emperor's own elephant—the chief of its species—appeared in an infuriated (*mast*) condition before her. Her attendants wanted to turn it back. But the *mahuts* as a class are vicious, and this one was further proud of being the Emperor's own driver. So he urged the elephant rashly onward. Her escort pulled out their arrows from the quivers ; but the brute flung its trunk on the *chaudol* to seize and trample it down. The porters dropped it and fled. Quick as thought Sahibji jumped out, ran into a money-changer's shop hard by, and shut the door. This was no common feat of agility, as a Muslim noblewoman travelling on the public road must have been securely wrapped up like a parcel sent by post in the rainy reason.

She had saved her life, but alas! she had broken *pardah*,—an unpardonable offence against Indian etiquette. Amir Khan was angry at her audacity, and for a few days lived in separation from her. Then the Emperor Shah Jahan told him frankly, "She has played a man's part ; she has saved her own and your honour at the same time. If the elephant had seized her and exposed her (bare body) to the public, what privacy would have been left?"

So she was taken back by her husband. Amir Khan might have cried out to his heroic wife,

> "Bring forth men children only!
> For thy undaunted mettle should compose
> Nothing but males."

But, alas! she was childless like Lady Macbeth. Her

husband, in fear of her, durst not take another wife, but kept a secret harem and had children by them. At last Sahibji discovered it, but recognised and lovingly brought up her step-sons. She had adopted a little girl who was reputed to be a Sayyid's daughter, and afterwards gave her in marriage to a Persian emigrant from Mashhad named Mir Muhammad Husain, who founded a curious new sect and declared himself its Pope (*Beguk*, midway between a Prophet and an Imam) with the title of *Namud*. (For a detailed account of him, *Siyar*, ii. 63—67.)

On being relieved of the government of Kabul, the widowed Sahibji made a pilgrimage to Mecca and Medina, where she gave away large sums in charity and was highly honoured by the Sharif and other people of the holy cities. [*M. U.* i. 277—287.]

XI

SHAISTA KHAN IN BENGAL (1664—1666.)

THE MANUSCRIPT SOURCE.

When Mir Jumla invaded Kuch Bihar and Assam, he had in his train an officer named Shihabuddin Talish, who has left a detailed history of the expedition, named by the author the *Fathiyyah-i-ibriyyah.* A long abstract of it was given by Blochmann in the Bengal Asiatic Society's *Journal* for 1872, Part I, No. 1 pp. 64-96. This Society has a fine old Ms of this work (D. 72), and the Khuda Bakhsh Library has three others. All these end with the death of Mir Jumla, 31st March, 1663.

But the Bodleian Library possesses a Ms of the work (No. Bod. 589, Sachau and Ethe's *Catalogue,* Part I, No. 240), supposed to be the author's autograph, which contains a continuation (folios 106*a*—176*b*), relating the events immediately following Mir Jumla's death and bringing the history down to Buzurg Ummed Khan's victorious entry into Chatgaon (Chittagong), 27 January, 1666. This portion is absolutely unique and of the greatest importance for the history of Bengal.

The internal evidence is overwhelming in favour of the *Continuation* being regarded as Shihabuddin Talish's work. The style is marked by the same brilliancy of rhetoric ; many favourite phrases and turns of expression are common to both the works ; and one peculiar sentence, which I have found in no other Persian history, occurs in both (*Conquest of Assam*, p. 58 of Ms D. 72, and *Continuation*, folio 124*a*). We have here (*f.* 156*b*) one instance of the author's imitation of Amir Khusrau's vicious rhetorical trick of running the variations of a single simile through a whole page of which there are three examples in the *Conquest.* The writer is the same hero-worshipper, only Shaista Khan here takes the place of Mir Jumla.

The author evidently died while writing the *Continuation*, for it ends abruptly, without carrying on the campaign in the Chatgaon District to its conclusion. He had no time to give it his finishing touches : the material is loosely arranged ; there is no regular division into chapters as in the *Conquest*, but only three headings (*surkhi*), these being on *ff.* 150*b*, 153*a*, and 161*b*. Moreover, the author has left blanks for dates in two places (*ff.* 149*b* and 175*b*), which he evidently meant to fill up after consulting other sources. Wrong dates are given on 106*a* and 167*a*, and some obscurity has been introduced into the narrative by his passing over the first day of the siege of Chatgaon (25th January, 1666) in absolute silence.

The *Continuation* supplies us with useful and original information on the following four subjects :—

(1) Shaista Khan's administration of Bengal up to January, 1666. (2) The system of piracy followed by the Feringis of Chatgaon, and a record of the various Magh incursions into Bengal and Bengal attacks on the Maghs. (3) A description of Sondip island and the history of its

conquest. (4) A description of Chatgaon and the history of its conquest by the imperialists.

I shall here deal with the first.

SHAISTA KHAN'S CIVIL ADMINISTRATION.

(*Translation*)

[117*a*] The mansabdars had their jagirs situated in different parganahs, and the multiplicity of co-partners led to the humble ryots being oppressed and the parganahs desolated. Large sums were wasted [in the cost of collection] as many *shiqdars* and *amlas* had to be sent out by [every] jagirdar. Therefore, the Nawwab ordered the *diwan-i-tan* to give every jagirdar *tankha* in one place only; and, if in any parganah any revenue remained over and above the tankha of a jagirdar [117*b*], it was to be made over to the jagirdar for collection and payment into the public treasury. Thus the department of Crown-lands would make a saving by not having to appoint collectors [of its own in the parganahs of jagirdars]; and, secondly, it was not good for one place to have two rulers [*viz.*, the jagirdar's and Government collectors]. The *diwan-i-tan* set himself to carry out this work.

Next, Shaista Khan learnt the truth about the appointments and promotions made after Mir Jumla's death by the acting subahdars. Most of these men were now dismissed; a few, who were really necessary for the administration, were retained in service. I have noted this difference between Shaista Khan and other servants of the Crown, in the matter of saving Government money, that they desire solely to gain credit with the Emperor, while his aim is pure devotion and loyal service. He considers the least parading of this fact as akin to hypocrisy and remote from true devotion and fidelity.

At this time the *aimadars* and stipend-holders of the province of Bengal began to flock to the Nawwab to make complaints [118*a*]. The facts of their case were:— After the reign of Shah Jahan, the late Khan-i-khanan [Mir Jumla] confirmed in his own jagirs many of these men who were celebrated for devotion to virtue and love of the Prophet's followers, and some who had got *farmans* of the Emperor. All other men who had been enjoying *madad-i-m'aāsh* and pensions in the Crown-lands and the fiefs of jagirdars, were violently attacked by Qazi Rizvi, the Sadr; their *sanads* were rejected and their stipends and subsistence cancelled. It was ordered that the *aimadars* should take to the business of cultivators, till all the lands they held in *madad-i-m'aāsh,* and pay revenue for them to the department of Crown-lands or to the jagirdars. And, as in carrying out this hard order these poor creatures could not get any respite, many who had some means sold their property, pledged their children [as serfs], and thus paid the revenue for the current year [118*b*], preserving their lives as their only stock for the next year. Some, who had no property, brought on themselves torture and punishment, gave up their lives, and thus escaped from all anxiety about the next year.

(*Verse*)

Like fire they ate sticks [*i.e.*, received beating] and
gave up gold [or sparks],
And then, through loss of strength, they fell down
dead in misery.

And now even by the resumption of the cultivated lands sufficient gain in the form of produce cannot be collected, because the *aimadars* abstain from tilling the lands that have been escheated to the State ; and even the chastisement and pressure of the *amlas* cannot make them engage in cultivation. And so the land remains waste and the *aimadars* poor and aggrieved. Owing to the great distance and the fear of calamities, these poor perplexed sufferers could not go to Delhi to report their condition fully to the Emperor and get the wicked and oppressive officials punished [119*a*]. Hence their sighs and lamentations reached the sky.

One Friday, the Nawwab, as was his custom, went [to the mosque] to offer his Congregation prayer. After it was over he learnt that an old *aimadar* had suspended himself upside down, his head one yard above the ground, from a tree near the mosque, and that he was on the brink of death and was saying: (*Verse*)

Shall my life return [to my body] or shall it go out,—
what is thy command?

The Nawwab ordered the author to go and ask him the reason. I went to the old man and inquired. He replied, "My son, who held thirty *bighas* of land in *madad-i-m'aāsh*, has died. The *amlas* now demand from me one year's revenue of the land. As I have no wealth, I shall give up my life and thus free myself [from their oppression]." I reported the matter to the Nawwab, who gave him a large sum, and then confirmed his son's rent-free land on him. (*Verse*)

> God favours that man,
> Whose life gives repose to the people. [119*b*.]

The wise know that the resumption of the lands of *aimadars* and the cutting off of the subsistence of stipend-holders bring on great misfortunes and terrible consequences [on the wrong-doer]. I have seen some among the rulers of this country who engaged in this wicked work and could not live through the year. (*Verse*)

> The dark sigh of sufferers, in the heart of dark nights,
> Snatches away by [God's] command the mole
> of prosperity from the cheek of the oppressor.

It is a lasting act of virtue and an undying deed of charity to bestow *imlak* on the needy and *idrar* on the poor. The hindering of such liberality and the stoppage of such charity does not bring any gain in this world and involves one in the Creator's wrath in the next.........

[120*a*] One day there was a talk on this subject in the Nawwab's court. As "the words of kings are kings among words," he remarked, "If a man has not grace enough to increase the gifts made to these [poor] people, he should at least not deprive them of what others gave them [120*b*], because . . . . these people, too, should be counted among the needy. And one should not

through his own meanness of spirit and vileness of heart resume the charitable gifts of others."

In short, the Nawwab's natural kindness having been excited, he ordered that Mir Sayyid Sadiq, the Sadr, should fully recognise the *madad-i-'aash* and *wazifa* which these men had been enjoying in the Crown-lands according to the reliable *sanads* of former rulers. As for what was held [rent-free] in the fiefs of jagirdars, if it amounted to one-fortieth of the total revenue of the jagirdar, he should consider it as the *zakat* (tithe) on his property and spare it. But if the rent-free land exceeded one-fortieth [of the total jagir], the jagirdar was at liberty to respect or resume [the excess]. Whosoever held whatever rent-free land in the parganahs of the jagir of the Nawwab, on the strength of the *sanad* of whomsoever, was to be confirmed in it without any diminution, and was on no account to be troubled [by any demand of revenue]. As for those who had no means of subsistence and now, for the first time, begged daily allowances and lands in the jagir of the Nawwab, the *diwani* officers were ordered to further their desires without any delay.

The Sadr carried out the above order in the case of the Crown-lands and the jagirs of [other] jagirdars [121*a*]. In the jagir of the Nawwab his *diwan-i-bayutat*, Khawajah Murlidhar,—who had been brought up and trained in the Nawwab's household, was marked by honesty and politeness, possessed his master's confidence and trust, and, in spite of his still being in the flower of youth, had the wisdom and patience of old men,—displayed in this work of benevolence such zeal and exertion as, I pray, God may favour all Musalmans with. Every day two to three hundred *aimadars* presented their *sanads* to him and then departed. Next day, in the presence of the Nawwab, he passed them through the Record office and sealed them, and then gave them back to the *aimadars*. In short, he exhibited such great labour and praiseworthy diligence in this business, that every one of this class of men got what he desired. And the aforesaid Khawajah gained a good name and respect for himself, temporal and spiritual welfare for his master, and prayers for the perpetuaton of the empire for the Solomon-like Emperor. (*Verse*) [121*b*]

> That man's influence with the king is a blessed thing,
> Who forwards the suits of the distressed.

SHAISTA KHAN'S GOOD DEEDS.

(*Translation.*)

[127*a*] I. His exertions for conquering the province and fort of Chatgaon ; the suppression of the pirates, and the consequent relief of the people of Bengal.

II. Every day he held open *darbar* for administering justice, and quickly redressed wrongs. He regarded this as his most important duty.

III. He ordered that in the parganahs of his own jagir everything collected by the revenue officers above the fixed revenue should be refunded to the ryots. [127*b*].

IV. The former governors of Bengal used to make

monopolies (*ijara*) of all articles of food and clothing and [many] other things, and then sell them at fanciful prices which the people in need of them had no help but to pay. Shaista Khan restored absolute freedom of buying and selling.

V. Whenever ships brought elephants and other [animals] to the ports of the province, the men of the subahdar used to attach (*qurq*) them and take whatever they selected at prices of their own liking. Shaista Khan forbade it.

VI. His abolition of the collection of *zakat* (*i.e.*, one-fortieth of the income) from merchants and travellers, and of custom (*hasil*) from artificers, tradesmen and new-comers,* Hindus and Musalmans alike. The history of it is as follows :—

From the first occupation of India and its ports by the Muhammadans to the end [128*a*] of Shah Jahan's reign, it was a rule and practice to exact *hasil* from every trader,—from the rose-vendor down to the clay-vendor, from the weaver of fine linen to that of coarse cloth,—to collect house-tax from new-comers and hucksters, to take *zakat* from travellers, merchants and stable-keepers (*mukāri*). As Sadi has said, "At first oppression's basis was small ; but every successive generation increased it," [so it happened], till at last in all provinces, especially in Bengal, it reached such a stage that tradesmen and

* *Khush-nashin*, which may also mean 'well-to-do men.'

merchants gave up their business, and householders took to exile, saying—(*Verse*)

> "We shall flee from the oppression of the Age,
> To such a place that Time cannot track us there."

The rulers, out of greed for *hasil*, gave them no relief. On the roads and ferries matters came to such a pass that no rider was allowed to go on unless he paid a *dinar*, and no pedestrian unless he paid a *diram*. On the river-highways if the wind brought it to the ears of the toll-collectors (*rah-dars*) that the stream was carrying away a broken boat without paying *hasil*, they would chain the river with waves [128*b*]. If the ferry-officers heard that the wave had brought to the bank a broken plank as *zakat*, they would pat it on the back of its head in the form of a gentle breeze. They might be considered as acting with unparalleled leniency if no higher *zakat* was taken from rotten clothes actually worn [on the body] than from mended rags, and with extreme graciousness if cooked food was charged a lower duty than uncooked grain. None of the Delhi sovereigns, in spite of their efforts to strengthen the Faith and follow the rules of the Prophet, put down these wicked and [canonically] illegal practices, but connived at them. Only, we read in histories, Firuz Shah forbade these unjust exactions. But after him they were restored, nay increased. But when, by the grace of God [129*a*] Aurangzib ascended the throne, he sent orders to the governors of the provinces and the clerks of the administration not to do such things in future. He thus gave relief to the inhabitants of villages and travellers by [129*b*] land and sea from these harassments and illegal demands. The learned know that no other king of the past showed such graciousness, made such strong exertions, and remitted to the people such a large sum—which equalled the total revenue of Turan. (*Verses*)

O God! Keep long over the heads of the people,
This King, the friend of holy men,
Whose shadow gives repose to the people.
Through the guidance of [Thy] worship, keep his heart alive.

I strongly hope that, just as the peasants and merchants have been released from oppression and innovations [in taxation], so someone would fully and freely report to the Emperor the distress among the soldiery and the fact of their being harassed and crushed by the oppression of the thievish clerks, and thereby release the soldiers from the tyranny of these godless men [130*a*]. The army is treated by the Hindu clerks, and drowsy writers as more degraded than a fire-worshipping slave and more unclean than the dog of a Jew. Whenever that forked-tongued cobra, their pen, brings its head out of the hole of the ink-pot, it does not write on the rent-roll (*tumar*) of their dark hearts any letter except to pounce upon and snatch away the subsistenc of the soldiers. Indeed, when their tongue begins to move in the hole of their mouth, it does not spit out anything except the curtailment of the stipends of the soldiery. At times they would senselessly split a hair, and do not abstain from numerous unjust fines.

Again, if after life-long exertion and the showering of bribes, they are induced to sign the descriptive roll (*fard-i-čhehra*) of any soldier, then, at the time of branding (*dagh*) they designate a charger worthy of Rustam as a mere pack-horse, and on the day of verification (*hashiha*) they describe [in the records] a horse that stands erect as one fit for the yoke, a horse that bends its leg as lame, a horse that shies as doubtful, a horse that lacks a particle of hair as *Taghlibi.* They call a Daudi coat of mail the film of a was" and a steel helmet itself a small linen cap. They regard a Rustam as a Zal, and a Zal as a mere child. May God the Giver [130*b*] reward with the long life of Noah, the patience of Job, and the treasures of Corah that valiant man, brave like Asfandiar, who after traversing these hill-tops (=hindrances) gets his *tasdiq yad-dasht qabz* and *barat* passed through the Haftkhan of the accounts department, so that his business may be done. In the shambles of the office of Crown-lands, stipend-holders have to flay themselves [before getting their dues], and at the sacrificial altar of the office of the *diwan-i-tan, tankha-dars* find it necessary to root out their own lives. O ye faithful! Did man ever hear of such tyranny as that each letter of the identification-marks in the record office should be written by a [different] clerk? O ye Muslims! Did man ever see such oppression as that one word has to be written by ten men? In [making out] the pay assignment-paper (*barat*) they decrease the *tankha* due and magnify the deduction to be made. If, through a mistake, the balance is entered in the receipts (*qabuz*), they treat it as a true record and appropriate the amount to themselves. And they think that they have conferred a great obligation if they consent to [issue such a paper as] this:—"In the parganah of Wiranpur (City of Desolation) in the *sarkar* of Adamabad (Depopulation), tracts are assigned on the revenue in jagir [to the duped soldier?] and [he should] demand from the jagirdar *Khana-kharab* (Ruined) the arrears of many years at this place." A day's difference in the verification (*tashiha*) is seized upon as a ground for making a year's deduction [from the trooper's pay.] If a man has entered service on the 1st Farwardi, they assign *tankha* to him from the end of the coming Asfandiar. For the single grain of wheat (=fruit of the tree of knowledge, in Muslim mythology) which Father Adam, in his jagir of the *sarkar* of Jannatabad (Paradise), ate without [131*a*] authorisation, they demand from his progeny refund amounting to an ass's load. If a man's pay is due for 3 years, they designate it as one for many years and then write [only] one-half of it (?). The faces of the clerks of the *taujih* (register) are disagreeable. The answer of the author of this journal is, "The state of not being in need is better, without the need of taking oaths [to it]." No harm has been done to me by these men (the clerks), and no confusion has been introduced into my affairs by them ; but [I write] from seeing and hearing what they have done to the helpless and the weak in the court [of the Nawwab] and in the provinces far and near. (*Verse.*)

> My heart is oppressed, and the pain is so great,
> That so much blood gushes out of it.

In short, the Emperor's orders for abolishing *zakat* and *hasil*, sent to Bengal, were for abolishing them in the parganahs of the Crownland. The Nawwab had a free choice in his jagir with regard to all exactions except the *rahdari* and the prohibited cesses (*abwabs*). But this just, God-fearing, benevolent governor, out of his sense of justice and devotion to God, abolished the *hasil* amounting to 15 lakhs of Rupees which used to be collected [131*b*] in his own jagir, and he thus chose to please God, relieve the people, and follow his religious master (Aurangzib).

VII. In many parganahs the despicable practice had long existed that when any man, ryot or newcomer (*khush-nashin*), died without leaving any son, all his property including even his wife and daughters was taken possession of by the department of the Crownlands or the jagirdar or zamindar who was in authority; and this custom was called *ankura* [=hooking]. The Nawwab put down this wicked practice.

VIII. In the *kotwali chabutras* (police stations) of this country it was the custom that whenever a man proved a loan or claim against another, or a man's stolen property [was recovered], the clerks of the *chabutra,* in paying to the claimant his due, used to seize for the State one-fourth of it under the name of "fee for exertion." The Nawwab abolished it.

IX. When the plaintiff and defendant presented themselves at the magistracy (*muhakuma*), both of them were kept in prison until the decision of their case, which was wilfully delayed. And the summons-servers (*itlaq-goian*) took daily allowances from the prisoners and paid them into the State. This evil custom, too, was now abolished.

X. The courtiers [132*a*] used daily to present to the Nawwab many needy persons, and he made them happy with gifts of money. When he set out on a ride or dismounted at a stage or took a walk, and also on the day of *Id* and other holy days, in addition to [supporting] the established almshouses, he used to invite the populace and feed vast numbers to satiety at the tables he spread. His profuse charity so thoroughly removed poverty and need from Bengal that few hired labourers or workmen could be had [for money] to do any work . . . . . Every year he used to send to all the provinces vast sums for the benefit of the faqirs, orphans, and motherless children, and thus laid in *viaticum* for his last journey.

XII

THE FERINGI PIRATES OF CHATGAON, 1665 A.D.

[*from the contemporary Persian account of Shihabuddin Talish, in the Bodleian Ms.* 589.]

ARRACAN DESCRIBED.

[153*a*]. The fort of Chatgaon is an appurtenance of the kingdom of Arracan, which is a large country and great port of the east. One side of it is enclosed by high hills which join the mountains of Kashmir, China, Cathay, and Mahachin. Another side is bordered by the ocean. Deep rivers and wide oceans enclose the western side, which adjoins Bengal. The land and water routes alike for entering the country are very difficult. Its conquest is an extremely hard task. The people of the country are called Maghs,—which is an abbreviation of *Muhamil-i-sag* (=despicable dog), according to [the proverb] "The name descends from heaven." They do not admit into their country any other tribe than the Christians, who visit it by the sea-route for purposes of trade. Good elephants abound ; horses are totally wanting. This writer has heard from the Khan-i-Khanan [Mir Jumla] that the elephants of Arracan surpass all other elephants in beauty of appearance and character. Some mines of metals are said to exist in the country. The inhabitants have no definite faith or religion, but incline rather to the Hindu creed.

Their learned men are called *Rawlis*; they do not transgress the guidance of the latter in their earthly affairs. The *Rawlis* have the ways of the *Sewrahs* [=Shwetambar Jains]. The Rajahs of this country hold pre-eminence over other lower rulers, by reason of their large forces, spacious country, and great splendour. The governors of the ports and islands of the east always show respect and meekness to them. These Rajahs are so proud and foolish that so long as the sun does not decline from the zenith they do not put their heads out of the doors of their palace; they say, "The sun is our younger brother. How can we hold Court while he is over our heads and we below him?" In their decrees and letters they give themselves the titles of "Elder brother of the Sun, Lord of the Golden House and White Elephant." Of their offspring that base-born son is considered the proper heir to the throne whom they have begotten on the person of their own sister. After the conquest of Chatgaon [by Shaista Khan] it was found from the records of the place that the year was written as 1127.* On being asked to account for the date, the people said that the beginning of the era was the beginning of their royal dynasty, and that the aforesaid years had passed since the establishment of the rule of these Rajahs. This fact makes it clear that in this long period [of 1127 years] no foreigner had succeeded in conquering the country, and no outsider had got into it. Their cannon are beyond numbering, their flotilla

* This should be 1027. In the Burmese vulgar era, used also in Arracan, 1027 corresponds to 1665 A.D. (*Bengal and Agra Gazetteer.*)

(*nawwara*) exceeds the waves of the sea [in number]. Most of their ships are *ghurabs* and *jalbas ; khalus* and *dhums* are larger than *ghurabs ;* these are so strongly made of timber with a hard core (*az chob-i-qalbdar*) that the balls of *zamburaks* and small cannon cannot pierce them. [Latterly] the Rajah appointed the Feringi pirates to plunder Bengal, and hence he did not send the Arracan fleet for the purpose.

OLD CHATGAON DESCRIBED.

[162*a*.] Chatgaon is a tract adjacent to Bengal and Arracan alike. From Jagdia, where there was a [Mughal] outpost, to Chatgaon lay a wilderness. On the skirt of the hill was a dense jungle, without any vestige of habitation or living being. The river Feni, rising in the hills of Tipperah, passes by Jagdia* and falls into the ocean. Ninety-nine *nalas*, which contain water even in seasons other than the monsoons, intervene between Feni and Chatgaon. After the capture of Chatgaon, bridges (*pul*) were built by Shaista Khan's order over all these *nalas*. From Dacca to Chatgaon six creeks (*bahar*) have to be crossed in boats ; one of them is the river of Sripur, which is so broad that a boat can perform only one trip across it and back in the whole day.

On the bank of the Karnafuli river are some hills, high and low, situated close to each other. The lower hills have been heaped over with earth and raised to the level of the higher ones ; all these hills have been scarped cylindrically, fortified, and named the fort [of Chatgaon].

* In Rennell's *Atlas*, Sheet 1, Jagdia is on the Little Feni River.

In strength it rivals the rampart of Alexander, and its towers (*burj*) are as high as the *falak-ul-baruj*. [163*a*] Fancy cannot sound the depth of its moat, imagination cannot reach its niched parapet.

In the fort has been dug a deep ditch, about eight yards in breadth ; on the eastern side, close to the edge of the ditch, flows the river Karnafuli, which descends from the Tipperah hills to the sea. On the north side is a large wide and deep tank close to the ditch. Behind the tank, along the entire north side and a part of the western side, are hills. The hills are so high and the jungle so dense, that it is impossible to traverse them even in imagination. Within the fort two springs flow, the water of which runs into the Karnafuli river in the monsoons, when the channel of the springs becomes so broad that a *jalba* boat can easily pass through it. As the people of the fort use all the water [that issues] in seasons other than the rainy, they dam the springs and block the outlet to the Karnafuli river. On a height within the fort is a tomb, known as the *astana* of Pir Badar ; the attendants of the shrine perform prayer and fast. The Magh infidels . . . . have settled some villages in *waqf* on this tomb ; they make pilgrimage to the holy dead and offer presents. It is said that if one could perform the impossible feat of dragging a large gun to the top of the hill at the western corner which adjoins Tipperah, its balls would fall within the fort. On the other side of the Karnafuli there is a lofty and strong fort, opposite the fort of Chatgaon ; it is full of defence-materials.

Every year the Rajah of Arracan sends to Chatgaon a hundred ships full of soldiers and artillery munitions, with a new *Karamkari* (commandant, superintendent), when the former *Karamkari*, with the ships of last year, returns to Arracan. There is always some trustworthy relative or faithful clansman of the Rajah in charge of the government of Chatgaon. He issues gold coins stamped with his own name at this place and its dependencies. [164*a*.]

In bygone times, one of the Sultans of Bengal named Fakhruddin fully conquered Chatgaon, and built an embankment (*al*) from Chandpur across the river, opposite the outpost of Sripur, to Chatgaon. The mosques and tombs which are situated in Chatgaon were built in Fakhruddin's time. The [existing] ruins prove it.

CHATGAON IN MAGH HANDS.

When Bengal was annexed to the Mughal empire, and included in the records of the *qanungo* department, Chatgaon was entered in the papers of Bengal as one of the defaulting unsettled [districts]. When the *mutasaddis* of Bengal did not really wish to pay any man whose salary was due, they gave him an assignment on the revenue of Chatgaon! Towards the end of the rule of the Bengal kings and the early years of the conquest of Bengal by the Mughals, when great confusion prevailed in the country, Chatgaon again fell into the hands of the Maghs, who did not leave a bird in the air or a beast on the land [from Chatgaon] to Jagdia, the frontier of Bengal, increased the desolation, thickened the jungles, destroyed the *al,* and closed the road so well that even the snake and the wind could not pass through. They built a strong fort, and left a large fleet to guard it. Gaining composure of mind from the strength of the place, they turned to Bengal, and began to plunder it. None of the viceroys of Bengal [before Shaista Khan] undertook to put down this trouble and punish them. Only Ibrahim Khan Fath Jang, in the Emperor Jahangir's reign, resolved to conquer Chatgaon and destroy the wicked Maghs. [This expedition failed.]

[122*b*.] DOINGS OF THE PIRATES OF CHATGAON.

From the reign of the Emperor Akbar, when Bengal was annexed to the Mughal empire, to the time of the conquest of Chatgaon during the viceroyalty of Shaista Khan, Arracan pirates, both Magh and Feringi, used constantly to [come] by the water-route and plunder Bengal. They carried off the Hindus and Muslims, male and female, great and small, few and many, that they could seize, pierced the palms of their hands, passed thin canes through the holes, and threw them one above another under the deck of their ships. In the same manner as grain is flung to fowls, every morn and evening they threw down uncooked rice from above to the captives as food. On their return to their homes, they employed the few hard-lived captives that survived [this treatment] in tillage and other hard tasks, according to their power, with great disgrace and insult. Others were sold to the Dutch, English, and French merchants at the ports of the Deccan.

Sometimes they brought the captives for sale at a high price to Tamluk and the port of Baleshwar, which is a part of the imperial dominions and a dependency of the province of Orissa. The manner of the sale was this:—The wretches used to bring the prisoners in their ships, anchor at a short distance from the shore off Tamluk or Baleshwar, and send a man ashore with the news. The local officers, fearing lest the pirates should commit any depredation or kidnapping there, stood on the shore with a number of followers, and sent a man with a sum of money to the pirates. If the terms were satisfactory, the pirates took the money and sent the prisoners with the man. Only the Feringi pirates sold their prisoners. But the Maghs employed all their captives in agriculture and other kinds of service. Many high-born persons and Sayyids, many pure and Sayyid-born women, were compelled to undergo the disgrace of slavery, service or concubinage (*farash wa suhabat*) of these wicked men. Muslims underwent such oppression in this infidel land (*dar-ul-harb*) as they had not to suffer in Europe. It was less in some governors' time and more in others'.

As they for a long time continually practised piracy, their country prospered, and their number increased, while Bengal daily became more and more desolate, less and less able to resist and fight them. Not a householder was left on both sides of the rivers on their track from Dacca to Chatgaon. The district of Bakla,* a part of

* *Bakla* included Backerganj and part of Dacca (*P. A. S. B.*, Pt. I., 1873, p. 209).

Bengal, lying in their usual path, was [formerly] full of cultivation and houses, and yielded every year a large amount to the imperial Government as duty on its betel-nuts. They swept it with the broom of plunder and abduction, leaving none to inhabit a house or kindle a fire in all the tract. Matters came to such a pass that the governor of Dacca confined his energies to the defence of that city only and the prevention of the coming of the pirate fleet to Dacca, and stretched some iron chains across the *nala* of Dacca and set up some bridges of bamboo (*nai,* reed) on the stream (*nahar*) of the city.

DEMORALISED BENGAL NAVY.

[124 *a.*] The sailors of the Bengal flotilla were in such a fright, that I may say without exaggeration that whenever 100 war-ships of Bengal sighted four ships of the enemy, if the distance separating them was great the Bengal crew showed fight by flight, considered it a great victory that they had carried off their lives in safety, and became famous in Bengal for their valour and heroism! If the interval was small and the enemy overpowered them, the men of the Bengal ships—rowers, sepoys, and armed men alike—threw themselves without delay into the water, preferring drowning to captivity.

Once Ashur Beg, an officer of Prince Shujā was cruising with about 200 boats, when a few of the enemy's fleet, in number not even one-tenth of the imperial flotilla, came in sight. Ashur Beg was mortally frightened; in great agitation he cried to the *mānjhi* or captain of his ship, "*Ai bāi āsh bedeh*!"* The *manjhi* in perplexity asked, "*Mir-jiu*! whence can I get broth at such a time? Just now these pirates will cook a nice broth for you!" Ashur Beg in agitation and bewilderment kept up crying, "You confounded fellow, give *āsh*," and the *mānjhi* went on replying, "I have not got it with me. Whence can I bring it?" [The fact is] sailors use the term *wars* to mean, 'backing the boat'; Ashur Beg in his terror had forgotten the word and used *āsh* instead! In no other part of the Mughal empire has any neighbouring infidel [king] the power to oppress and domineer over Muslims; but rather do [infidel kings] show all kinds of submission and humility in order to save their homes and lands, and the [Mughal] officers of those places engage in making new acquisitions by conquest. In Bengal alone the opposite is the case; here the mere preservation of the imperial dominion is considered a great boon. Those governors in whose times these piracies were less frequent, congratulated themselves and exulted at it. None of them tried to stop the path of oppression and domination of this wicked tribe through their fear of the necessary expenditure and exertion, weakness of faith and trust, and the [false] notion of their lack of power.

ROUTES OF THE PIRATES.

[107*b*.] In Jahangir's reign, the Magh pirates used to come to Dacca for plunder and abduction, by the *nala* which leaves the Brahmaputra, passes by Khizirpur, and

* "Ho, brother, give [me] broth." *Bai* is the Dacca pronunciation of *Bhai*.

joins the *nala* of Dacca. Khizirpur is situated on the bank of the Brahmaputra, on a narrow embankment (*āl*). In the monsoons all the land except the sites of the houses is covered with water. The governors of Dacca, therefore, at the end of the monsoons and during winter, which was the season of the coming of the pirates, used to go to Khizirpur with an army and encamp there. After some years, the *nala* dried up, and many places in the track of the pirates in the Brahmaputra river also became fordable. Thus their [water] route to Dacca was closed on this side, and restricted to the side of Jatrapur* and Bikrampur. Recently as the pirates could more easily carry out their chief design of kidnapping men in the villages of Dacca and other parganahs, they did not exert themselves to reach Dacca town.

[139*a*.] When the pirates came from Chatgaon to molest Bengal, they passed by Bhalua, a part of the imperial dominions, on the right, and the island of Sondip, belonging to the zamindar Dilawwar, on the left, and reached the village of Sangramgarh. [From this point] it they wished to plunder Jessore, Hughli, and Bhushna, they moved up the Ganges ; if they wanted to raid Bikrampur, Sonargaon, and Dacca, they proceeded up the Brahmaputra. Sangramgarh† is the land at the extremity

---

* In Rennell, Sheet 1, Jatrapur is given 30 miles west of Dacca.

† No trace of Sangramgarh is found in Rennell. The *Alamgirnamah*, p. 943, says that its name was changed to Alamgirnagar, and that it was 21 *kos* from Sripur (p. 944). It must have been near Rennell's *Mendigunge*. Khafi Khan calls it Sangramnagar, ii. 188.

of the island (*i.e.*, delta) which contains Dacca and other towns and villages. In front of it the Ganges and the Brahmaputra unite. The mingled stream, after passing by Bhalua and Sondip, falls into the sea. In ancient times, a man named Sangram had built a fort here to repel the Magh raids into Bengal. In Hindi a fort is called a *garh*. By the combination of these two words the name of the place has been formed. If a fort were built here and stored with weapons, munitions, and materials of defence, and a large force and well-equipped flotilla kept here, the oppression of the pirates and the raids of the Maghs into Bengal could most probably be prevented.

FERINGI PIRATES.

[150*b*.] Many Feringis lived happily at Chatgaon* and used to come to the imperial dominion for plunder and abduction. Half their booty they gave to the Rajah of Arracan, and the other half they kept. This tribe was called *Harmad*.† They had 100 swift *jalba* boats full of war-materials. The governors of Bengal were disturbed by their robbery and were too weak to prevent it. As the Harmads [=Feringi pirates] were not in need of the help of the Arracan fleet, the king of Arracan did not send his ships to practise piracy in Mughal territory (Bengal). He considered the Feringi pirates in

* Their settlement was called *Feringi-bandar* or *Bandar*, on the south bank of the Karnafuli, very close to its mouth.

† This word is evidently *armad*, a corruption of *armada*. *Armad* is used in the sense of fleet in *Kalimat-i-tayyibat* and in Marathi.

the light of his servants, and took the booty they brought [as his share].

[In December, 1665, the Feringis of Chatgaon, partly in fear of Arracanese treachery and partly won over by Shaista Khan's tempting overtures], came with all their families in 42 *jalbas* and took refuge with Farhad Khan, the Mughal *thanahdar* of Noakhali. The Khan sent their chief naval captain,* with a few of their great men to Shaista Khan at Dacca, while he kept all the others with their ships at Noakhali, showing them great attention and kindness. The captain and other leaders of the Feringis had audience of the Nawwab at night, and received splendid robes of honour and other unexpected favours. The Nawwab asked them, "What did the zamindar of the Maghs fix as your salary?" The Feringis replied, "Our salary was the imperial dominion! [152*b*]. We considered the whole of Bengal as our *jagir*. All the twelve months of the year we made our collection [*i.e.*, booty] without trouble. We had not to bother ourselves about *amlas* and *amins*; nor had we to render accounts and balances to anybody. Passage over water was our [field-] survey. We never slackened the enhancement of *our* rent, *viz.*, booty. For years we have left no arrears of [this] revenue. We have with us papers of the division of the booty village by village for the last 40 years." One can infer from this answer the condition of things and the weakness of the governors of Bengal. The coming over of the Feringis gave composure to the hearts

* *Capitao mor* is a Portuguese phrase meaning 'chief naval officer' and not a Captain named Moor.

of the people of Bengal. Two thousand Rupees were presented from the Nawwab's own purse as reward to this chief captain and the other Feringis who had come from Chatgaon, and from the imperial Treasury a monthly stipend of Rs. 500 was settled on the captain, and other comfortable salaries on others of the tribe.

XIII

THE CONQUEST OF CHATGAON, 1666 A.D.

(Shihabuddin Talish's account and the Alamgirnamah.)

DECAY OF THE BENGAL FLOTILLA.

[113*a*] During the viceroyalty of Prince Shuja, when great confusion was caused by his negligence, the extortion ,and violence of the clerks (*mutasaddis*) ruined the *parganahs* assigned for maintaining the *nawwara* (=flotilla). Many [naval] officers and workmen holding *jagir* or stipend were overpowered by poverty and starvation. Day by day their distress and ruin increased. When Mir Jumla came to Bengal as viceroy, he wished to make a new arrangement of the expenditure and *tankhah* of the flotilla, which amounted to 14 lakhs of Rupees. After abolishing the old system, and just before beginning the re-organisation, he was overcome by the spells of Assam [*i.e.*, died of the Assam queen's witchcraft]. Many naval officers and men too perished in the expedition ; so that at Mir Jumla's death the flotilla was utterly ruined.

[122*a*] [Early in 1664] the pirates came to Bagadia, a dependency of Dacca, and defeated Munawwar Khan, zamindar, who was stationed there with the relics of the *nawwara*—a few broken and rotten boats—and who bore the high title of cruising admiral (*sardar-i-sairab*).

Munawwar fled in confusion. Ismail Khan Tarin and other Nawwabi officers, whom [Shaista Khan's son and deputy governor at Dacca] Aqidat Khan had sent with a small force to Munawwar, prevented the crew of their own boats from retreating by turning them round. The crew, on seeing their passengers averse to flight, jumped into the sea and swam ashore to safety. Ismail Khan and his comrades boldly made a firm stand and repelled with their bows and guns the enemy who had advanced to seize them. A musket-shot grazed the leg of Ismail Khan. The current drove their sailorless boats to the bank, and they escaped destruction. The few boats that still belonged to the *nawwara* were thus lost, and its name alone remained in Bengal.

SHAISTA KHAN'S RESOLVE TO SUPPRESS PIRACY.

On 8th March, 1664, the new viceroy, Shaista Khan, entered Rajmahal [the western capital of Bengal]. [115 *b*]. When he learnt that the cause of the ravages of the pirates was the power and equipment of their fleet and the dilapidation of the Bengal fleet, he gave urgent orders to Muhammad Beg [Abakash, the *darogha* of the *nawwara*] to restore the flotilla, wrote to Aqidat Khan also [on the subject], accepted the suggestions of Muhammad Beg, appointed at his request Qazi Samu as *mushrif* of the *nawwara*, and sent them back to Dacca with robes of honour and presents. As timber and ship-wrights were required for repairing and fitting out the ships, to every *mauza* of the province that had timber and carpenters, bailiffs (*muhasal*) were sent with warrants (*parwanah*) to take them to Dacca. It was ordered that at the ports of Hughli, Baleshwar, Murang, Chilmari, Jessore, and Karibari, as many boats should be built as possible and sent [to Dacca]. The Nawwab spoke to the Captain of the Dutch, who was present at the audience, "You make vast amounts every year by your trade in the imperial dominions, for which you have to pay no duty or tithe. For this reason, the path of the profit of Muslim and Hindu *beparis* and merchants in the imperial dominions, especially in Bengal, has been closed. In gratitude for such favour and bounty you should call for ships from your country, and co-operate with the imperial forces in the expedition against Arracan for extirpating the Maghs, which I have in view. Abolish the factories (*kothi*) that you have in Arracan. Otherwise, know for certain that trade and traffic with you will be forbidden all over the empire, and your gains stopped." The Captain replied, "I cannot agree to this great and serious proposal without first writing to our head, the General [Governor-General of the Dutch Indies], and getting his consent." [116 *b.*] The Nawwab, accepting the Captain's entreaty, said, "Write and call for a reply," and entrusted to the Captain a *parwanah* on the above subject, one suit of *khilat* and one jewelled saddle-cover, for the General. Through God's grace, their help was at last found unnecessary.

As the Feringis engaged in piracy, kidnapping and plundering the inhabitants of Bengal, lived at Chatgaon under the protection of the zamindar of Arracan, giving half their booty from Bengal to him, the Nawwab sent Shaikh Ziauddin Yusuf, one of his own officers, as *darogha* of the port of Ladhikol,* which is near Dacca and where Feringi merchants, engaged in the salt trade, live; he ordered the Shaikh to manage that these Feringis should write to their brethren, the pirates of Chatgaon, offering assurances and hopes of imperial favours and rewards, and thus make them come and enter the Mughal service. Ziauddin, too, was to send conciliatory letters [of his own] to them.

SHAISTA KHAN CREATES A NEW FLOTILLA.

[137 *a*] On 13th December, 1664, Shaista Khan first entered Dacca. He devoted all his energy to the rebuilding of the flotilla: not for a moment did he forget to mature plans for assembling the crew, providing their rations and needments, and collecting the materials for ship-building and shipwrights. Hakim Muhammad Husain, mansabdar, an old, able, learned, trustworthy and virtuous servant of the Nawwab, was appointed head of the ship-building department. The *mushrifi* of the flotilla was given, *vice* Qazi Samu, to Muhammad Muqim, an expert, clever, and hardworking officer serving in Bengal, whom Mir Jumla had left at Dacca in supervision of the *nawwara* at the time of the Assam expedition. Kishor Das, an imperial officer, a well-informed and experienced clerk, was appointed to have charge of the *parganahs* of the *nawwara,* and the stipend of the jagirs assigned to the [naval] officers and men. To all posts of this department expert officers were appointed.

* In Rennell, Sheet 1, *Luricool,* 13 miles west of Chandpour.

Through the ceaseless exertions of the Nawwab, in a short time nearly 300 ships were built and equipped with [the necessary] materials. Those who had seen the [sorry] plight of the *nawwara* after the death of Mir Jumla, can understand the great change effected by Shaista Khan in a short time.

SECURING BASES FOR THE WAR.

[139 *b*] Sangramgarh is situated at the point of land where the Ganges and the Brahmaputra unite. The Nawwab ordered Muhammad Sharif, the late *faujdar* of Hughli, to go to Sangramgarh as *thanahdar,* with many men, officers, and guns, and build a fort there. Abul Hasan was posted there with 200 ships to patrol and check the pirates. Muhammad Beg Abakash, with a hundred ships, was stationed at Dhapa, with orders to go and reinforce Abul Hasan whenever he heard of the coming of the pirates.

A wide high road (*al*) was built from Dhapa* to Sangramgarh, so that even in the monsoons horse and foot could proceed on land from Sangramgarh to Dacca, a distance of 18 *kos*.

[Sondip was a halfway house between Sangramgarh and Chatgaon, and formed an excellent base. Hence the Nawwab decided to wrest it from its zamindar Dilawwar before sending the expedition to Chatgaon. On 12th

---

* The site of Dhapa is given in Rennell (sheet 12) as *Dhape ki Kila,* 6 m. s.e. of Dacca.

November, 1665, Sondip was conquered and a Mughal *thanah* established there. [142 *b*—150 *a*.]

THE FERINGIS DESERT TO THE MUGHAL SIDE.

[151 *a*] Ever since his coming to Bengal the Nawwab had been planning how to put down the root of disturbance, the Feringi pirates, either by winning them over or by slaying them. As already narrated, Shaikh Ziauddin Yusuf told the Feringis of Ladhikol what the Nawwab had said, and they wrote to their piratical brethren of Chatgon reassuring them and asking them to visit the Nawwab. When the Nawwab was making his progress [from Rajmahal] to Dacca, the [Portuguese ?] Captain of the port of Hughli interviewed him on the way. The Nawwab, after gracing him with favours, asked him to write to the Feringi pirates of Chatgaon tempting them to come over to the Nawwab's service. When he reached Dacca, the Captain of Tamluk also was ordered to write letters of invitation to them. When these successive letters arrived at Chatgon, and the news of the conquest of Sondip and the establishment of a Mughal *thanah* there spread abroad, spies reported these matters to the king of Arracan. The news threw him into terror, and he wrote to his uncle's son, the governor of Chatgaon, to look carefully to the defence of the country and fort, conciliate the Feringi pirates, and send to Arracan their families and children, and informed him that a large fleet equipped for battle was being shortly sent to Chatgaon for reinforcement. As he had from the above causes come to entertain suspicion [of the fidelity] of the Feringis, he really wished

to lure their families to Arracan and massacre the Feringis themselves at Chatgaon at an opportune time. The hearts of the Feringis were distracted and shaken by the arrival of the tempting letters and the news of the Mughal establishment at Sondip. On learning of the wishes of the Magh chief, they fled with their families in 42 *jalbas* to Farhad Khan at Noakhali for protection.* [They were taken into imperial service and liberally rewarded by the Nawwab.]

INVASION IMMEDIATELY DECIDED ON.

The chief naval captain or Feringi leader, reported to the Nawwab, "Owing to their pride and folly, the king and counsellors of Arracan have neglected the defence and munitions of the fort, and mostly depended on us [for this purpose]. But now that they have heard of the conquest of Sondip. [157 *a*] they have ordered a large army and fleet to reinforce [the defence of Chatgaon]. If the Mughal force attacks the fort before the arrival of this reinforcement, its capture will probably be very easy." The Nawwab, who had been day and night thinking how to realise this object, regarded the coming over of the Feringis as the commencement of the victory, and decided not to let this opportunity slip away.

* The *Alamgirnamah*, p. 947, says: "The Feringis, learning [of the intended Arracanese treachery,] resisted and fought the Arracanese, burnt some of the ships of the latter, and started for service in Bengal with all their goods and ships. On 19th December, 1665, fifty *jalbas* of the Feringis, full of guns, muskets, and munitions, and all the Feringi families, reached Noakhali."

From Jagdia, the frontier of Mughal Bengal, to Chatgaon, a distance of 30 *kos,* is an utterly desolate wilderness. The expeditionary force would have to be supplied with provisions [from Bengal] till after Chatgaon was reached, besieged, and captured. As the Bengal crew were mortally afraid of the Magh flotilla, provisions could not be sent by water, though the means of transport in this province are confined to boats. Hence, when in Jahangir's reign, Ibrahim Khan Fath Jang decided to attack Chatgaon, for two years before setting out he collected provisions at Bhalua and Jagdia.

COMPOSITION OF THE EXPEDITION.

It was decided that the Nawwab's son, Buzurg Ummed Khan, with 4,000 troopers should conduct the campaign, while the Nawwab would look after the work of keeping the army supplied with provisions. If the siege were protracted he would quickly go and join his son. On 24th December,* 1665, at a moment auspicious for making a beginning, Buzurg Ummed Khan started [158 *b*] from Dacca. Under him were appointed Ikhtisas Khan, a commander of 2,500 (1,000 extra troopers), Sarandaz Khan, a commander of 1,500 (800 troopers), Farhad Khan, a commander of 1,000 (150 troopers), Qarawwal Khan, a commander of 1,000 (800 troopers),

* The *Alamgirnamah,* p. 948, gives 25th December as the date, and says that the expeditionary force was composed of "Buzurg Ummed Khan with *two* thousand troopers of the Nawwab's own *tabinan* (followers), Sayyid Ikhtisas Khan Barha, Subal Singh Sisodia, Miana Khan, Karn Khaji and some others."

Rajah Subal Singh Sisodia, a commander of 1,500 (700 troopers), Ibn Husain, *darogha* of the *nawwara*, a commander of 800 (200 troopers), Mir Murtaza, *darogha* of the artillery, a commander of 800 (150 troopers), other imperial officers with their followings, all the *naqdis* and *ahadis* except a few who were engaged in special works, and 2,500 troopers in the Nawwab's pay. All the *amirs*, *mansabdars*, *sardars*, and *jamadars* were presented with robes of honour, horses, swords, and shields, according to their ranks. Mir Abul Fath was appointed *diwan* and Muhammad Khalil pay-master and news-writer of the force. From Dacca Mir Murtaza, and from Sondip Ibn Husain, Muhammad Beg Abakash, Munawwar Khan zamindar and other zamindars of the *nawwara*, and Haiat Khan *jamadar* with the Nawwab's soldiers, who had accompanied him to the conquest of Sondip, were ordered to go to Noakhali, join Farhad Khan and the chief captain and other Feringi pirates who had come from Chatgaon and entered the imperial service, and then proceed by land and sea as the van of Buzurg Ummed Khan's army.

Askar Khan, who had been posted to Ghoraghat, returned opportunely and was stationed at Dacca.*

* The *Alamgirnamah*, p. 948, adds: "Kamal, a former Arracanese king's son, who in Shah Jahan's reign had fled to Dacca from the oppression of the present king, was ordered to accompany Mir Murtaza with a band of the Maghs who lived at Dacca, on the assurance that he would be made chief of his tribe. A letter (*parwanah*), inviting submission to the Mughals and offering conciliatory favours from the imperial Government, was written to the governor of Chatgaon and sent to him with one of the Maghs."

The imperial fleet under Ibn Husain consisted of 288 ships, as described below:—

Ghurab	... 21	*Jalba*	...	96
Salb	... 3	*Bachari*	...	2
Kusa	... 157	*Parenda*	...	6
		[Not specified]		3
				288

NAWWAB'S VIGOROUS EXERTIONS.

Before this Mir Murtaza had collected many axes at Dacca. From the *parganahs,* too, axes had been brought by issuing *parwanahs,* so that several thousands of them had been collected. These were sent with the expedition for clearing the jungle. Every day the Nawwab wrote to the officers of the expedition letters full of plans and advice, and inquiries addressed to the Khan about the condition of the enemy and the state of the road. On the first day [when the expedition left Dacca] the Nawwab stayed outside [the harem] till noon, and again from the time of the *asar* prayer to one *prahar* of the night, and supervised this business. Even when he was in the harem, if any good plan struck him, he at once sent word to the officers to carry it out. Muhammad Khalil was ordered to keep him daily informed of the occurrences. Shaikh Mubarak, an experienced and trusted servant, appointed to command the Nawwab's retainers accompanying Buzurg Ummed Khan, was ordered to report all the daily events, great and small, to the Nawwab, and give the Khan every advice that he considered fit.

FEEDING THE ARMY.

The officers of the *golahs* (granaries) were ordered that one-half of all the grain that *beparis* brought into Dacca should be sent to the army. To the *faujdars* of all parts of Bengal urgent *parwanahs* were issued directing that every kind of provision that they could secure should be despatched to the expeditionary force. *Yasawwals* were appointed by the Nawwab to see to it. So excellent were the Nawwab's arrangements that from the beginning till now the price of grain in the army has been to the price in Dacca as ten to nine.

MUGHAL ADVANCE BY LAND AND SEA.

Buzurg Ummed Khan moved quickly on, carried his entire army over the deep river in a few days, crossed the river of Feni,* entered the Magh territory, and

* The *Alamgirnamah*, p. 949, describes the movements of the expedition thus: Farhad Khan, appointed a force of pioneers, wood-cutters, and some infantry armed with bows and muskets for making a road and clearing the jungle. On 12th January, 1666, marching from Noakhali with Mir Murtaza and other comrades, he reached the outpost of Jagdia. Ibn Husain and his comrades on board weighed anchor. On the 14th, Farhad Khan and his party crossed the Feni river and advanced cautiously. On the 20th, he reached a tank, from which Chatgaon was one day's journey, and waited for Buzurg Ummed Khan's arrival. That general, after crossing the Feni on the 17th . . . . arrived on the 21st at a place 8 *kos* behind the position of Farhad Khan and Mir Murtaza, which [latter] was ten *kos* from Chatgaon fort, and where the jungle was very thick and the road very bad,—and halted there. Farhad Khan daily advanced a little, cutting the jungle and levelling the road.

advanced cutting the jungle and making a road. According to the Nawwab's command a *thanah* was established on the river of Feni, under Sultan Beg, *mansabdar,* with a contingent of horse and foot. As the river of Feni joins the sea, it was feared that the enemy's ships would pass up the river and harass the imperial army's passage. It was, therefore, decided that out of the commanders at Noakhali, Ibn Husain should advance with the *nawwara* by the sea and Farhad Khan, Mir Murtaza, and Haiat Khan by land, in aid of the *nawwara.* If they could, they should enter the Karnafuli river and occupy its mouth, and also attack Chatgaon. Otherwise they should stay in the neighbourhood and wait for Buzurg Ummed Khan's arrival. The jungle was thereafter to be cut along the sea stage by stage, the flotilla to advance by sea and the Khan by its coast ; in march and halt the land and sea forces were never to be separated.

These officers started from Noakhali. Ibn Husain with the flotilla soon arrived at the creek of Khamaria, two stages from Chatgaon, and began to cut the jungle *before* towards Chatgaon and *behind* towards the advancing army. Farhad Khan, Mir Murtaza and other commanders [161*b*] of the land force too advanced cutting the jungle, and joined hands with Ibn Husain on 21st January, 1666. Buzurg Ummed Khan who was hastening clearing the jungle, arrived with the [main] army within three *kos* of Khamaria.

The flotilla waited for the army at Dumria, a dependency of Chatgaon, which was about 20 *kos* from the halting-place of Buzurg Ummed Khan.

FIRST NAVAL BATTLE, *23rd January.*

In the evening of the 22nd,* the scouts (*qarawwals*) of Ibn Husain [167*b*] brought news that the enemy's flotilla having come from Chatgaon was staying in the creek of Kathalia, six hours' journey from their place. Ibn Husain, after informing the imperial and Nawwabi servants who were on board most of the ships, got ready for action. At night he sent a few ships to the mouth of the creek, telling the passengers to keep a good look out. Next morning, the scouts reported that the enemy's flotilla had started from Kathalia to fight the imperial *nawwara* and might come up immediately. Ibn Husain, after sending a man to inform Buzurg Ummed Khan of the matter, set out to meet the enemy, though the wind had freshened, and the sea was raging in billows threatening to sink the imperial ships. Abul Qasim, who was in the ship of Muhammad Beg Abakash, narrates that when in this tempest he unmoored his ship to join Ibn Husain, one of the Turkish soldiers standing on the bank cried out to Md. Beg Abakash in Turki, "Are you mad, that you put your boat out during tempest in such a deep and terrible sea?" He replied, "Brother, if I were not mad, I should not have become a soldier!" Farhad Khan, Mir Murtaza, and Haiat Khan advanced by land to co-operate with the navy, following the road cleared by the men of the ships. Beyond the clearing they could not go on account of the density of the jungle.

---

* Text gives the 24th, which is wrong. *Alamgirnamah*, p. 950, mentions the 23rd as the day of the *battle*.

Ten *ghurabs* and 45 *jalbas* of the enemy hove in sight and began to discharge their guns. The Chief Captain and other Feringis, who led the van, boldly steered their ships up to the enemy, Ibn Husain coming behind them. The enemy could not resist the onset ; the men of their *ghurabs* jumped overboard, and the *jalbas* took to flight. Ibn Husain, seizing the *ghurabs,* wanted to pursue. But the Bengal sailors, who had never even seen in their minds the vision of a victory over the Magh fleet, objected, saying that that day's victory—the like of which even centenarians had not seen—ought to content them. Ibn Husain had to yield ; but advancing a little from the spot where the *ghurabs* had been captured, he decided to stay there till evening and to return to the creek of Khamaria at night.

Suddenly two or three ships with flags (*bairaq*) were seen afar off. The Maghs, when they left the Kathalia creek that morning for fight and reached the creek of Hurla close to Khamaria, in their pride left their large ships—called *khalu* and *dhum,*—and [some] other ships here, and sent on only ten *ghurabs* and 45 *jalbas* as sufficient for [defeating and] capturing the imperial flotilla. The two or three ships with flags now seen were among those *khalus* left in the creek.

Ibn Husain encouraged his crew, saying, "Now that the fugitive *jalbas* have joined their larger fleet, the enemy have surely been seized with terror. It behoves [us] as brave men not to give the enemy time, nor let the opportunity slip out of our grasp, but attack them in full reliance on God." These words had effect on the Bengal crew ; they agreed and started for Hurla. The enemy learning of it issued from the creek and stood at sea in line of battle. Ibn Husain arriving there found their line stronger than Alexander's rampart. He felt that to run his smaller ships against the [enemy's] larger ones,—whose many guns would, at every discharge, command [his ships],—was to court needless ruin, but that he ought to stop in front of the enemy, engage in firing, and wait for the arrival of his larger ships (*salbs*,) when he would put the latter in front and attack the enemy. He therefore began firing his guns and sent a man to hurry up the *salbs*. These arrived at the time of the evening prayer. From that time to dawn, there was cannonade between the two sides.* [169*b*.]

---

* The *Alamgirnamah*, p. 950, says:—"[After the first naval battle] the enemy fled. Ibn Husain, with his light and swift ships gave chase and captured ten *ghurabs* and three *halias* [=*jalbas*] from them. Soon afterwards, the larger ships (*nawwara-e-buzurg*) of the enemy came in sight, for a second time fought a long and severe fight, and at sunset fled from the scene of action. Ibn Husain pursued them, [p. 951] but as the enemy's ships entered the Karnafuli, and his own larger ships had not come up with him, he thought it inadvisable to advance, but withdrew his fleet to a suitable place, and passed the night in keeping watch.

When Buzurg Ummed Khan heard of it, he wrote strongly urging Farhad Khan and Mir Murtaza not to wait for clearing the jungle and making a road, but to hurry up and join hands with the *nawwara*. He himself gave up road-making and advanced quickly. Next day [24th January,] Farhad Khan arrived at the bank of the river [Karnafuli]. The enemy lost heart at the sight of the Islamic army."

SECOND NAVAL ENCOUNTER, *24th January.*

Next morning, the Muslims flying their victorious banners, beating their drums, and sounding their bugles and trumpets, advanced towards the enemy, firing guns and in this order: First the *salbs*, then the *ghurabs*, and last the *jalbas* and *kosas* side by side. The enemy lost all courage and firmness, and thought only of flying. They turned the heads of their larger ships away from the imperialists, attached their *jalbas* to them, and began to tow back these big ships, fighting during their flight.

Ibn Husain without throwing away caution or making rash haste, advanced in his previous formation. At last at about 3 P.M., the enemy entered the mouth of the Karnafuli, reached the island in mid stream in front of Chatgaon fort, and drew up their ships off the bank on which Chatgaon stood. The imperial fleet too came to the Karnafuli and seized its mouth. On the [further] side of the Karnafuli, near the mouth and close to the village called Feringi-bandar, where the Feringi pirates had their houses, the enemy had built three bamboo stockades on the brink of the water, and filled them with artillery, many Telingas (as the fighting men of Arracan are called) and two elephants, in preparation for fight. When the imperial flotilla entered the mouth of the Karnafuli, these forts opened fire on them with muskets and guns. Ibn Husain sent most of his ships up the river and many of the soldiers by the bank, and attacked them. After making some vain efforts the garrison of the stockades took to flight. The Mughals burned the forts and returned.

ARRACAN NAVY ANNIHILATED.

Now with a strong heart and good hope, Ibn Husain dashed upon the enemy's ships. The Chief Captain and other Feringi pirates, the Nawwab's officers [such as] Muhammad Beg Abakash and Munawwar Khan zamindar, came swiftly from different sides. A great fight was fought. Fire was opened [on the Mughals] from the fort of Chatgaon also. At last the breeze of victory blew on the banners of the Muslims. The enemy were vanquished ; some of their sailors and soldiers jumped overboard ; some remaining in their ships surrendered as prisoners. Most of the former carried off their lives, only some being drowned. Many were slain by the swords, arrows, and spears of the victors. A few, reaching the bank, carried the news to the fort. Many of the enemy's ships were sunk by the fire or ramming of the Mughal fleet ; the rest, 135 ships, were captured by the imperialists* and consisted of :—

---

* The operations in the Karnafuli are thus described in the *Alamgirnamah*, p. 952 :—"[On 24th January,] Ibn Husain with the imperial fleet entered the Karnafuli river and attacked the enemy's fleet that had fled there. A second terrible battle was fought for two *prahars* of the day. At last the imperialists gained the victory, and the enemy fled, many of them being killed, many others taken prisoner, and many drowned after jumping overboard."

Khalu	... 2	*Kosa*	...	12	
Ghurab	... 9	*Jalba*	...	67	[Should be 68]
Jangi	... 22	*Balam*	...	22	

Meantime, Buzurg Ummed Khan, hearing of the naval battle, hastened to the neighbourhood of Chatgaon. The *choukidars* of the fort informed the garrison of the near approach of the Mughal army. This news and the spectacle of the victory of the imperial fleet struck such terror into the hearts of the garrison and soldiers of the country, that in spite of their large number they fled.

NIGHT AFTER BATTLE.

That night† Ibn Husain, sending to the fort two trustworthy men out of those taken prisoner in the ships, wrote to the *qiladar* who represented the Rajah of Arracan, "Why should you needlessly destroy yourself

† The *Alamgirnamah*, p. 951, says:—"After the victory the imperial fleet halted in the Karnafuli below the fort of Chatgaon. Some of the Feringis of Chatgaon who had remained there, and many [p. 952] other Feringis who at this time had come from Arracan to aid them, interviewed Ibn Husain. The Chief Captain, who accompanied the imperial forces in this expedition, did excellent service. Next day [25th January,] Buzurg Ummed Khan arrived at the foot of the fort of Chatgaon with the rest of the army. The imperial forces by land and sea encircled the fort. The garrison, after making great exertions, found that they could not resist the Mughal army, and at last sought safety. The second day of the siege, 26th January, 1666, the imperial army gained possession of the fort, the whole province of Chatgaon, and the entire artillery and navy of the place . . . [p. 953]. The governor of Chatgaon, who was the son of the Arracan king's uncle, was taken prisoner with one son and some other relatives, and nearly

and your family? Before you are forcibly seized and sacrificed to our swords, give up your fort, and save your life and property." The *qiladar*, feeling himself helpless and in need of protection, sent back the reply that he [172*a*] should be granted respite for the night and that next morning he would admit them.

CHATGAON FORT SURRENDERS.

In the morning of 26th January, 1666, which was the sunset of [the glory of] the Maghs, the commandant opened the fort gate and informed Ibn Husain, who started for the fort. But Munawwar Khan zamindar had entered it before him, and his companions had set fire to it. Ibn Husain entered soon afterwards, and tried his best to put out the fire, but in vain. The fire was so violent that he could not stay there, but came out bringing the *qiladar* away with himself.

When the fire went out, he again proceeded to the fort and attached the property. He sent the *qiladar* with the news of victory to the Nawwab at Dacca, and also informed Buzurg Ummed Khan of the happy event.

The Maghs who were in the fort on the other side of the river, fled, and that fort, too, fell into Mughal hands. The peasantry on the further side of the river,

---

350 men of the tribe, 132 ships of war, 1,026 guns made of bronze and iron, many matchlocks and *zamburaks* (camel pieces), much shot and powder, other artillery materials, and three elephants, were captured. Large numbers of the peasants of Bengal who had been carried off and kept prisoner here, were now released off the Magh oppression and returned to their homes."

who were mostly Muslims kidnapped from Bengal, attacked the Maghs that fled yesterday and to-day, slew one of their leaders, captured two of their elephants, and brought them to Ibn Husain. Of the four elephants in the fort of Chatgaon, two were burned in the fire and two were secured by the Mughals.

REWARDS TO THE VICTORS.

On 29th January the news of the conquest reached Dacca. The Nawwab after thanking God, began to give to all the army liberal rewards consisting of robes, horses, and elephants, distributed alms to the poor, and ordered the music of joy to play. Wealth beyond measure was given to the Feringi pirates and one month's pay as bounty to his own officers and the crew of the *nawwara*. [173*a*.]

That very day the Nawwab sent a despatch on the victory to the Emperor. When it arrived at Court,* the Emperor ordered joyous music to be played. Rewards were given to all concerned in the conquest: the Nawwab was presented with a costly jewelled sword of the Emperor, two elephants, two horses with gold trappings, a special *khilat*, and an imperial *farman* of praise. Buzurg Ummed Khan, Farhad Khan, Mir Murtaza, Ibn Husain, and Muhammad Beg Abakash were promoted. Ibn Husain got the title of Mansur† Khan, and Mir Murtaza that of Mujahid Khan.

* "At the end of Sh'aban [February 1666]" according to the '*lamgirnamah*, p. 956. "The Emperor ordered Chatgaon to be named Islamabad."

† *Muzaffar* according to the *Alamgirnamah*.

NEW GOVERNMENT OF CHATGAON.

[175*b*.] On 27th January,* 1666, Buzurg Ummed entered the fort of Chatgaon, reassured the people that their lives were safe, and firmly forbade his soldiers to oppress the people, in order to cause the place to be well-populated and prosperous.

[Here the Bodleian Ms. ends abruptly on f. 176*b*. I give the concluding portion of the campaign from the *Alamgirnamah*, pp. 953-956.]

Buzurg Ummed Khan stayed at Chatgaon for some time to settle its affairs. Miana Khan was sent to the north of Chatgaon to reassure the peasantry and to establish a *thanah*. Taj Miana, with his followers and 100 musketeers, was appointed as *thanahdar* and guard of the roads from Chatgaon to the bank of the Feni river.

RAMBU TAKEN AND ABANDONED.

The port of Rambu† is four days' journey from Chatgaon, and midway between Chatgaon and Arracan. A large body of the enemy defended its fort. Mir Murtaza was ordered to that direction, to win over the peasantry, learn all about the paths and ferries of that region, and, if he found it possible, to go to the place and besiege it. The Mir, after traversing difficult roads, dense jungles, and terrible rivers, at the end of 12 days arrived within one *kos* of Rambu. Next day, at morn

* The date is left blank in the Bodleian Ms. I have supplied it from the *Alamgirnamah*.

† *Ramoo* in Rennell, Sheet 1.

he stormed the fort. The Arracan king's brother named Rawli, who held the government of the place, tried his best to oppose, but being worsted, he fled with the garrison to a jungle close to a hill near the fort. Mir Murtaza giving chase slew many of them and captured many others. Some of the enemy, who had taken refuge in the hill, came out to surrender, and were made prisoner. Many Muslim ryots of Bengal, who had been kept as captives here, were liberated and returned home.

Buzurg Ummed Khan hearing of the victory and learning that the king of Arracan was sending a force by land against Rambu, despatched Miana Khan, Jamal Khan Dilzaq, and many others to reinforce Mir Murtaza. The Mir, after his victory, had posted a company of musketeers on the bank of the river one and a half *kos* from Rambu, to keep watch for the enemy's arrival. One day a large force of the enemy with seven elephants suddenly issued from the jungle, fell upon the musketeers, and dispersed some of them. Mir Murtaza hearing of it, rode with a force to the bank of the river, and in spite of its water being deep and the enemy having begun to make entrenchments on the [other] bank, boldly plunged in with his comrades and crossed over in safety. The enemy, after a hard fight, fled. The victors pursued, slew and captured many of them, and seized 80 guns, many muskets, and other war material.

As the space between Chatgaon and Rambu is very hard to cross, full of hills and jungles, and intersected by one or two streams which cannot be crossed without boats, and as in the rainy season the whole path is flooded, and this year there was only a small store of provisions and the rainy season was near,—therefore the sending of the Mughal army into Arracan was put off. Buzurg Umed Khan, in view of the roads being closed and reinforcements and provisions being cut off by the rains, very wisely ordered Mir Murtaza to evacuate Rambu and fall back with the chiefs, zamindars, prisoners, and peasants of Rambu, on Dakhin-kol,* which is close to Chatgaon. He did so.

---

* *i.e.*, 'The southern bank of the river.'

XIV

ORISSA IN THE SEVENTEENTH CENTURY.

1. SOURCES OF INFORMATION EXTANT.

In his *Account of Orissa Proper or Cuttack,* writen in 1822, Alexander Stirling complains, "The slender information extant of the proceedings of the Mughal officers from the retirement of Raja Man Singh in A.D. 1605 to the diwanship of the famous Nawwab Jafar Khan Nasiri (A.D. 1707 to 1727), has to be gleaned from a few scattered notices in Persian histories of Bengal and scarcely intelligible revenue accounts, though the century in qustion must be regarded as a *most important period* in the annals of the country, when we consider the deep and permanent traces impressed on the state of affairs, by the arrangements, institutions, offices, and official designations, introduced by the imperial government during that interval."

From Persian works, not indicated by Stirling, it is now possible to fill, though partially, this gap in our knowledge of Orissa during the seventeenth century, which Stirling rightly calls "a most important period in the annals of the country." Our sources of information are :—

(i) The Memoirs of Jahangir and the official annals of the reigns of Shah Jahan and Aurangzib, which throw light only on the conquests and changes of officials but not on the administration or the condition of the people. (ii) The *Muraqat-i-Hasan,* or Letters of Maulana Abul Hasan, who served the *subahdars* of Orissa as secretary for about 12 years (1655—1667), and put this collection together in 1080 A.H. (1669—1670). Only one manuscript of this work is known to exist, which belongs to the Nawwab of Rampur in Rohilkhand. (iii) Letters addressed by Aurangzib to Murshid Quli Khan when *diwan* of Bengal, Bihar and Orissa, about 1700—1705, included in imperial secretary Inayetullah Khan's *Ahkam-i-Alamgiri.* (iv) *Baharistan-i-Ghaibi* or memoirs of Shitab Khan, giving the history of Bengal and Orissa during the reign of Jahangir. (Paris MS.).

By means of these sources the middle and close of the century are brightly lit up for the historian, but the other portions of it will remain dark till some other happy discovery among Persian manuscripts.

2. LIST OF MUGHAL SUBAHDARS.

Hashim Khan, appointed 26th September, 1607 (*Tuz.* 60), transferred to Kashmir by order, dated 24th May, 1611, but continues in Orissa for some time. (*Tuz.* 97).

Rajah Kalyan (son of Rajah Todar Mal), appointed 1611 (*Tuz.* 98), removed and recalled to Court to answer charges (which were found on inquiry to be false), 1617. (*Tuz.* 192 and 199).

Mukarram Khan (son of Muazzam Khan), appointed 1617 (*Tuz.* 214).

Hasan Ali Kh. Turkman, appointed 1620. (*Tuz.* 308).

Jalayer Khan, (*Baharistan,* 273*a*).

Mirza Ahmad Beg Kh., app. 1621. (*Tuz.* 332), fled away 1624. Then interregnum.

Baqar Khan Najam Sani, 4th February, 1628-1632.

The order removing him from Orissa was dated 24th June, 1632, but he reached the imperial Court on return on 13th January, 1633.

Mutaqad Khan (Mirza Maki), 1632-1641.

The order removing him from Orissa was issued on 9th March, 1640, but he reached the imperial Court on 29th July, 1641.

Shah Nawaz Khan, 1641-1642.

Appointed to Orissa on 9th March, 1640, but went there about the middle of 1641, removed by order dated 8th March, 1642, but continued in the province till the end of that year.

Muhammad Zaman Tihrani (as agent of Prince Shuja), 1642-1645.

Order of appointment dated 8th March, 1642, removal dated 21st November, 1645.

Mutaqad Khan, 1645-1648.

Appointed 21st November, 1645. Recalled to Court in the 22nd year of Shah Jahan's reign (July 1648—June 1649).

Tarbiyat Khan (Shafiullah Birlas, vilayet-za) as agent of Prince Shuja, 1655-1656.

Anarchy, 1658-1659.

Ihtisham Khan, November 1659—September, 1660.

Khan-i-Dauran, September 1660—May 1667.
Tarbiyat Khan, June 1667—October 1669.
Safi [or Saif] Khan, October 1669—?
Rashid Khan, ?—March, 1676.
Shaista Khan, March 1676—December 1676 (?)
Nurullah (as agent of Prince Azam), June, 1678—?
Ghaznafar Khan, June 1698—
Kamgar Khan, ?—1704.
Azim-ush-shan, 1704-1712 (absentee).
Murshid Quli Khan, 1712-1727.*

3. SIEGE OF THE TEMPLE OF JAGANNATH.

When the rainy season arrived, Hashim Khan, the subahdar of Orissa, and all other officers thought that after the rise of Canopus, when Islam Khan and the officers posted in Bengal would set out against Masnad-i-ala Musa Khan and the famous "twelve Bhumiyas" of Bengal, they too should march out against Rajah Purushottam Dev and other zamindars of Orissa, and either force them to offer voluntary submission, or seize and send them to

---

* The *Alamgirnamah* says that the Emperor learnt of Khan-i-Dauran's death on 7th December 1667 (page 1067), but on page 1050 he is represented as dead in the preceding June. I have accepted the latter date. From 1704 to 1712, while Prince Azim-ush-shan was the governor of Bengal (including Orissa) and Bihar, Murshid Quli acted, first as diwan and later as deputy subahdar and *de facto* ruler. In 1712 he became, full governor of Bengal and Orissa. Ghaznafar's name is found only in *Fort St. George Diary*, 24 May 1698.

the imperial Court. But Rajah Keshodas Maru [a Rathor of Merta] thought that it would be cowardice on his part to wait for the co-operation of others and therefore he should undertake the exploit himself. He planned to set out from Katak, his own jagir, on the pretext of offering worship to the idol of Jagannath, reach the temple or monastery and after finishing his devotions treat the entire temple (enclosure) as a strong fort for himself, occupy it, seize all the property of the temple, which was worth more than two or three krores of Rupees, and torture the Brahman (servitors) to make them divulge the rest. It was done. When the news of it reached Rajah Purshottam Dev he thought it wise to punish Keshodas before the end of the monsoons and the arrival of other imperial commanders from Katak to reinforce him. . . Purushottam Dev came from Khurda with 10,000 cavalry, three or four *lakhs* of infantry and many *raths,* laid siege to the temple and pressed Rajah Keshodas hard. Some 500 to 1000 soldiers mounted each *rath,* which was driven forward by two to three thousand men. He brought ten to twenty such *raths** and pushed them on to the outer wall of the temple, making things intolerable for the men within. Rajah Keshodas, taking away the long poles—literally, pillars—from under the roofs of the houses and wrapping (their ends) with *shamianas, qanats* and apparel from the *farashkhanah,* which were then steeped in *ghee* and

* Maulana Shaikh in his masnavi on the sieze ascribed to the Rajah "more than 500 *raths*"—an incredible number. Each *rath* (he says) was made of wood, looked like a tall house, had 1,000 legs and was pushed forward by 1,000 men.

mustard oil, set fire to them and dashed them on the *raths* when the latter came close to the wall, so that a hundred or two hundred men on the top of the *raths* were at once burnt or killed, while two to three hundred others were trampled under one another's feet (in their hurried flight). The Uriyas, unable to resist, fled leaving the *raths* burning. Keshodas and his Rajputs defended themselves heroically. But many of his followers were slain in the struggle, and only 400 soldiers were left with him in the temple enclosure.

The Rajah of Khurda, on hearing of the defeat of his army, was disheartened, and took counsel with his wise wazir Bijadhar (Bidyadhar or Gajadhar ?)—who advised him to make peace. An ambassador was accordingly sent to Keshodas, but the negotiations were protracted.

In the meantime Islam Khan, the governor of Bengal, on hearing of Rajah Keshodas's adventure, sent strict orders urging Hashim Khan and other officers at Katak to go immediately to the aid of Keshodas. Rajah Purushottam Dev, on hearing of this new danger, agreed to make peace, promising (*a*) to send his daughter to the imperial harem (*dolah*), (*b*) to pay three *lakhs* of Rupees as tribute, (*c*) to give his sister in marriage to Rajah Keshodas and (*d*) pay him and his men one *lakh* of Rupees as a present (*nāl-bandi*). His officers induced Keshodas, in view of the severe loss of his men, to accept these terms, instead of holding out for more.

So, Keshodas left Puri with only forty horsemen (in order not to alarm Purushottam Dev), went to Khurda, and was there married to the Rajah's sister. But after the marriage, as Purushottam gave him only a lean worthless elephant, Keshodas grew angry, seized the big elephant and five female elephants which stood as guards at the palace gate and set off without taking leave. He sent his bride away (in advance) on a horse. The Uriyas crowded on all sides ; Keshodas Maru, fighting and slaying many of them, crossed the pass (between Khurda and Puri), reached the temple of Jagannath, and sent one of his officers to the Rajah demanding the *dolah* and tribute promised. The officers from Katak reached Puri and escorted Rajah Keshodas back to Katak . . . . The Emperor, at the recommendation of Islam Khan, promoted Keshodas to be a commander of 4000 and presented him with standards, a robe of honour, a sword, a dagger and a horse. (*Baharistan*, 12*a*-14*a*).

4. RAJAH KALYAN'S RAID ON KHURDA, 1611.

On being appointed subahdar of Orissa (*Tuz*. 98 says "*sardar* of the *sarkar* of Orissa"), Rajah Kalyan, the son of Rajah Todar Mal, decided to conquer Khurda and thus gain the Emperor's favour. After the country had been greatly sacked and devastated, Purushottam Dev made his submission, begged permission to come and wait at the Court in person, and agreed to send his daughter to the imperial harem (*dolah*) and present a tribute of three *lakhs* of Rupees and his famous elephant named Sheshanāg. These were delivered, and (also) one *lakh* of Rupees in cash with the *dolah*, and were duly sent to the Emperor by way of Bengal. (*Baharistan*, 57b-58a).

We read in the *Tuzuk* (p. 193) that shortly after 24th August, 1617, the Emperor viewed eighteen elephants sent to him by Rajah Kalyan from Orissa.

5. THE CONQUEST OF KHURDA BY THE MUGHALS, 1617.

In 1617, Mukarram Khan, the new governor of Orissa, invaded and conquered the kingdom of Khurda, of which the Rajah fled to the Rajah of Rajmahendri. Khurda was now annexed to the imperial dominions ,though the descendants of its last independent Rajah continued to enjoy some land as mere zamindars. The victorious subahdar was promoted to be a commander of 3000 (*Tuzuk*, 214-215).

The last notable event of Orissa in Jahangir's reign was the occupation of the province by the rebellious prince Shah Jahan and the flight of its imperial governor Mirza Ahmad Beg Khan in 1624. (*Bah.* 291*b*, *Tuz.* 382).

6. THE EXPANSION OF THE MUGHAL PROVINCE OF ORISSA.

In the sixteenth century the independent Rajahs of Orissa were crushed between the upper mill-stone of the Afghans advancing southwards from Bengal and the nether mill-stone of the Qutb-Shahi power (of Golkonda) expanding northwards from the Madras side. Under Akbar the Mughals held only the northern portion of Orissa, while the central portion was ruled by native princes with semi-independent powers, but bearing the title of *mansabdars* in the Mughal peerage. The Qutb-Shahis held the southern extremity of the province. In the reign of Shah Jahan the power of Golkonda was broken by the Mughals in 1636 and 1656, and Qutb Shah became a loyal feudatory of the Emperor of Delhi, paying him an annual tribute. Early in Aurangzib's reign Malud was the southernmost outpost of Mughal Orissa, and beyond it lay the Qutb-Shahi district of Chicacole, from which the Golkonda tribute "appertaining to the province of Orissa," about Rs. 20,000 a year, was sent to the Mughal subahdar of Orissa (*Muraqat*, 51, 160).

This result, however, was achieved after much fighting. On 13th Bahman, 12th regnal year (about the end of January, 1618), Jahangir records in his Memoirs: "At this time it was reported to me that Mukarram Khan, the governor of Orissa, had conquered the country of Khurda, and that the Rajah of that place had fled and gone into Rajmahendra. Between the province of Orissa and Golkonda there are two zamindars, one the Rajah of Khurda and the second the Rajah of Rajmahendra. The province of Khurda has come into the possession of the servants of the Court. After this it is the turn of the country of Rajmahendra. My hope in the grace of Allah is that the feet of my energy may advance further. At this time a petition from Qutb-ul-mulk reached my son Shah Jahan to the effect that as the boundary of his territory had approached that of the King [*i.e.*, the Mughal Emperor], and he owed service to this Court, he hoped an order would be issued to Mukarram Khan not to stretch out his hand, and to acquire possession of his country" (Rogers and Beveridge, i. 433).

In the winter of 1629-30, Baqar Khan, the governor of Orissa, marched to Khiraparah, 4 miles from Chattar-duar, a very narrow pass on the frontier between the Qutb-Shahi kingdom and Orissa, and 24 miles from Raj-mahendri, and plundered and laid waste its territory. The approach of the rainy season compelled him to retire without doing anything more. In the autumn of 1630 he set out again, with friendly levies from the zamindars of Khalikot, Kudla and Ala, and on 3rd December arrived in the environs of Mansurgarh, a fort built by a Golkonda officer named Mansur, 8 miles from Khiraparah. The enemy offered battle in the plain outside the fort, but were routed, and then the commandant of the fort, a Naikwar, capitulated. Baqar Khan returned, after leaving garrisons at Khiraparah and Mansurgarh (Abdul Hamid's *Padishahnamah,* I.A., 333). The Qutbshahis assembled in force to recover the fort, but Baqar Khan on hearing of it made a forced march and defeated the Deccan army. The news of this second victory reached the Emperor on 23rd April, 1631 (*Ibid,* 373).

7. BAQAR KHAN'S ADMINISTRATION.

Complaints against Baqar Khan's oppression of the peasantry and zamindars repeatedly reached Shah Jahan's ears, and at last on 24th June 1632 an order was issued removing him from the post. It is said that the governor called all the zamindars of the province together and then threw them into prison to extort revenue. By his order seven hundred of the captives were massacred, and only one escaped to carry the tale to Shah Jahan's Court. This fugitive produced a list (*tumar*, rent-roll) showing that Baqar Khan had collected forty lakhs of Rupees from the province. The Khan was in consequence recalled, and ordered to account for the money (*Masir-ul-umara*, iii. 484). His successor Mutaqad Khan ruled the province long and well, and died in retirement on 17th October, 1651 in extreme old age.

8. Interregnum and Ihtisham Khan's Administration.

From September 1657, when Shah Jahan fell ill and a war of succession broke out among his sons, to 6th May 1660, when Shuja fled from Dacca and Aurangzib became the sole master of Eastern India, there was anarchy in Orissa. The troops and most of the officers were withdrawn by Prince Shuja for his two advances on Agra and latterly for his prolonged struggle with Mir Jumla in the Rajmahal and Malda districts. Taking advantage of this state of things, all the Orissa zamindars withheld the revenue, and several of them built forts and looted their neighbourhood, for which they had afterwards to pay a heavy penalty, as we shall see in the section on Khan-i-Dauran's administration. But, by the autumn of the year 1659, Mir Jumla had established himself in Western Bengal in sufficient strength to enable him to detach from his army Ihtisham Khan to take charge of the governorless province of Orissa. Ihtisham Khan's stay there was too short to enable him to restore orderly government. That arduous task fell to the lot of Khan-i-Dauran, who in April 1660, was transferred from Allahabad to Orissa and worked there as *subahdar* till his death in May, 1667.

Ihtisham Khan's first acts were to issue a proclamation that the *khutba* should be read in all the mosques of Orissa, in the name of the new Emperor Aurangzib (*Muraqat,* 45), and to send a *parwanah* to all the *mansabdars, zamindars, chaudhuris, qanungoes,* etc., of the province announcing his own appointment as *subahdar* and ordering them to meet him at Narayangarh, whither he would march from Medinipur, the northern frontier of the province, some time after 14th November, 1659 (*Ibid,* 47-49).

When, less than a year afterwards, he was replaced by Khan-i-Dauran, and sent to Bengal to serve under Mir Jumla, he tried to carry away with himself as prisoners for default of revenue, the brothers of Rajah Nilkantha Dev, Gopinath, the brother of Bharat Patnayak and chief officer of Rajah Mukund Dev, and the other zamindars of the environs of Katak. As their zamindaris could not be administered nor any rent collected in the absence of these men, the Mughal faujdar of Katak secured the release of Gopinath Patnayak by himself signing a bond for Rs. 14,000 to Ihtisham Khan. And the other captives were similarly released. For this the faujdar was severely censured by Khan-i-Dauran, who insisted that they should be unconditionally delivered up to him as Ihtisham Khan's successor in office (*Muraqat,* 183-184, 156-157).

9. Mughal Reconquest of Orissa under Khan-i-Dauran, 1660-1663.

The first part of Khan-i-Dauran's viceroyalty was devoted to a task that was practically equivalent to the reconquest of Orissa for the Mughal Government, as imperial authority had disappeared from the province during the late War of Succession. The state of anarchy is very graphically described in the letters of this subahdar: "All the zamindars are refractory, owing to the slack rule of my predecessors" (page 134). The "zamindars on the further side of the Katjhuri, in the jurisdiction of Sayyid Sher Khan, have refused tribute and declared war against him" (page 59). "Krishna Bhanj, of Hariharpur, the leading zamindar of this province, during the interregnum spread his power over the country from Medinipur to Bhadrak, a distance of 50 or 60 *kos*, seizing the property of the inhabitants and wayfarers and severely oppressing the people" (pages 72 and 107). "The fort of Panchira was wrested from Shuja's men by Lakshmi Narayan Bhanj, the Rajah of Keonjhar, during the time of disorder" (pages 52, 58, 129). "For the last three years, the zamindars on the further side of Katak have been collecting vast forces and getting ready for war" (page 72)." Bahadur the zamindar of Hijli is in rebellion" (page 130). "Chhut Rai has dispersed the ryots of Medinipur, and is building a fort in the jungles with evil intentions" (page 190). It is useless to give a list of the names of the other rebel zamindars here, as they will be mentioned in detail in the history of Khan-i-Dauran's campaigns which follows.

The *farman* appointing Khan-i-Dauran to Orissa was sent from the imperial Court on 3rd April, 1660 (*Alamgirnamah,* 474). He received it at Allahabad, where he was subahdar, and soon set out for his new province "at the very height of the monsoons, defying the raging storms, excessive mud, and flooded rivers, which had closed the paths" (*Muraqat,* 85). On 26th September he entered Medinipur, the first town after crossing the Orissa frontier (page 130). After spending some days here to settle the district, organize the civil administration and revenue collection and station faujdars in all directions, he set out for Jaleshwar, in the meantime writing to the zamindars of northern Orissa to meet him on the way and pay their respects as loyal subjects (page 134). His intention was to "finish the Hijli business" first. Bahadur, the zamindar of that port, had rebelled, and had to be subdued before the Mughal route from Medinipur *via* Narayangarh and Jaleshwar to Baleshwar could be rendered safe. But "the other zamindars report that the country of Hijli is now covered with mud and water, and, not to speak of cavalry, even foot soldiers cannot traverse it. After a time, when the roads of the district become dry again, the campaign should be opened" (pages 132 and 134). So, Khan-i-Dauran put off the idea, and went direct to Jaleshwar, which he reached in the latter half of October (page 156).

At the news of the governor's approach, both Bahadur and Krishna Bhanj, the Rajah of Hariharpur (*i.e.,* Mayurbhanj), wrote to him professing submission and promising to wait on him at Jaleshwar (pages 133, 136 and 181). The Mughal faujdar of Remuna, on the Mayurbhanj frontier, wrote to the new governor that the agents (*wakils*) of these two zamindars had reached him to arrange for their masters' interview. He was ordered in reply to reassure them with kindness and send them back to their masters that they might come without fear or suspicion and see Khan-i-Dauran at Jaleshwar (page 181).

10. HARIHARPUR (MAYURBHANJ) AFFAIRS.

Bahadur evidently changed his mind and held off; Krishna Bhanj* came, but met with a terrible fate, which is best described in the governor's own words: "When I reached Jaleshwar, which is near his zamindari, Krishna Bhanj saw me after wasting a month on the pretext of choosing a lucky day [for the visit], and offered false excuses [for his late disloyal conduct]. During the inquiry and discussion for settling the amount of the revenue to be paid by him, he, inspired by pride in the largeness of his force, drew his dagger and rushed towards me. His companions, too, unsheathed their swords and made repeated charges. The grace of the Emperor saved my life. We slew Krishna Bhanj and many of his men. The rest fled. Some chiefs, such as Udand, the zamindar of Narsingpur, Chhattreshwar Dhol,

* His offences are thus summed up: "He kept one thousand horse and ten or twelve thousand foot soldiers, and was obeyed and helped by all the zamindars of this country. [During the anarchy] he had plundered the tract from Bhadrak to Medinipur, carried off the ryots to his own territory, increased the cultivation there, and ruined the imperial dominions" (page 107).

the zamindar of Ghatsila, and Harichandan, the zamindar of Nilgiri, threw away their weapons and delivered themselves up as prisoners" (pages 72 and 107-109).

"The relatives of the slain Rajah [of Mayurbhanj] raised disturbances, molesting the royts. So, I started for Hariharpur to punish them and halted at Remuna on the frontier of his dominion. His brother, Jay Bhanj, submitted, begged pardon, and brought to me his mother and son and three elephants and some money as a present (*peshkash*), and begged the *tika* of the Rajahship and zamindari for the son. I agreed, and then started to punish the rebels near Katak" (page 109).

11. KHURDA RAJ AFFAIRS.

When the Khan reached Katak, Rajah Mukund Dev of Khurda, "the leading zamindar of this country, whose orders are obeyed by the other zamindars"—"whom all the other zamindars of this country worship like a god* and disobedience of whose order they regard as a great sin" (pages 77 and 102)—waited on him with due humility, accompanied by the other zamindars and Khandaits [of Central Orissa] (page 110). Then, "owing to the badness of the climate, a severe malady seized the governor and he was confined to bed for two months, unable to move

* *Cf.* Stirling: "The title of sovereignty has been always acknowledged, by the general voice and feeling of the country, to vest in the Rajahs of Khurda. Down to the present moment the Rajahs of Khurda are the sole fountain of honour in this district" (86).

about." "The rustics [*i.e.*, uncultivated local zamindars] seized the opportunity and caused disorder. Rajah Mukund Dev absented himself from the force sent by me to punish the rebels, and himself caused lawlessness. The Mughal troops subdued many of the rebels and took several forts. After recovering a little I (*i.e.*, Khan-i-Dauran) on 7th February 1661 set out from Katak against the other forts which my subordinates were too weak to capture" (page 77). "On 16th February I arrived near the forts of Kalupara, Mutri, Karkahi, Khurdiha and [three] others,—seven forts close to each other on the side of a high hill. An assault was ordered next day. When our troops appeared near the forts, the enemy in a numberless host, consisting of *paiks* and infantry, both *Khudshan* (?) and zamindars of Banki and Ranpur, and other *Bhumiahs* and *Khandaits*,—offered us battle. Our men slew many of them and carried their trenches at the foot of the hill and after repeated charges entered their [main?] lines. The enemy fought with matchlocks, arrows, *khandahs, sablis, duars, dhukans, sintis*, etc., but being unable to resist fled away with their families. A great victory—unequalled by that of any former *subahdar*—was won. The seven forts were captured. Two or three days were spent in settling the conquered district and appointing *thanahs*" (pages 99-101).

"On 20th February, 1661, I left for the conquest of Khurda, the ancestral home of Mukund Dev, situated in the midst of a dense jungle and lofty hills (page 78). On the 23rd, I encamped a mile from Khurda. The Rajah had fled from it, and we seized a vast amount of booty and many prisoners at his capital" (page 102). "During the last 50 years, no other *subahdar* had reached these places. They were all conquered by my army! and the rustics became the food of the pitiless sword. I gave Mukund Dev's throne to his younger brother Bhramarbar" (page 78). The victorious *subahdar* halted at Khurda for some days. The fate of the premier Rajah of the province struck a salutary terror in the hearts of the other evil-doers. "All lawless men are now waiting on me with every mark of abject submission. The zamindar of Banki and Khand Narendra (the zamindar of Ranpur) have sent trusty agents to arrange for their interview with me. The path for collecting the revenue has been opened in all places and mahals. Rajah Mukund Dev, who had been ill-advised enough to defy my authority and withhold tribute, finding no way of escape from our heroes, saw me penitently on 18th March. The rebel Bharat [Patnayak], too, has done the same" (pages 158-159). Mukund Dev was afterwards restored to his throne, as we know from other sources.

An interesting bit of the history of the Khurda Rajahs is furnished in a letter of Khan-i-Dauran to his agent at the imperial Court. "Received your letter reporting that a counterfeit Gangadhar has gone to the Court and secured an interview with Kumar Ram Singh [Kachhwa, son of Mirza Rajah Jay Singh] through the mediation of Rai Brindaban-das, the *mushrif* of the elephant department, and offered to pay every year 12 lakhs of Rupees as tribute if the State is given to him. When I arrived in this province, Mukund Dev was the

Rajah of Khurda. As he caused disturbances, I expelled him from his zamindari and gave the *tika* of Rajahship to his younger brother and reported the case to the Emperor. I have learnt the following facts from trustworthy men:—when the late Mutaqad Khan was *subahdar*, he slew Narsingh Dev and made his nephew Gangadhar Rajah. Balabhadra Dev, the elder brother of the slain, became Rajah after killing Gangadhar with the help of the officers of the State. When he died, Mukund Dev succeeded at the age of four years only. During the administration of Muhammad Hayat, the agent of Shuja, a pretended Gangadhar appeared and created a disturbance. He was slain by a confederacy of the zamindars near Katak. After my arrival in the province, another man claiming to be the same (Rajah) appeared in Talmal (in South Orissa). Muhammad Jan, the faujdar of that district, arrested him and sent him to me, and he is still confined in the fort of Mankhandi at Katak. They say another man assuming the same name is roving in the jungles" (pages 186-187).

12. More Conquests by Khan-i-Dauran.

On 8th March 1661, the *subahdar* left Katak to chastise Lakshmi Narayan Bhanj, the Rajah of Keonjhar, who had wrested the fort of Panchira from Shuja's men (pages 58-59). His territory was ravaged and the fort in question recovered (pages 52 and 129).

At a subsequent date (probably), Bahadur, the rebel zamindar of Hijli, was captured with his family (page 116).

After Khan-i-Dauran had expelled Mukund Dev from Khurda, "Khand Narendra, the zamindar of Ranpur, and the zamindars of Malhipara and Dompara, who had never before waited on any *subahdar,*" saw him and agreed to pay tribute (page 103). "The zamindars on the further side of the Katjhuri, who had withheld tribute and fought the faujdar, Sayyid Sher Khan, were defeated" (page 59).

At the same time the Mughal faujdar of Malud, on the southern frontier of Orissa, was engaged in suppressing the rebellion of Pitam, the zamindar of Andhiari, and Kumar Guru, the zamindar of Malud (page 158).

The zamindari of Kanika was conquered by Mian Muhammad Jan, and the Rajah was driven out to a fort named Rika (?) on an island in the ocean. In order to besiege him there, *chhamp* boats of the river Mahanadi and larger boats too were sent to Muhammad Jan, with the help of Gopali, the zamindar of Kujang (pages 167 and 168).

Rao Tara [or Rawat Rai],* the zamindar of Kuyilu Madhupur, was thrown into prison for heavy arrears of revenue to the imperial exchequer for the parganah of Awlas. Gopali of Kujang also suffered the same fate (pages 170 and 172).

Khwajah Khalid Naqshbandi laid siege to the fort of Kulrah and carried mines under its walls. Then Sri Chandan [or Harichandan?], the *qiladar,* begged quarter. He was promised his life, but thrown into prison and

* On page 172 the name is spelt as *Bar-avatara*?

the fort was taken possession of. So also was another fort named Katkal (page 176).

Chhut Rai, the zamindar of Kailikot,* evidently in the neighbourhood of Narayangarh, had dispersed the ryots of (the parganah of) Medinipur and built a fort in the jungle with evil intentions (page 190). But his sons were thrown into prison, and he seems to have submitted, for we read in another letter how a *parwanah* was sent to him to stop the horse-dealers who used to deviate from the imperial road and take their horses by way of Banpur. They were to be sent to the provincial governor in future (page 160).

Rajah Nilkantha Dev was a loyal servant of the empire and fought under the Mughal banners with his contingent (page 143). Parganah Qutbshahi was his *jagir*, which he administered through his agent Gajadhar. Rs. 4,400 were due from the Rajah as arrears of revenue (pages 145 and 165). His brothers were placed in confinement by Ihtisham Khan for default, but Khan-i-Dauran secured their release (page 156).

The result of these operations was the restoration of imperial authority in Orissa. The country again enjoyed peace and order and the imperial revenue, which had entirely dried up during the interregnum, began to be realized again. Khan-i-Dauran could legitimately boast of his military successes, which in his own words were "unrivalled by any preceding *subahdar*." As he wrote in his despatches to the Emperor Aurangzib, "I have

---

* I am doubtful about this locality. Page 160 seems to refer to another *Kalikot* which was in the extreme south of Orissa.

punished all the usurpers, oppressors, and lawless men of the province and made them obedient. The revenue is being collected by our officers. The people are enjoying peace and happiness and plying their trades" (page 49). And, again, a year later, about April, 1662, he wrote, "The province is being well administered" (page 54).

13. Revenue collection.

After taking effective possession of the province and restoring order in this way, Khan-i-Dauran, early in 1662, sent five elephants as his present to the Emperor on the occasion of the marriage of two of his (the Khan's) sons, together with two other elephants presented by the Sultan of Golkonda. (*Muraqat,* page 53.) These, as we know from the official history (*Alamgirnamah,* 751), reached the Court at the end of May. The forests of Telingana, immediately west of Orissa and lying in the Golkonda territory, were famous for elephants, and these animals formed the usual present from the governors of Orissa to the Padishah. In May, 1628, Shah Jahan received five elephants from Baqar Khan and in September 1636 eight others from Mutaqad Khan. (Abdul Hamid's *Padishahnamah,* I.A. 201 and I.B. 216.)

Elephants, however, were occasional presents. The normal revenue also began to be sent to the imperial Court regularly from this time. Having "punished all the usurpers, oppressors, and lawless men of the province, and made them obedient," Khan-i-Dauran could report to the Emperor, "the revenue is being collected by our officers" ; and, as a proof of it, he at once transmitted to the exchequer at Delhi "the accumulated revenue of 15 lakhs of Rupees, kept at Katak and the parganahs, together with seven pieces of cloth (*parchah*), one piece of broad cloth, and two caskets of *Chhani* decorated in the Dutch style." These were escorted by his own men as far as Rajmahal,* whence they were to be sent to Court with the revenue of Bengal. (*Muraqat*, page 50.)

He next devoted himself to realizing the portion of the Golkonda tribute which "appertained to the province of Orissa," being paid from the Golkonda district of Chicacole. This money had naturally remained unpaid during the civil war between Aurangzib and his brothers. Its exact amount was also in dispute. The Qutbshahi agent at Chicacole (Haidar Khan) asserted that he had paid the fixed sums of Rs. 12,000 and Rs. 1,000 during every year of Shuja's viceroyalty. But the papers sent from Delhi put the tribute at Rs. 20,000 a year. Khan-i-Dauran succeeded in collecting Rs. 80,000 out of the arrears under this head, and sent an agent to Chicacole to dun for the balance. (Page 51.)

Evidently all the financial records of Shuja's time had been lost or destroyed by dishonest officers (page 60), and this produced uncertainty about the imperial dues also. For example, the Emperor knew the tribute of the zamindars of Saranghara to be Rs. 8,000 a year, but could not say what additional sum they used to pay as succession fee. Khan-i-Dauran wrote in reply, "I find from the

---

* Later, the Orissa revenue used to be delivered to the faujdar of Bardwan for transmission to Court. (Page 189).

old records of the *subah* that they used to pay Rs. 10,000 as succession fee, but then their annual tribute was nothing like what your Majesty represents it. They used to pay something as *nazar* at intervals of two or three years [but no regular tribute]. I have now laid on Purushottam Dev Rs. 10,000 as fee for succeeding his brother [in the zamindari], which has been fully realized." (Page 61.)

Severe measures had to be taken with the revenue collectors and zamindars lest they should defraud the Government of its dues. Khan-i-Dauran writes thus to Muhammad Jan, a former diwan of the province, whom he had appointed (page 196) land-steward or factor (*sahib-i-ihtamam*) for his fiefs from Bhadrak to the southern limit of Orissa:—"Balabhadra and Brajanath *qanungoes*, who have been released from prison, and Paramananda, the zamindar of Rahmachnan (?), are sent to you in chains under a bailiff (*sazawal*) as asked for by you......If you fear that before my arrival near Katak the zamindars will carry off the crops, then write urging the *amils* to collect the dues and attach the standing crops. Appoint men to guard the grain." (Pages 163, 164). And, again, to Man Singh, the faujdar of Remuna: —"Send select men to hasten the gathering in and guarding of the crops and the collection of the Government dues......Send them quickly that the revenue (*i.e.* Government share) of the autumn harvest may not be removed." (Page 182).

The inference naturally suggested by the above passages, namely, that in Mughal times the revenue of

Orissa was collected in the form of rice, is definitely supported by a letter from Murshid Quli Khan to Aurangzib written about 1704: "The revenue-collection of Orissa depends on the autumn harvest, which has to be kept stored for a long time, and, in spite of all my devices, cannot be sold." To this the Emperor replied, "I have heard that traders take the crop and in return for it they bring from the ports whatsoever is in demand." (Inayetullah's *Ahkam-i-Alamgiri*, Rampur MS., 219*b*.) Khan-i-Dauran says the same thing,—"In this country the realization of the land-revenue of the whole year depends on the three months of autumn." (Page 65.) "As for the *malangi* boats for loading rice in, they have not been procured owing to the bad conduct of the darogha of the port. Get boats from the zamindars of the mahal, and send the rice to the port to be shipped in the sailing season." (Page 165, see also page 146.)

Some incidental light is thrown on the State purchase of local industries. Khan-i-Dauran writes to Muhammad Jan, "The officers of the imperial Government have reported that 210 *kudi* of cloth, of the *sahan, barbarah, do-suti* and *thati* varieties, 20,000 maunds of rice, 300 maunds of mustard oil ('yellow oil'), 260 maunds of sesamum, and 100 maunds of *galmosafr* are required for provisioning the ships [of the State]. According to the schedule attached to this letter, urge the officers of Jajpur, Bhadrak and other mahals in your faujdari to get them ready quickly and send them before the sailing season to the port of Baleshwar to Muhammad Baqar, the darogha of ship construction." [This is evidently a reference to Shaista Khan's vigorous naval construction programme with a view to his conquest of Chittagong in 1665.] "The price of these things will be deducted from the amounts due from the *amlas.*"

"The *amlas* should advance to the weavers, artisans, oil-vendors, etc., money for the things ordered. First, settle the price with the help of brokers. Then, take bonds with the attestation of the brokers for the delivery of the goods in time. Send the *do-suti* before the other articles to the darogha that he may make sails with them. All the *kalapatis* and *najars,*—master craftsmen and blacksmiths,—living at the port of Harishpur and other places, should be won over and sent to Baleshwar, to engage in shipbuilding [for the Government] there. Dated 28th December, 1664." (Pp. 173—175.)

We also learn that "Rs. 39,000 was due from the chaudhuri and qanungo of Chakla Medinipur, on account of the *taqavi* loan and *pattan* to the peasants." (Page 189.) A much larger amount must have been granted by the State for this purpose.

14. Comparative Revenue Returns.

No useful or very reliable return of the total revenue of Orissa during the seventeenth century can be constructed, first because the area under imperial rule varied considerably from time to time, and, secondly because the Persian statistical books (*Dastur-ul-aml*) now extant are very badly written and occasionally drop certain figures out of a sum and thus give palpably wrong amounts. In these MSS. arithmetical figures are not represented by the Arabic numerals (as in all modern countries), nor by letters of the alphabet (as in the Roman system of notation and the Arabic *abjad*), but by *raqaim* or groups of symbolic marks suggestive of Chinese writing. The slightest carelessness or indistinctness in writing these *raqaim* may turn 20 into 2,000. The following comparative study of the revenue of Mughal Orissa at different periods is placed before the reader with the warnings that (*a*) the area assessed was not always the same, (*b*) these figures give only the standard or paper assessment, while the actual collection fluctuated from year to year and was always short of these amounts, and (*c*) some of the figures quoted below are probably unreliable or incorrectly transcribed in the Persian MSS.

Revenue of Orissa.

1594 A.D.	Rs.	31,43,316	(Ain-i-Akbari ii. 141-144)
1648 ,,	Rs.	50,00,000	(Abdul Hamid's Padishahnamah ii-711)
1654 ,,	Rs.	56,39,500	(Dastur-ul-aml used by Thomas)
1665 ,,	Rs.	72,70,000	(Bernier, 457)
c 1690 ,,	Rs.	35,70,500	(Dastur-ul-aml Br. Mus Or. 1641 f. 5*b*)
c 1695-1700	Rs.	43,21,025	(Dastur-ul-aml used by Thomas)
c 1695 A.D.	Rs.	1,00,02,625	(Khulasat-ut-tawarikh, 32*a*)
c 1697-1707	Rs.	57,07,500	(Manucci, ii. 414)
1707 A.D.	Rs.	35,70,500	(Ramusio)
1707 ,,	Rs.	35,70,275	Jagjivandas. in India Office MS. 1799, p. 5,
Tieffenthaler,	Rs.	35,70,525	

It will be seen that the 5th, 9th, 10th and 11th of the above figures are all derived from the same source, *viz.*, an official return. The amount mentioned in the *Khulasat-ut-tawarikh* is clearly wrong. The rather high figures given by Bernier and Manucci are not necessarily incorrect, but may be due to the efficient administration of Khan-i-Dauran and Murshid Quli Khan respectively.

15. THE DIWANS AND THEIR METHOD OF REVENUE ADMINISTRATION.

List of Diwans of Orissa.

Mian Muhammad Jan, ?—1657 ; dismissed, lived at Baleshwar, afterwards (1661) appointed land-agent of the subahdar, Khan-i-Dauran.

Mir Ismail, ?—October, 1660.

Mirza Ibrahim, Bakhshi, officiates as diwan also, October, 1660—March, 1661, dismissed.

Muhammad Hashim, March 1661—*c.* 1663, dismissed.

Muhammad Tahir, died in the province.

Muhammad Taqi, *c.* October, 1664— 1665 ?

Khwajah Muhammad Mumin, *c.* 1665—?

Owing to the political disturbances through which the province had passed at the end of Shah Jahan's reign, the loss of financial papers, and the appointment of an almost entirely new staff of officials, the revenue department was in a very unsatisfactory and confused condition during the first few years of Aurangzib's reign. Some of the provincial diwans seem to have been inefficient, slack or dishonest ; otherwise we cannot account for their rapid succession and frequent dismissal. A permanent diwan arrived in March 1661 in the person of Muhammad Hashim. This man set to work with the proverbial energy of a new broom. Proud of having been appointed from the Court by the officiating Imperial Chancellor (Rajah Raghunath), and no doubt charged with a mission to reform the administration of the department and realize the State dues fully, he reached the province with a contempt for his predecessors in office and a deep-rooted suspicion that the subahdar had been robbing the State in collusion with the local diwans.

Muhammad Hashim, diwan, started by rudely quarrelling with Khan-i-Dauran. The subahdar wrote to him on 1st July, 1661, "Your predecessors were Muhammad Jan and Mir Ismail. You have called for their papers. What objection can I possibly have to giving them to you? Muhammad Jan gave up his office long ago, and has since then been living at Jajpur on account of ill-health. You complain that Mir Ibrahim, Bakhshi, has usurped and appropriated to himself some villages in the parganah of Sarsatibisi. What his agents have collected from that parganah will be paid into the imperial treasury. You write that the amil of parganah Karmul has misappropriated some money collected in that mahal. I order an inquiry to be made, and in case the allegation is found true, the man will be beaten to make him disgorge the money." (Pp. 141, 142, see also 142—145.)

The new diwan seems to have set himself up as a centre of defiance to the provincial governor's authority, and introduced confusion into the executive government. As Khan-i-Dauran wrote to him, "You have summoned the employees of the Mint to Hariharpur. Have you received any order from the Emperor to set up a Mint there? If not, send the men immediately back to Katak to do their former work." [Then follows a censure of the diwan's conduct.] "The men of the imperial artillery, starving through non-payment of their salary, have come away from the outposts where they were stationed. You should come here quickly and grant them *tan* (cash pay) according to the regulations." (Pp. 146, 147.) We learn a little later that their pay had been stopped on the plea of checking the accounts!

Even in the department of revenue collection, the inconsiderate and capricious methods of Muhammad Hashim spelt ruin to the imperial administration. As Khan-i-Dauran wrote to Aurangzib:—

"The mahals of crown-land (*khalsa*) have been reduced to desolation and their affairs have fallen into confusion, by reason of the harsh assessment (*tashkhis*) of an unsuitable amount of revenue and the neglect of attention to details by Muhammad Hashim, the diwan. The villages have been ruined by his harsh exactions. He used to transact business in this way: when a candidate for revenue-collectorship (*krori*) accepted the post, Hashim Khan used to impose on him the (paper) assessment of the parganah and send him there, before he could learn about the (actual) yield of the place. After a short time, another man was secured for the same post, and

Hashim Khan, taking money for himself from this man, dismissed the former collector, appointed the second man and made him promise in writing to pay a larger revenue than the first *krori* had engaged for. After a little more time, a third man appeared, offering a still higher sum to the State, and he was sent as collector to the parganah, on his giving a bribe to Hashim Khan and signing a bond (*muchalka*) for the payment of a larger revenue! The Khan never informed the zamindars, headmen (*chaudhuris*) and ryots about this assessment (*jama-bandi*), but kept them full of anxiety and distraction as to the State demand. He has thus increased the revenue [on paper] two-fold in some places and three-fold in others, while the ryots, unable to pay, have fled [from their homes] and the villages have turned into a wilderness... When Muhammad Hashim arrived in person to make a settlement (*band-o-bast*), the ryots, already brought to death's door by his oppression and harsh exactions, [mostly] fled on hearing the news of it. Some of them, unable to pay the demand, have died under blows; most others are in prison. It is impossible for me to report [fully] the grievances of the ryots, who, having sold their wives and children, have barely succeeded in keeping body and soul together." (Pages 63, 64.)

As Muhammad Hashim refused to follow the advice of Khan-i-Dauran and reform his ways, the latter wrote to the Imperial Chancellor to remove him and appoint another *diwan* (page 65). This was done, either late in 1662 or early in 1663 (as Rajah Raghunath, to whom the governor's letter was addressed, died on 2nd June, 1663).

16. Islam in Orissa.

The pro-Islamic ordinances issued by Aurangzib early in his reign and described in my *History of Aurangzib*, Volume III, Ch. 28, were enforced in Orissa also. On page 203 of the *Muraqat-i-Hasan* is given the text of the proclamation by which "the *faujdars, thanahdars, gumashtahs* of *jagirdars, amils, kroris*, ferrymen, road-guards, *chaudhuris, qanungoes* and *zamindars*, of the entire *subah* of Orissa" are told that His Majesty the Emperor had abolished the duty on "the commodities mentioned in the following schedule," for the good of his subjects, and that these officers should abstain from levying the taxes and should keep the roads open for the transit of goods, on pain of imperial displeasure and chastisement. The schedule is not given in my MS., but we know from other sources what the abolished duties were. (See my *Mughal Administration*, Ch. 5.)

The beginning of Aurangzib's reign saw the strict restoration of the offices of Canon Law Judge (*qazi*) and Censor of Public Morals (*muhtasib*) enjoined by Islamic rule and precedent, in every province and important town. Shaikh Junaid was appointed *muhtasib* of Katak, and his duties are described on page 196. (See also *History of Aurangzib*, III, Ch. 28, § 2.) Of the *qazis* of Katak we find two names: Rahmatullah, who was dismissed for misconduct and violation of canon law, and Sayyid Muhammad Ghaus, who succeeded him both as *qazi* and *mir-i-adil*, on a salary of Rs. 4 daily, in 1665. (Pages 192—195 and 125.)

At the end of the sixteenth century, Orissa, like many other parts of Eastern India, was notorious for the castration of children and their sale as eunuchs by their mercenary parents. (Jarrett's *Ain-i-Akbari*, ii, 126.) In 1668 Aurangzib issued a general order forbidding this wicked practice throughout his empire. (*Masir-i-Alamgiri*, 75.) Even some years earlier he had made the Imperial Chancellor, Rajah Raghunath, write to the governor Khan-i-Dauran, a "letter by order" telling him that in Orissa many people used to castrate their sons, that Shujà had forbidden it during his viceroyalty, and that the *subahdar* should put a stop to the practice immediately on the receipt of this imperial order. Khan-i-Dauran replied, "I have made careful inquiries, but found no trace of this practice. They say that it has never been done in this province from ancient times to this." (Pages 75, 76.)

The Muhammadan rulers of India used to make grants of rent-free land to the holy men and scholars of their own faith as "help to subsistence" (*madad-i-mash*). Several instances of this system are given in the *Muraqat*. "Shaikh Abul Khair lives like a *darvish* in a monastery in the village of Qutbpur in *sarkar* Goalpar. For the last 24 years he has been enjoying as his *madad-i-mash* a village named Darbast-Jasra in parganah Kasijurah in that *sarkar*, in accordance with the *sanads* of former governors. The papers sent by the Khan-i-Khanan (*i.e.*, Mir Jumla) to the diwan of this *subah* show the village as resumed to the State. Please move the Emperor to restore this faqir's grant." (Khan-i-Dauran to the

Imperial Chancellor, pages 78, 79.) "Shaikh Barkhurdar, a member of the Naqshbandi order and a holy monk of Katak, enjoys as his *madad-i-mash* a village yielding Rs. 317 a year, named Nur-tank in parganah Karmul, in *sarkar* Katak. I recommend for him the additional grant of one Rupee daily from the income of the *chabutra* of the *mir-i-bahar* (admiral or *ghat* officer) of Katak." (Khan-i-Dauran to the Chief Sadar of the empire, page 124.) We also have a *parwanah,* dated 13th December, 1665, conferring a *madad-i-mash* village in parganah Baqarabad, *sarkar* Katak, on Hakim Muhammad Rafi. (Page 200.)

The *Muraqat* also throws light on Aurangzib's policy of temple-destruction. On page 172 the governor writes to his agent Muhammad Jan: "The destruction of the temple of Kendrapara and the building of a mosque there has greatly pleased me." Page 202 gives the following general order for the demolition of Hindu places of worship:

"To all *faujdars, thanahdars, mutasaddis,* agents of *jagirdars, kroris,* and *amlas* from Katak to Medinipur on the frontier of Orissa. The imperial Paymaster Asad Khan has sent a letter written by order of the Emperor, to say that the Emperor, learning from the news-letters of the province of Orissa that at the village of Tilkuti in Medinipur a temple has been [newly] built, has issued his august mandate for its destruction and the destruction of all temples built anywhere in this province by the... infidels. Therefore, you are commanded with extreme urgency that immediately on the receipt of this letter you should destroy the above-mentioned temples. Every idol-house built during the last 10 or 12 years, whether with brick or clay, should be demolished without delay. Also, do not allow the...Hindus and...infidels to repair their old temples. Reports of the destruction of temples should be sent to the Court under the seal of the *qazis* and attested by pious Shaikhs."

17. Topographical Notes.

The following *faujdaris* or sub-divisions, each under a *faujdar*, are incidentally mentioned in the *Muraqat*:—

1. Chakla Medinipur, from Medinipur to Narayangarh. (Pp. 38, 188.)

2. Remuna, on the frontier of Mayurbhanj. (Pp. 181, 109). Five miles north-west of Balasore.

3. Katak. (P. 137.)

4. Pipli Niur, beyond the Katjhuri river. (P. 52.) Twenty-two miles due north of Puri.

5. Padishahnagar, beyond the Katjhuri river. (P. 52.)

6. Pachhera (P. 62.) *Panchira*, west of the Baitarani, 24 miles west of Bhadrak and 3 miles west of Killah Amboh ; it stood at the gate of the kingdom of Keonjhar when proceeding from the east.

7. Sarang-garh and Sandhahpur ['Sarangerh and Santrapur' of Stirling, page 49.] (Page 82.)

8. Talmal. (Pp. 145, 156, 163.)

9. Malud, "on the frontier facing the Deccan." (Pp. 81, 158, 160, 162.) South of Lake Chilka, 19.33N. 85.19E.

All the above are mentioned by Stirling (48, 49) as Mughal thanahs, with the exception of *Padishahnagar*, the nearest approach to which in Stirling's list is *Alemghir Shirgerh*.

We also learn that Soroh was on the frontier of Bhadrak and Lakhanpur on that of Keonjhar (*Muraqat*, pp. 41, 59.) As to *Khalikot* or *Kailikot*, Stirling (page 45) mentions the zamindari of *Kalicote* as "a Hill Estate, now under the Ganjam District. Separated from Orissa about 1730." Fifteen miles due north of Ganjam Town.

Mansurgarh.—I find a *Mansur-Kota* 12 miles south-west of Ganjam and 8 miles due east of Berhampur.

Hariharpur.—Nine miles south of Baripada (in the Mayurbhanj State.)

Narsinghpur.—North of the Mahanadi, 20.27N. 85.7E.

Nilgiri.—Eleven miles south-west of Balasore.

Soroh.—On the railway line, midway between Balasore and Bhadrak.

Khurda.—The old fort stands 5½ miles west of the Khurda Road station.

Kujang.—20.14E. 86.34E. on the seacoast.

Dompara.—19 miles south-west west of Katak.

Malipara.—Eleven miles south-east of Dompara.

Kalupara.—"Gurr Kalloparra" of *Indian Atlas*, sheet 116, 5 miles south-east of the Khurda Road station.

Mutri.—"Mootooree" of the *Atlas*, 1 mile north-west of Kalloparra.

Khurdiha.—"Gurr gorodhea" of the *Atlas*, 2 miles south-west of Kalloparra.

Bani.—On the south bank of the Mahanadi, 23 miles south-west west of Katak.

Ranpur.—20.4N. 85.25E.

Talmal.—At the north-east corner of Lake Chilka, 15 miles north-west west of Puri.

Harishpur Garh.—On the seacoast, 20.4N. 86.29E.

Kanika.—Along the seacoast, north of Point Palmyras and south of 21N. Latitude.

Kulrah.—"Khulardah" of *Atlas*, 8 miles south south-east of Katak.

Bhanpur.—Fourteen miles north of Kalikot. (Sheet 107.)

Rawata.—There is a parganah "Raootrah" in *Atlas*, due north-east of Balasore, across the river. (Sheet 115.)

XV

A GREAT HINDU MEMOIR-WRITER.

I. Family History.

The complete official history of the reign of the Emperor Aurangzib (1658-1707 A.D.) was written from State papers and personal recollections by Muhammad Saqi Mustaid Khan only three years after that Emperor's death. It is invaluable for dates, names of persons and places, the proper sequence of events, and official changes and administrative regulations. But it is a small volume, devoting on an average only ten pages to the affairs of one year of the reign of a sovereign who was one of the most active and ambitious rulers of the world and effected such momentous changes in Northern India and Southern India alike. A chapter of this work is therefore usually a dry list of official appointments and changes (exactly like the Government Gazettes of the present day) and a bare summary of events following one another in rapid succession. It tells us nothing about the real circumstances under which the events took place, their true causes and effects, the condition of the people and the state of the country.

For these latter points the most valuable contemporary history of Aurangzib is the *Nuskha-i-Dilkasha* written by a Hindu named Bhimsen ,who was a hereditary civil officer of the Mughal Government, passed his life in the Mughal cities and camps of the Deccan, and visited most places of India from Cape Comorin to Delhi. This work contains very important, and often unique information about many historical personages and events of the time and topographical details. The British Museum, London, has a complete manuscript of the *Dilkasha,* hastily but correctly written (*Or.* 23). The copy belonging to the India Office Library, London, is less correct and covers only the first half of the book, ending abruptly with the capture of Golkonda in 1687. (No. 94, Ethe's Catalogue 445.) The Bibliotheque Nationale, Paris, has another and a complete copy (Suppl. 259, Blochet's Catalogue 602.) One other MS of it is known to exist, in Bihar. An abridged and incorrect English translation of a part of it was published under the title of *Journal of a Boondelah Officer,* in Jonathan Scott's *History of the Deccan,* (Shrewsbury, 1794.)

Bhimsen's father, Raghunandandas, was one of the six sons of Jivmal ,a Kayastha of the Saksena section, the other five being Bhagwandas, Shyamdas, Gokuldas, Haridas and Dharamdas. Of these Bhagwandas rose to the highest position then open to a Hindu. He was appointed *Diwan* (Chancellor) of Mughal Deccan with the title of *Dianat Ray* (=Baron Honesty) in 1657, accompanied Aurangzib from the Deccan during his march northwards to contest the throne of Delhi, and lived at that capital with the Court till his death in 1664. He had every expectation of being appointed chief Diwan of the Empire, but when Aurangzib confined his old father in Agra Fort (June, 1658), Ray-i-rayan Raghunath Rai, the Assistant Diwan, who had been doing all the duties of the Imperial Diwan, deserted to the prince, and his timely submission was rewarded by his being given the post of the chief Diwan of the Empire, though without the title. Thus Dianat Ray lost his highest hope.

Raghunandan was *mushrif* of the imperial artillery of the Deccan, a post which he resigned about 1670, in order to pass his old age in religious meditation, dying at Aurangabad in 1674.

Genealogy of the family:—

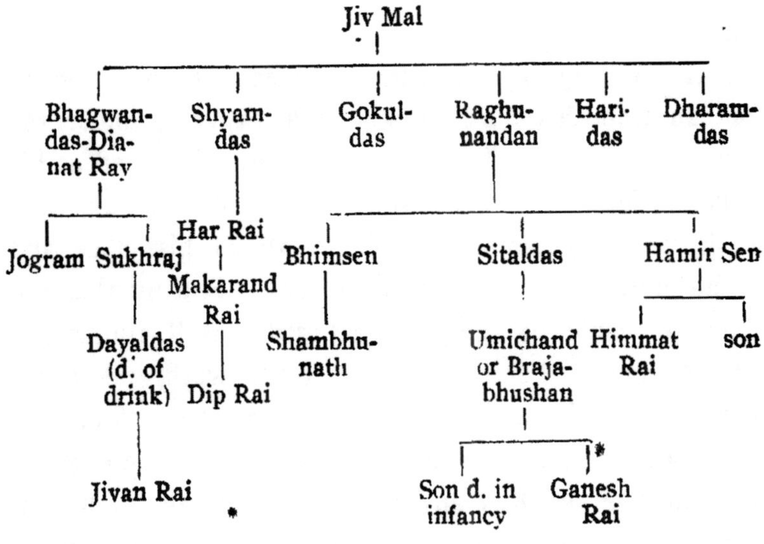

II. Early Life.

Bhimsen was born at Burhanpur on the Tapti (the capital of Khandesh) in Samvat 1705 (1649 A.D.), and at the age of eight he left this place to join his father at Aurangabad. That was an eventful year (1657). The crown of Delhi was changing hands and the boy retained a vivid recollection of the "rumours of war" in Northern India that agitated the citizens of Aurangabad. At the age of ten he paid a visit to the Nasik caves and Trimbak fort in his father's company. The death of Dianat Ray at Delhi (1664) dashed down to the ground all the hopes of high promotion cherished by his family. His eldest son Jogram was appointed by the Emperor *mushrif* of the Elephants,—no very high post; but died in a few years. Then Sukhraj, the younger son of Dianat Ray, was appointed *mushrif* of the Imperial Drink and Betel leaf Departments.

At Aurangabad Bhimsen received his education in Persian from his ninth to his fifteenth year, under the care of his father. Then, for seven years he acted as his father's deputy. Raghunandan was growing old and weak, and felt himself unable to attend his office and do his duties as *mushrif* of Artillery. Fearing that the Emperor would be angry if he heard that Raghunandan was staying at home, while his office work was being actually done by a youth of 21, he resigned (1670.)

Young Bhimsen had now to look out for some employment and turned to many patrons of his family, but in vain. At last he secured the post of *mushrif* of muster and branding of horses in the division of Daud Khan Quraishi, immediately under Mir Abdul Mabud, the Paymaster (*bakhshi*) of that general. He had to pay a large bribe to get the post and had also to run into debt to engage and equip followers in a manner worthy of his post and *mansab*. He started for Daud Khan's camp at Junnar, but met him on the way and returned with him to Aurangabad to the Court of Prince Muazzam, then viceroy of the Deccan. But now a bitter quarrel broke out between the prince and his general Dilir Khan, the latter being supported by Daud Khan. Thus the projected expedition under Daud Khan was abandoned, and Bhimsen's new post was abolished. But Maharajah Jaswant Singh very kindly took him into his service, and they set off together northwards to the Tapti in pursuit of Dilir Khan. Bhimsen took this opportunity of revisiting his birthplace Burhanpur, and then returned to Aurangabad, in September 1670.

III. Official Employment.

A few days afterwards, Daud Khan was detached by the prince to intercept Shivaji on his return from the second loot of Surat. Bhimsen accompanied this army as clerk (*peshdast*) to the Bakhshi in addition to his former post, and was present at the battle of Dindori (17 Oct. 1670) in which the Mughals were defeated by Shivaji with heavy slaughter. Then he went with Daud Khan's force to Nasik and Ahmadnagar.

After some time the Khan marched to Ankai Tankai (near the Manmad railway junction) to check the Marathas who were active near the forts of the Chandor range, such as Dhodap. Thence he hastened into Baglana to raise the siege of Salhir. During this march our author was separated from the army and in great danger of being cut off; but he was saved by Nur Khan, a Muhammadan mercenary of the Maratha army, who had formerly been befriended by his father at Aurangabad. Daud Khan arrived too late to save Salhir from being captured by Shivaji, but continued fighting near the Chandor range for some time and took the fort of Ahivant.

A letter now arrived from the Emperor accepting the prince's recommendation that Bhimsen should be appointed *mushrif* of muster and branding. Jaswant had induced the prince to make this proposal. But through the machinations of the Hindu favourites of Mahabat Khan, the new commander-in-chief of the Deccan, the post was conferred on a son of Brindaban (the son of Dara's diwan). The cup was thus snatched away from the lips of Bhimsen and he had to pass a long time in unemployment and distress, but his high-placed friends helped him with money.

After a time Bahadur Khan, the new viceroy of the Deccan, (1672) gave that post to Bhimsen and he held it for many years afterwards.

In the course of the pursuit of the Marathas who had raided Ramgir (110 miles north-east of Haidarabad) in November, 1672, Bhimsen had a marvellous adventure with a *darvish* which reads like a romance. For the next two years he made much money and lived in great happiness and comfort; "even great nobles could not live in that style" as he brags! But a succession of bereavements overtook him soon afterwards: he lost his uncle Gokuldas (a few years earlier), his brother Sitaldas, and his father Raghunandan, then Har Rai and Har Rai's father Shyamdas.

For a long time Bhimsen had been childless. So, he

adopted as his own, a son of his younger brother Sitaldas, who was born in 1671 and named Umichand by the astrologers and Brajabhushan by our author. In 1678 this little child was married.

In 1686 Bhimsen, tired of work, left his office duties in the imperial army to be discharged by his agents (*gumashtas*) and went to live with his family at Naldurg, a fort 25 miles north-east of Sholapur. Here in 1688 a son was born to him and named Shambhunath ; but Brajabhushan, whom he had adopted as his son, continued to be cherished as a member of his family, like his eldest son.

IV. Serves Dalpat Rao Bundela.

Soon afterwards, Bhimsen left Naldurg and joined the Mughal army at Sholapur. At this place he was taken into the service of Dalpat Rao, the Bundela chieftain of Datia and an important general in Aurangzib's army, as his private secretary and "man of business." Lands yielding Rs. 12,000 a year were given to him as his salary, evidently in Bundelkhand. [Bhimsen does not seem to have resigned his post in the imperial army.] The connection thus begun continued till Dalpat's death eighteen years later.

In the company of Dalpat Rao, who was lieutenant to Aurangzib's foremost general Zulfiqar Khan Bahadur Nusrat Jang (the son of the *wazir* Asad Khan), our author marched through jungles to Jinji (in the South Arcot District) in 1691. The siege of this fort by the Mughal army was soon abandoned (for a time), and Dalpat with

Bhimsen went to Wandiwash and then to Madras for treatment under the celebrated European doctors of the place. The Rao was not cured and returned after losing much money. The Italian traveller Niccolao Manucci, who had set up as a doctor without any medical knowledge, says that Dalpat's agent was deceived by a selfish middleman and did not consult him but went to some other quack, and hence his failure to be cured! (*Storia do Mogor*, iii. 139.)

The business of Dalpat Rao brought Bhimsen from Madras to the imperial camp at Brahmapuri on the Bhima river, 18 miles south-east of Pandharpur. After finishing it, he returned quickly to Jinji, only to come to Naldurg again for the marriage of his son Shambhunath (celebrated at Haidarabad.) Soon after going back to Jinji he retraced his steps and travelled to Agra on a mission of Dalpat Rao, and on his return he stopped at Naldurg. To this district Dalpat Rao came after the fall of Jinji in 1698, and our author joined him. During the journeys of these eight years, Bhimsen visited most of the famous temples and cities of the Madras Presidency and Northern India, and he has left short but extremely valuable descriptions of them as they were two hundred and fifty years ago.

Towards the end of 1700 the Mughal army laid siege to Panhala, a fort 14 miles north of Kolhapur. During the enforced idleness of the siege, Bhimsen began to write his History in his tent at the foot of the fort. But the long wars of Aurangzib had made the Deccan desolate, famine and disorder raged everywhere; the government seemed to have collapsed. It was not safe to live amidst such anarchy. Bhimsen, therefore, sent his whole family from Naldurg, at first to Aurangabad and then to Dalpat Rao's capital Datia (1706).

V. Last Years.

Next year Aurangzib died; his third son Azam crowned himself in the Deccan and set out with his army to seize Delhi and Agra. But at Jajau, 20 miles south of Agra, he was defeated and slain by his elder brother Bahadur Shah I. (8th June, 1707.) On that fatal field, a cannon ball passed through the body of Dalpat Rao killing him and wounding Bhimsen, who was sitting on the same elephant behind the Rao, in the arm. Our author, though wounded, burnt his master's body at Dhamsi, 16 miles south of Agra, and then retired to Datia with all his hopes crushed. To make matters worse, a war broke out between the two sons of Dalpat for the *gadi*. Bhimsen in disgust left Datia with his family and came to Gwalior. As the right-hand man of Dalpat, who was a most influential partisan of Azam Shah, Bhimsen had been created by that prince a commander of five hundred, and he would have risen still higher if his patron had triumphed at Jajau.

But now he was thrown out of employment and put to great distress for his daily bread. After trying in vain for a post under Bahadur Shah I., he succeeded in getting his sons Brajabhushan and Shambhunath enrolled (as petty clerks) in the service of Prince Khujista Akhtar Jahan Shah, through the kind help of Ray-i-rayan Gujar

Mal, and returned home to lead a life of religious meditation. We know nothing of his death, nor of the after-history of his family. But the genealogical tree given above may be the means of tracing his living descendants, if my readers at Datia, Gwalior, Burhanpur and Aurangabad make inquiries.

VI. As a Writer.

The value of Bhimsen's History lies in his extensive and accurate personal observation and his position. As a clerk in the Mughal army of the Deccan and the friend of many generals and other high officers, he secured correct official information and learnt many a State secret, while his situation at a distance from the throne and the fact of his History not having been written for the Emperor's eyes placed him above the temptation to omit or disguise facts discreditable to the Government or write a fulsome eulogy on the Emperor and his courtiers. He is thus free from the worst defects of the official histories of the Mughal emperors. Bhimsen knew the truth and could afford to tell it. He has also given true sketches of the characters of various historical personages of the time and pointed out their defects. His reflective mind and Hindu creed enabled him to look with the eyes of a neutral spectator at the events of Aurangzib's reign and to narrate their true causes and effects. Above all, his account of many incidents of the Mughal warfare in the Deccan is as valuable as the reports of the "Eye witness" in the Great European war. Indeed, he is our only source of detailed information about them.

Things which the pompous official historians of the day scorned to mention,—such as the prices of food, the amusements of the people, the condition of the roads, and the social life of the official class,—are described here only. For Deccan history in the late 17th century, he is invaluable.

The character of Bhimsen as a man is unfolded in his Memoirs without any disguise. We see his weakness, but we also see his strong fidelity to friend and master, his devotion to his kith and kin, his love of children and his devout faith in Hinduism. Bhimsen was a charming character, tender, unpretentious, frank and serene, loving social gaiety but also deeply touched by sorrow. If it be true that "the style is the man," then we must highly praise this master of a simple business-like prose, in which there are no useless flowers of rhetoric, no profuse wordiness, no round-about expression, but plenty of accurate observation and concise but clear statement of all essential points. These are rare qualities in a Persian writer.

XVI

AN OLD HINDU HISTORIAN OF AURANGZIB.

There are two extremely valuable contemporary histories of Aurangzib's reign (1657-1707 A.D.), written in Persian but by Hindus. One is the *Nuskha-i-Dilkasha* by Bhimsen, a Kayastha, born at Burhanpur, and the other is the *Fatuhat-i-Alamgiri* composed by Ishwar-das of Patan in Gujrat. Of the latter only one manuscript is known to exist in the world, *viz.*, British Museum Pers. MS Additional No. 28884. It contains 329 pages of 11 lines each. The great importance of these two historians lies not only in their looking at the reign through the eyes of contemporary Hindus, but also in their living near enough to the great Mughal officers to learn the historical events of the time accurately, but not near enough to the throne to be lying flatterers.

Ishwar-das, a Nagar Brahman and inhabitant of the city of Patan in the *subah* of Gujrat (now in the Gaikwar's dominions), served Shaikh-ul-Islam from his youth up to his 30th year. This Shaikh, as the Chief Qazi of the Empire, used to accompany the Emperor Aurangzib in camp and Court alike, and Ishwar-das in the train of his master got good opportunities of learning the true facts of Indian history directly from the chief officials of the time or their servants. We know from the official record of Aurangzib's reign (entitled the *Masir-i-Alamgiri*) that Shaikh-ul-Islam acted as Chief Qazi in succession to his deceased father Abdul Wahhab (a Borah) from December 1675 to November 1683, when he resigned his post on account of the Emperor rejecting his advice not to fight with brother-Muslims like the sultans of Bijapur and Golkonda, as that would be a sin according to the *Quran*. In December 1684, the Shaikh set out on a pilgrimage to Mecca, and Ishwar-das now took service under Shujaet Khan who was viceroy of Gujrat from 1685 to 1701. As he was in his 30th year at this time he must have been born in 1655 A.D., and his history was completed in 1730, when he was seventy-six years old. It is interesting to note that Khafi Khan's famous history of the Mughal Empire was also completed within four years of this latter date.

Shujaet Khan employed Ishwar-das as *amin* and *shiqdar* (revenue-collector) in certain *mahals* of the Jodhpur *parganah* which the Emperor had annexed on the death of Jaswant Singh in December, 1678. This position brought Ishwar-das into frequent contact with the Rathors and, as he tells us in his History, a strong friendship sprang up between him and them. From this cause came his life's chance of official reward and elevation to the rank of a *mansabdar*.

We all know, that Aurangzib's fourth son, Muhammad Akbar, rebelled in 1681, but being defeated fled to the Maratha Court (and finally to Persia), leaving his infant son Buland Akhtar and daughter Safiyat-un-nisa in the hands of the Rajputs. These were tenderly brought up in a secret nook by Durgadas Rathor, the guardian and champion of Ajit Singh, the young heir to the Jodhpur throne. Aurangzib was ever eager to recover his grand-children and thus preserve his family-honour. At the same time, Durgadas was worn out by the constant war with the Mughals and the devastation of his country.

The rest of the story we shall give in the words of Ishwar-das :—

"His (*i.e.*, Durgadas's) period of suffering was over and his happy days arrived. So (in 1698) he sent a letter to the author of this book,......stating that if Shujaet Khan gave him a safe-conduct and spared his home from harm pending the Emperor's orders on his petition (for forgiveness), he would send Safiyat-un-nisa Begam to the imperial Court. The Emperor at once acceded to the proposal......The author (*i.e.*, Ishwar-das), on the arrival of the Emperor's reply, by order of the Khan visited Durgadas, who was living in a place extremely difficult of access, persuaded him with wise advice, confirmed him in his good resolution, and returning to the Khan, took proper escort and conveyances back with him for conducting the princess to her grandfather. As the Begam had been pleased with this slave's services and arrangements, she asked him to accompany her to the imperial Court......Arrived there, the Begam informed Aurangzib that Durgadas had been so attentive to her as to get for her a Muhammadan tutoress from Ajmir, under whose tuition she had already read the *Quran*, and committed it to memory. This fact convinced the Emperor of Durgadas's devotion and induced him to forgive all his past offences. The imperial grace gushed forth and he asked, "Tell me what Durgadas wants." The Begam answered that Ishwar-das knew it. His Majesty at once ordered me to be presented to him in his private chamber by Qazi Abdullah, the friend of Shujaet Khan. Next day, I was honoured with an audience and reported Durgadas's prayer to receive a *mansab* and allowance. It was granted; and this humble atom (*i.e.*, Ishwar-das) was also created a commander of 200 horse in rank (*zat*), invested with a robe of honour (*khilat*), and sent to bring Buland Akhtar and Durgadas to the presence......On my return to Ahmadabad I was rewarded by Shujaet Khan, too. Repeatedly visiting Durgadas, I took solemn oaths on behalf of the Khan, and reassured his mind with promises. Durgadas, on getting *parwanahs* conferring *jagirs* on himself and being put in actual possession of the *mahals* assigned to him, came with me to Ahmadabad. The prince and Durgadas were conducted by the author to Surat, where many officers deputed by the Emperor met the prince in advance, both to welcome him and also to teach him Court-etiquette. But the prince continued to behave like a dumb and awkward clownish lad, and the Court doctors failed to remedy his defect.

When Durgadas arrived at the portico of the Audience Hall, the Emperor ordered him to be ushered unarmed (like a prisoner or suspect). Durgadas, without a moment's hesitation or objection, took his sword off. Hearing this, His Majesty ordered him to come in with his arms on! When he entered the tent, [the finance minister] Ruhullah Khan was ordered to meet him in advance and present him. The Khan conducted him to the Emperor after binding his wrists together with a handkerchief. [This was a mummery by which the offender had to beg the royal pardon, appearing like a captive of war or criminal under arrest. The reader will remember how the representatives of the citizens of Calais had to make submission to Edward III, by appearing with halters round their necks. It was, in Mughal India, a merely theatrical action, intended to soothe the imperial dignity].

His Majesty now graciously ordered Durgadas's arms to be untied, promoted him to be a commander of 3,000 horse (in rank, with an actual contingent of 2,500 troopers), and gave him a jewelled dagger, a *padak* (gold pendant), and a string of pearls,—and an order on the imperial Treasury for one *lakh* of Rupees.

The author, too, was favoured by the Emperor with a robe of honour and a promotion of 50 horsemen in rank and ten troopers in his actual following, and was given a *jagir* in Mairta (in Marwar, west of Ajmir.)"

So, Ishwar-das became a commander of 250 horse in rank, in reward of his success in diplomacy. This account of himself is also supported by the Persian history, *Mirat-i-Ahmadi* (i. 333.) We know nothing further of our author. The colophon of his book tells us that it was written "as a memorial of Mehta Ishwar-das of the Nagar caste,......and completed on 21st Rabi-ul-awwal, 12th year of the reign of Muhammad Shah, 1143 A. H. (23 September, 1730 A.D.), for the information of Lala Khushhal." Now, a Persian work entitled *Dastur-ul-aml-i-*

Shahanshahi mentions a certain Lala Sahib, the son of Braja Rai, the son of Ishwar-das. If this Lala Sahib was Lala Khush-hal, we can conclude that our author in his old age composed his reminiscences of the grand times in which he had lived, for the information of his grandson, who must have pressed him to tell the story of the famous Aurangzib's reign.

Contents of Ishwar-das's History:—

XVII

INDUSTRIES AND FOREIGN COMMERCE OF AURANGZIB'S EMPIRE.

Throughout the 17th and part of the 18th centuries, Indian industries were kept alive and developed by three agencies, namely (*a*) the Emperors of Delhi, (*b*) the nobility, and (*c*) the export traders. These export traders were mostly foreigners ; not only did European nations like the Portuguese, Dutch, English and French take a leading part in our sea-borne commerce, but Arabs Persians and men of Zanzibar also were largely engaged in the traffic. Several Muhammadans of India, especially in Lower Sindh, Gujrat, Kanara and Malabar, as well as some at Masulipatam on the East Coast, had ships of their own which sailed to the Near East and the Far East, trading on their own account. The Maratha king Shivaji had a mercantile marine of his own, though it was very small in tonnage and value and mostly carried on coastal trade.

It would be a mistake to suppose that the Emperor and the nobility concerned themselves with nothing but articles of luxury or art products. The bad state of transport in that age did not permit the export, or inland distribution over long distances, of any article of heavy bulk and low price. Only costly articles of comparatively small bulk could be profitably exported or moved within the country very far from the places of their origin. The cheap water transport down the Ganges enabled cargoes of saltpetre to be sent from North Bihar (Lalganj) to Calcutta and Chandarnagar for loading in ships bound for Europe. For the purpose of export Ahmadabad, Surat, Masulipatam, and in Bengal Hijli, Satgaon near Hughli, Sripur near Dacca, and Chatgaon were very advantageously situated, because of their nearness to the sea. And Patna also shared this advantage for all the year by reason of its position on the greatest river-highway of India.

A certain amount of fabrics of ordinary use and foodstuffs could, therefore, be profitably exported from some of our ports to other Asiatic countries, and such articles also found customers in the households of the Emperor and the nobility. The imperial palace contained a variety of factories or work-shops, called *Karkhanahs*, on which detailed information will be found in my book the *Mughal Administration*, Chapter 10. But it would be a mistake to imagine that the sovereign selfishly kept to himself the goods produced or the artistic skill developed in his *Karkhanahs*. For one thing, the greater portion of the articles turned out in them was periodically presented to the nobles as a matter of administrative practice, and the surplus left over after satisfying the wants of the imperial household and official needs, was sold to private persons. Skilled artisans trained in these imperial workshops, especially apprentices after completing their technical education, found employment with the nobles and Rajahs, as all of them were not required by the Mughal Government. In this way their skill was transplanted all over the country. The most notable instance of this diffusion of talent and elevation of the cultural level of the country by the action of the Court, is supplied by the schools of Mughal painters and musicians.

The nobles had to present the rarest products, both natural and manufactured, of their provinces to the Emperor, the princes, and the ministers. It was not only a tactical blunder, but also a breach of social etiquette to approach the great empty-handed. The nobles therefore appointed the best local artisans to manufacture for them articles worthy of presentation in time for their next visit to the Court. Thus, though they maintained no *karkhanah* at their own expense in imitation of the sovereign, they caused fine stuffs to be manufactured for themselves by advancing money and materials to the local craftsmen and deputing one of their servants to watch the labourers at home and get the work done. In this consisted their encouragement of the arts and crafts within their jurisdiction.

The foreign traders, however, were the chief cause of the expansion of our manufactures, especially of articles of ordinary use as distinct from superfine articles of luxury and rare art-products, though a small quantity of the latter class of goods was also shipped by them. They followed the universal mediæval system of giving *dādan* or advances to individual workmen and looking after them in their cottages and securing the delivery of the goods in proper time (*i.e.*, just before the shipping season or westward monsoon winds.) For this supervision they had to keep an army of agents. They also bought extensively at big marts through their Indian brokers, usually under the supervision of a junior European factor. The suppliers at these marts were not big capitalist manufacturers, but a large number of individual producers, and a few wandering middlemen who had made their purchases in the villages of the cottage manufacturers and brought the goods to the central mart for sale. Only a small portion of the goods exported by the European Companies was manufactured in their own *kuthis* or factories. The goods there manufactured were the costlier or specially designed articles, and, therefore, formed an exceptional class in our export list.

In the case of the major portion of our exports, the European Company's agents (*gumashtas* and *peons*) regularly visited the workmen in their cottages, to see that the advance taken by them was being applied to the right use and that the things they had contracted to supply were in such an advanced state of production as to be delivered in time for the sailing of the Europe-bound ships. There was the constant risk that a rival company might seduce, or some high-handed official might intimidate the workman to abandon the work for which he had received the *dādan*, in favour of some other article, or to deliver the finished article to this third party instead of the company that had paid the advance. There was no legal means of punishing these breaches of contract, and the company's original agreement with the producers could be enforced only by bribing the *subahdar* or *faujdar* into putting pressure on the workmen to keep their word.

At Qasimbazar in Bengal, in the middle of the 17th century, the Dutch employed seven to eight hundred silk weavers, and the English and the French probably three to four hundred each, but mostly in the cottages of these men. [Bernier, 439.]

In spite of these disadvantages and risks, our foreign trade was a brisk one, except when a terrible famine war or extensive and long-continued civil disorder entirely deranged the economic life of the community. For example, the Maratha raids during the late 17th and early 18th centuries ruined the trade of Gujrat and Kanara, and their incursions into Bengal from 1742 to 1751 did that of Bengal, as we see from the graphic details given in the Factory Records of the English and the French in the last-named province.

Foreign trade occupied a negligible position in the economics of the Mughal empire till the end of the 17th century, on account of its small volume,—the total yield of the import duty being probably less than 30 lakhs of Rupees a year, while the land revenue brought to the State one hundred and eleven times that amount. The value of the Indian products exported by the English East India Company during the first sixty years of its trade with this country (1612-1672) did not average more than a hundred thousand pounds (equivalent to eight lakhs of Rupees) per annum, but by the year 1681 it rose to £230,000 for Bengal alone. The trade of the Dutch Company with India was at this time probably at least as large as that of the English Company, but the trade of the Portuguese was now reduced to negligible proportions.

There is no evidence to show that any very considerable volume of trade by sea was in the hands of native merchants, but a small amount of traffic continued to be carried on by the overland route to Persia and Turkey and also Tibet. "The fact is that the people of India at that time obtained little by international exchange except precious metals, together with a few articles of luxury enjoyed by the rich. The imports were in the main paid for by her export of cotton goods, supplemented by a small variety of raw produce, such as pepper, indigo, and saltpetre. India was thus economically almost self-supporting." "During the first half of the 17th century, the English E. I. Co.'s trade with the East was to a large extent confined to dealings in five classes of goods. In the English market the products most sought for were *spices* from the Archipelago and the Spice Islands, the *raw silk* of Persia, and the *saltpetre* and *indigo* of India. No doubt a fair quantity of the *finer cotton cloths* as well as a small quantity of manufactured silk goods were imported into England. But for the most part the English Company's purchases of cotton goods were made not for import into England, but for the markets of the further East and of Persia. India, indeed, possessed almost a monopoly in the manufacture of cotton goods in foreign markets, . . . but she had not even a considerable export trade in silk goods. Raw silk came [to England] chiefly from Persia and from China, while even in the first half of the 17th century China supplied the greater part of the manufactured silk articles imported into England." [C. J. Hamilton, *Trade between England and India.*]

The main exports of the Mughal empire in the 17th century were: (1) opium, (2) indigo, (3) cotton yarn and fabric, and (4) silk stuffs. Among the minor articles were (5) diamonds, (6) pepper, (7) ginger, (8) *ghee*, (9) sugar, (10) lac, (11) wax, and (12) saltpetre.

Opium was chiefly grown in Bihar, Malwa (where there was an immense local consumption of it and export to the neighbouring Rajputana), Berar, and Khandesh. It was carried "to numberless places by sea", as Bernier noticed (p. 440.) India's customers for this drug were Pegu (*i.e.*, Lower Burma), Java, the Malay world, and China on the one hand, and Persia and Arabia on the other. The Khandesh opium was exported through Surat, and the Bihar opium through Bengal.

Indigo was largely exported from Bengal, but we have no information whether it was grown in Bihar also. A cheap coarse species of this dye was produced in the western border of Khandesh ; but the best kind came from Biana and its neighbourhood in the Agra province, and the second best from Sarkhej in Gujrat and from Golkonda. Biana indigo sold at prices 50 per cent. higher than the varieties grown in other parts of India, namely, Rs. 36 to 40 per maund of 60 seers (=52 French *livres*) against Rs. 15 to 20 per maund of 42 seers (=34 French livres) fetched by Gujrat Indigo. [Tavernier, ii. 9.] In addition to what was exported, there was a large internal consumption of indigo, because it formed the basic material in washing and bleaching ordinary cotton cloths to a pure white colour. Thus, cotton cloths were sent from their places of origin to central spots for washing, such as Agra, Ahmadabad, Masulipatam, and certain places in Bengal, probably Dacca and Qasimbazar. [Tavernier, ii. 3.] No indigo was locally grown near Masulipatam, and therefore the cotton manufacturers of that district had to depend on Bengal exports of the dye. Ahmadabad drew its indigo from Khandesh and probably also from Bengal.

Cotton. The raw wool was exported only to the Persian Gulf and Arabia. It did not pay to send it to greater distances or to Europe. Khandesh and Berar were then, as now, the chief seats of this fibre, and the cotton grown here found its easiest way to Ahmadabad and Surat for embarkation. The extensive cotton spinning and weaving carried on in that age in Bengal and Masulipatam seem to have depended upon the local production of the raw material, and not on imports from Berar by way of the Western Coast.

Cotton yarn. The coarser counts were exported (from Ahmadabad and Surat) "in large quantities" to Europe to be made into the wicks of candles and into stockings and also to mingle with the web of silk stuffs. [Tavernier, ii. 8.] From St. Thome in Madras vast quantities of red-dyed cotton yarn were exported to Pegu, as Cæsar Frederick noted about 1575, the chief merit of the article being that "this colour will never waste, but the more it is washed, the redder it will show." [Hakluyt, v. 402.]

Cotton fabrics fell into five classes: (*a*) white ordinary and (*b*) coloured ordinary, both plain in texture and known in England as *calicoes*, (*c*) flowered, (*d*) printed, called *chintz*, and (*e*) muslin. Coarse white cotton cloths were exported from lower Sindh, Bengal, Orissa and other places on the East Coast of India, to many countries of Southern Asia and the Indian Archipelago, and in small quantities to Japan ; towards the end of the 17th century a market was found for them in England also.

Baftas, or cotton cloths dyed red blue or black at Ahmadabad and Broach, were exported largely to Mozambique, Abyssinia, the Philippine Islands, Sumatra and the Far East. [Tav. i. 72 and ii. 27.] The *baftas* which were dyed at Agra were mostly consumed inland in far-off places within India itself [Tav. i. and ii. 5.]

As for cotton cloths worked in gold and silver, Benares and Ahmadabad were the chief centres of their manufacture, and from these places they were exported to all parts of India and the world outside. [*Storia do Mogor*, ii. 83 and 125.] Bidar in the early 18th century was famous for this industry. [*Chahar Gulshan*, 94*b*.] At Agra it was fostered by royal patronage. [*Storia*, ii. 424 and *Khulasat-ut-tawarikh*, 25*a*.]

Very fine cotton fabrics, both white and coloured, were exported from Khandesh *via* Surat and Ahmadabad. [*Storia*, ii. 429.] They were also produced for foreign markets as well as home consumption at Patna and Ahmadabad. [*Ain-i-Akbari*, ii. 240.] The whole Madras Coast from Masulipatam to Pondicherry, and next to it but considerably behind, Kanara or the country from Hubli to Karwar, were the seats of the most productive cotton industry in India ; but the wars following the Mughal conquest of Golkonda (1687) and the expansion of the Maratha power completely ruined these regions and the primacy in cotton manufacture passed on to Bengal in the third decade of the 18th century.

The place of honour among the cotton stuffs exported from India was occupied by *muslin* or extremely fine white cloth, sometimes of a plain texture, but most often worked with flowers of cotton silver or gold thread. This was the most famous speciality of Indian commerce throughout the civilised world, and marvellous stories are told by the European travellers about the extreme delicacy, thinness, and transparency of the best muslins. Their centres of production were Dacca and Qasimbazar in Bengal, and in a lesser degree Agra, Sironj in Malwa, and Broach, Baroda, and Navsari in Gujrat. Europe, as well as the Far East, was our best customer for this article.

Chintz or hand-painted or printed calico. The most famous seat of its manufacture was Masulipatam, which supplied the imperial household of Delhi, though a large number of other places produced cotton-prints of lesser and varying degrees of excellence. The Masulipatam *chintz* used to line the walls of the imperial *darbar* hall, and, as screens in the palace, were so beautiful that the painted flowers looked like natural ; as if the spectators were gazing at a parterre in a garden. [Bernier, 270, 362, 403.] But very little stuff of this high quality was available for export, as the imperial household consumed the whole output, which was small. About 1580 Cæsar Frederick noticed among the *chintz* loaded at St. Thome, "fine bumbast cloth . . . . painted, which show as they were gilded with diverse colours, and the more they be washed the livelier the colour will show." [Hakluyt, v. 402.] At Masulipatam and some other dyeing centres, the brightness of the colour was popularly ascribed to the properties of the local water. Other places such as Multan, Sidhpur in Gujrat, Lahor, Burhanpur, Sironj, manufactured cheap *chintz* for popular consumption in India and foreign markets, one of the largest customers being Persia.

Silk. The yarn was the monopoly of Bengal. A good deal of the output was woven locally, but "enormous quantities" of the yarn were also exported to Gujrat, Tartary, and all parts of the Mughal empire for weaving. At Surat they manufactured carpets of silk, or of silk and gold and silver thread. At Ahmadabad all kinds of silk stuffs were woven, the specialities of the city being brocades and flowered silk pieces. These last were largely exported to the Malay world, as well as to all other parts of India. In Bengal, Qasimbazar was the chief seat of silk-weaving, and here as also in some other towns fabrics of all kinds were produced. [Bernier, Tavernier, ii. 2.] Benares was as famous in the middle of the 17th century for its silk stuffs and silk embroidery as it is today. In Asia, Burma was the chief customer of our silk goods. Towards the end of the 17th century Indian silk taffetas and brocades began to be exported to Europe in larger quantities, and a distinct improvement in the dyeing and weaving of silk was effected in Bengal by the English E. I. Co. bringing out experts in these arts from Home.

Tassar. "Cloth of herbs from a silk which groweth among the woods", or "grass cloth looking like silk," as the early European travellers quaintly describe it, was the speciality of Orissa and was extensively exported from the Orissa ports [Hakluyt, v. 409 and 482] and also from Bengal.

Diamond mines were distributed over the country stretching from Chota Nagpur (Sambalpur) southwards into the present Nizam's Dominions. The Golkonda kingdom (and not the city of that name nor its environs) had the most productive mines of this gem, as is well known. This precious stone made its way out of India through the ports of the West Coast. For a long time Goa was the chief diamond mart in the world ; afterwards Chaul, Surat and Bombay took its place. It is not generally known that immediately north of Bihar in the sub-Himalayan tract now lying in the Purnia district there was a region called *Gokra-desh* which was famous in Jahangir's time for its valuable diamond mines, but we lose all trace of these Himalayan mines after 1612.

Long **pepper** was extensively exported from Bengal and Hijli and also from the West Coast. As for black or round pepper, Kanara was the land of it, and supplied the whole world. It is this pepper which brought the English and the Dutch to the Malabar Coast in the 17th century.

Ginger was exported from Orissa and Bengal. But candied preserves made of this root were sent abroad by sea in vast quantities every year from Ahmadabad.

Ghee was exported from Orissa and probably, but to a lesser extent, from Bengal also, "to numberless places by sea."

Sugar. At Agra "very white sugar" was made, but it was locally consumed as Agra was the centre of a vast and flourishing population. Small quantities of white sugar were exported from Hughli in Bengal. But our foreign export of sugar in that age consisted mostly of what the European travellers call "moist sugar" (*i.e.*, molasses or *gur*) and dry brown sugar. Patna grew an enormous quantity of sugar, much of which was exported down the river through the Bengal ports of Satgaon (=Hughli) and Hijli. Cæsar Frederick noticed it about 1575 and Tavernier saw the same trade flourishing in Bengal eighty years later. Berar was another seat of the sugar industry. Malwa grew sugarcane, but probably for local consumption by chewing. The Madras coast depended on imported sugar.

Lac. Bengal and Orissa had a monopoly of it. It served a twofold purpose: first, a brilliant red dye was extracted from it, and then the shellac was used in varnishing toys and making women's bangles, of which there was an immense internal consumption. The Dutch exported it to Persia for the red colour. The lac bangle and toy industry flourished most in Gujrat (especially at Surat), but it must have been diffused more or less over every part of India.

Saltpetre was the monopoly of North Bihar and it had an immense sale in Europe, as a material for making gunpowder. This was particularly the case during the wars of the middle 18th century.

Slaves were exported from Bengal and Madras, and famines used to reduce the price of human flesh so much that about 1690 a boy could be purchased at Madras for two to five Rupees and in 1810 a grown up male slave fetched Rs. 15 in Purnia.

I shall here speak of a few Indian manufactures of that age which had no foreign market: paper, arms, leather-goods, wood-work, *shawls*, carpets, glass-ware &c.

Writing paper was well made at Rajgir (Bihar), Lahor, Sialkot, and Aurangabad. But the finest variety was the speciality of Kashmir, and owed its life to the fostering care of imperial patronage. There was usually a hamlet of paper-makers, called *Kāghazipurā* in the environs of most provincial capitals and of big towns where the Court was stationed for a long time. Their output was the ordinary coarse paper for daily use. Arms were manufactured in the cities of Lahor, Sialkot, Multan and Gujrat (in the Panjab), and also in certain towns of the provinces of Gujrat and Golkonda. The Panjab and Sindh were the homes of the leather industry of India,—fostered also in Jaipur in the middle 18th century.

Kashmir was famous for its wood-work of various kinds, which reached the highest excellence, in fineness of carving, beauty of design, perfection of varnish, and the inlaying of gold thread on wood (*kuft-gari.*) It was also, as all know, the home of *shawl* manufacture, though the Mughal Emperors attempted to introduce this industry at Agra, Lahor and Patna. [Bernier, 403.] Carpets were woven at Fathpur-Sikri, Alwar and Lahor, and woollen carpets at Jaunpur, Zafarwal and Kashmir. Glass-wares were made at Alwar and Bihar. [*Ain.*, ii. 152 and 181.] But we had to depend mainly on Europe for our supply of this article.

The chief imports into India in the Mughal age were silver and gold (in specie) and, to a lesser extent, copper and lead. We were practically dependent upon foreign countries for these metals, though not for iron and steel,—which however were imported as cheaper than the home output. For high class woollen clothing, Europe (notably France) was our sole supplier; and large quantities of imported broad cloths and other woollen fabrics (Arabic *saqarlat,* 'scarlet') were consumed in India by the imperial household, the courtiers and rich men. Next in value to these were horses, of which large numbers came by ship from the Persian Gulf, and by the land-route from Central Asia, Khurasan and Kabul through the north-western passes. Hill ponies, called *tangan* or *gunt,* were imported from the Eastern Himalayan States, Tibet and Bhutan, through Bengal, Kuch Bihar, Morang and Oudh. Large quantities of fruits,—fresh in winter and dry all the year round,—were consumed in Upper India and came from Central Asia, Persia and Afghanistan. Spices,—such as cloves, nutmegs, cinnamon and cardamon,—were supplied by the Dutch from the Spice Islands, which had a monopoly of these commodities. Articles of luxury like musk and porcelain came from China, pearls from Bahrain (Persian Gulf) and Ceylon, elephants from Pegu and Ceylon, superior brands of tobacco from America, glass-ware and curiosities from Europe, and slaves from Abyssinia; but the quantity of these was very small, as was to be expected from their high price and limited consumption. Superior kinds of European wine had a good but secret sale among the nobility of the

Mughal empire and the Hindu Rajahs, but were very often presented (both by the English and the French) as the most effective bribe to the Mughal and Maratha generals and ministers. European paper, at first imported by the Portuguese and later by the Dutch (but still popularly called 'Portuguese paper'), was largely consumed by the independent Sultans of the Deccan; but the Mughal Emperors used the very fine product of their own State-factories now known in Europe as "India paper." The European trading Companies very occasionally sold light artillery and munitions (in small quantities) to our local rulers in their sudden need; but there was no regular trade in these things, and, indeed, transactions in them were mostly done in secret as unlawful.

A thin stream of traffic entered India from the Himalayan regions by way of Oudh (and later through Patna); they sent to us, loaded on ponies and sheep (!), small quantities of gold, copper, musk, the tail of the Yak cow (for use as fly-whiskers), and short thin hill-ponies. The mountaineers, after selling these goods, took back salt, cotton, glass-ware &c.

Our imports may be classified in detail according to the countries of their origin.

From Europe. In 1611 the English Captain Downton noted that at Surat "they had extraordinary desire for our quicksilver, vermilion, velvet and lead." [Purchas, iii. 265.] The Dutch used to sell at Agra quantities of broad-cloths, large and small looking-glasses, plain laces, gold and silver laces, iron wares and spices. A century before this, the kingdom of Vijaynagar in the Deccan used to import through Goa, Arabian horses, velvets, damasks, and satins, armesine of Portugal, pieces of China, saffron and scarlet. [Hakluyt, V. 389.]

From Central Asia and Afghanistan,—dried and fresh fruits of an immense variety, amber, assafœtida, rough rubies, &c. [Bernier, 249, 118.]

From the Himalayan States and Tibet came caravans laden with musk, China wood, rhuburb, mamiron (a root, medicinal for the eye), crystal, jade, fine wool; also gold, copper, lead, the tail of the Yak cow (Hindi *chāmar*), honey, borax, wax, woollen stuffs and hawks. Patna and Oudh first received these goods, as nearest to Nepal and Tibet, from which they came. Hawks were the speciality of Kumaun, Garhwal, and other mid-Himalayan States, as well as of Afghanistan and Central Asia, and were highly prized by the Emperors and the nobility for falconry.

From the Malay world, spices were imported by the Dutch. From *Pegu* rubies came; from Persia and South Arabia pearls and some kinds of gems.

Our exports were paid for by the importation of silver from Europe and gold from China, Sumatra and Persia. These precious metals were absorbed by this country in large quantities. [Bernier, 202-204.]

The most important article of import in point of value in the 17th century was horses, as more than one hundred thousand of these animals were purchased every year from Persia, Arabia, and to a lesser extent from

Tartary. They mostly entered India from Persia *via* Qandahar and Southern Afghanistan, through the N. W. frontier passes. Arab horses and those of Southern Persia came by sea through Gujrat, especially the port of Surat. We can form some idea of the immense value of this trade when we learn that in Shah Jahan's reign the price of the finest horses reached up to Rs. 15,000 each, while an ordinary elephant could be purchased for Rupees one to two thousand. Another source of our horse supply was Morang (north of Purnia) and Kuch Bihar, from which hardy hill ponies, called *gunt*, were imported in large numbers. [Abdul Hamid's *Padishah-namah*, ii. 96, *Alamgirnamah*, 690.] These were bought by the middle and lower classes.

The main trade routes of India in the 16th and 17th centuries were:—

(*a*) From Lower Bengal and Orissa by ship to the Coromandel Coast and also to Gujrat and Europe.

(*b*) From Pegu and the Spice Islands to Bengal, the Orissa Coast and Masulipatam and back; also to Japan and China.

(*c*) From Masulipatam to other ports in India, as well as to the Far East and the Near East, and even Africa. [Our foremost eastern port.]

(*d*) From Kanara and Konkan (on the West Coast) to Jedda and Mocha in Arabia, Egypt,

Persia, Zanzibar, Europe and the Far East, especially the Malay country.

(*e*) From the Gujrat ports to the East Coast, Bengal, Persia, Arabia, Egypt, as well as Europe. Surat our foremost western port.

(*f*) From Lahor to Kashmir and Afghanistan (both these countries then belonging to the empire of Delhi), as well as Central Asia and Persia by land. Also from Multan through the Bolan Pass and Qandahar; some 14,000 camels laden with merchandise passed by this latter route in 1615, and 3,000 camels in normal years.

The great river highway of the Ganges was the finest artery of trade from Patna or even as far up as Benares to the Bay of Bengal nearly throughout the year.

Excluding Afghanistan, the empire of Delhi had a revenue of Rupees 13 *krores* and 21 *lakhs* under Akbar, and 33 *krores* and 25 *lakhs* under Aurangzib. This figure stood for the land revenue alone, and did not include the proceeds of taxes like *zakat* (one-fortieth of the annual income of Muslims, to be spent by the State solely in religious charity) and *jaziya* or income-tax on non-Muslims. A rough idea of the proportion of the different sources of State-income can be formed from the figures for Gujrat, about the year 1688, when the land-tax brought in 113 *lakhs, jaziya* five *lakhs,* and the custom-duties of the port of Surat alone 12 *lakhs* per annum.

XVIII

LETTERS OF AURANGZIB

"Letters", says a Frenchman of genius, "are the very pulse of biography." They show the core of an individuality, and reveal the relations of the character of the man to his work. [*Athenæum*, No. 4207.] The letters of historical import written during the period of Aurangzib that are still preserved run to several thousands; their number exceeds many times that of the surviving correspondence of any other Mughal sovereign's times. This was the natural result of the exceptional length of Aurangzib's reign, 51 lunar years (preceded by eight years of strenuous exertion as a provincial governor under his father), and of his character as a perfect "master of the pen as well as of the sword." The value of these letters to the historian cannot be exaggerated; along with the daily news-sheets sent from his Court or camp, but in a much greater degree than the latter class of documents, they form the most original source for the study of his reign.

Many of his letters, probably the greater part of them, have perished. We now possess only five definitely arranged collections of his epistles, varying widely in the volume of their contents and often overlapping. These are: (i) *Adab-i-Alamgiri* by Qabil Khan; (ii and iii) *Kalimat-i-Tayyibat* and *Ahkam-i-Alamgiri* by Inayetullah

Khan, (iv) *Raqaim-i-Karaim* by Sayyid Ashraf Khan, Mir Muhammad Al-Husaini, and (v) *Ahkam-i Alamgiri* imputed to Hamid-ud-din Khan Bahadur Nimcha-i-Alamgir-shahi. These illuminate only the beginning and the very end of this monarch's reign, leaving the intervening period of about 42 years (1660-1702) dark, so far as this source of information is concerned.

In addition to the above works, we possess a few fairly complete sets of his letters to certain persons, though these have not been edited with a view to forming any specific book. These are (vi) Aurangzib's letters to Mirza Rajah Jai Singh of Jaipur (with the replies of the latter), (vii) his letters to Murad Bakhsh during the war of succession, (viii) his letters to his rebel son Muhammad Akbar (with the replies of that prince), and (ix) his official orders and regulations sent to the governor or *diwan* of Gujrat. During the period of 42 years (1660-1702) intervening between Qabil Khan and Inayetullah, no imperial secretary's *collected letter-book* has been preserved. *Stray* letters from Aurangzib written during this interval have been found in many places or incorporated in miscellaneous works, but they amount to little in the aggregate compared with the first-named group of works.

The letters *from* Aurangzib after he had been well settled on the throne are not so rich in historical information as the despatches written *to* him by his sons and officers. As he was personally present in most of the important expeditions of his reign, there was no occasion for any official despatch to be written describing them, and hence we lack this primary source of information

19

about them and cannot get, with regard to many events of his reign (at which he was personally present), the copious and accurate details which an official gives of his own exploits for the information of his master.

The imperial *farmāns* and *sanads* granting land or stipends to persons, or rights to traders, were, from the nature of the case, isolated documents and no editor has collected them. Examples of them are constantly cropping up in India, among the descendants of the original donees, collectors of manuscripts, curio-dealers, and in museums. They are marked by a monotonous uniformity of style and contents and give us very little history. Forged grants of this period often come to notice.

Adab-i-Alamgiri.

Aurangzib's earliest known secretary (*munshi*) was Abul Fath, a native of Tatta or Lower Sindh, who was given the title of Qābil Khan, Munshi-ul-mamālik, with a purse of Rs. 4,000 at the first coronation of this monarch (21 July, 1658). He had served his master from the age of 14 to that of 40, and after spoiling his eyesight by excessive application to writing, was compelled by ill-health to resign his post in July 1659. He was given a pension of Rs. 5,000 a year besides a parting gift of Rs. 1,000. As his ancestral home, the province of Tatta, was now in a desolate state, Qabil Khan in his retirement elected to live in Lahor and begged from the Emperor a house in that city, a hundred bighas of waste land near it for himself, and 1,000 bighas of rent-free land in that province for his children, pleading that the sum of

Rs. 5,000 was inadequate for supporting his large family. In May 1662, he came from Lahor to Delhi at the Emperor's call and died there next month.

Abul Fath's younger brother was twenty years later given his title of Qabil Khan and became a close personal attendant and favourite of Aurangzib, holding the office of Superintendent of Posts and Intelligence. [By a misprint in the Bibliotheca Indica edition of *Masir-i-Alamgiri*, p. 190, he is called *Mir Munshi* or imperial secretary, which he never was.] This man during his 2½ years of favour at Court amassed a fortune of twelve lakhs of Rupees in cash, besides much property and a new mansion, by selling his influence with the Emperor to suitors. At last his misdeeds drew on him the Emperor's wrath; he was dismissed and banished to Lahor, where he died soon after his arrival (1680.)

Abul Fath Qabil Khan's letters are full drafts, written in a vigorous and at the same time flexible and elegant style. Their chief merit is that in them the sense is never buried under the flowers of rhetoric, nor is there any verbose heaping up of mere words. He left behind him 628 letters, mostly written in the name of Aurangzib to the Emperor Shah Jahan and other persons of the time, followed by some which Qabil Khan wrote in his own name, either to convey Aurangzib's orders or on his own behalf. They range in date from 26 November 1649 to June 1659. These letters were afterwards supplemented by a long history of the war of succession and Aurangzib's accession (slightly abridged from known works like *Alamgirnamah*) and 146 letters written in 1678-80 by

Shaikh Muhammad Sadiq Muttalibi of Ambala (pen-name *Nā-tamām*) on behalf of prince Muhammad Akbar, the fourth son of Aurangzib. Sadiq, at the request of his son Muhammad Zaman, edited the whole work, with the above three distinct parts in 1703 A.D. and gave it the title of *Adab-i-Alamgiri*. It is by far the largest and most important letter-book of Aurangzib. The editor died on 5th Dec. 1716. One British Museum MS. of this book, Or 177, was copied from the original in Delhi in 1713.

INAYETULLAH'S LETTER-BOOKS.

For the closing years of Aurangzib's reign we possess two letter-books of his trusted officer Inayetullah Khan Kashmiri, who, however, never held the post of imperial secretary (*Mir Munshi*), but was only a personal disciple (*murid-i-khās*) and great favourite of the old Emperor. Inayetullah traced his descent from Sayyid Jamāl of Naishāpur, but his family had been long settled in Kashmir. His father was Mirzā Shukrullah, and his mother Hafiza Mariam, a learned lady who served as tutor to the princess Zeb-un-nisā and taught her the *Quran* and Persian literature. After holding subordinate posts, Inayetullah was appointed steward of the household of princess Zinat-un-nisā in October 1688, rising in July 1692 to the high office of *Diwan-i-tan*, to which the *diwani* of *Khalsa* was added in April 1701. In March 1698, he had, over and above his revenue duties, officiated as chief *Sadr* of the empire. "He had the regulations on the tip of his tongue. The Emperor greatly liked his composition and spelling" and favoured him far in excess of his comparatively humble rank as a mansabdār of 1,500 (personal grade.) How the prime minister Asad Khan was ordered by Aurangzib to apologise to Inayetullah for a quarrel about the limits of their tents in Puna on 1st May 1703, has been told in *Masir-i-Alamgiri*, 475-476. In July 1706, the Emperor allowed Inayet to stand inside the golden railing of his Court, to which only the few highest ministers were admitted.

In Bahadur Shah's reign, Inayetullah rose to be Lord High Steward (*Khān-i-sāmān*), and in April 1717 he was reappointed *Diwan-i-Khalsa* and *tan*, besides being *subahdar* of Kashmir (which he governed by deputy.) He rose still higher, in February 1721, when he was created a 7-*hazari* and acted as wazir of the empire pending the arrival of Nizam-ul-mulk from the Deccan. He died in 1727.

Inayetullah idolised Aurangzib and saw in the restoration of this monarch's state policy and administrative rules the only hope of saving the decadent Mughal empire from ruin. After Aurangzib's death he induced Muhammad Sāqi Mustad Khan to write a full history of that Emperor's reign, the official annals of which (entitled *Alamgirnamah*) had been stopped at the end of the 10th year. To this fact we owe *Masir-i-Alamgiri*, the most complete and accurate guide to the events of this reign.

Inayetullah tells us in the preface to his letter-book that he had been brought up by Aurangzib and had served him till his death, after which he decided to gather in a volume and publish for the world's instruction the notes which the Emperor had at different times written to him to be worked up into fully drafted letters and sent to the various princes and nobles addressed, or issued for guiding the administration of affairs. To this work he gave the title of *Kalimāt-i-Tayyibāt*, and it was completed in 1121 A.H. (1709 A.D.) At a later date, probably shortly afterwards, he got together more orders dictated to him by his late imperial master and issued them under the name of *Ahkām-i-Alamgiri*. The author of *Masir-ul-umara* distinguishes between the two volumes by saying that *Kalimāt* contains the royal letters signed by the Emperor, while *Ahkām* contains the orders and replies sent through Inayetullah, *i.e.*, what is officially known as letters "By order" (*hasb-ul-hukm.*) In *Kalimāt* Aurangzib gives his hints to his secretary ; in *Akham* the secretary writes fully drafted letters to the officers addressed. The tone and general purport of the two collections are much alike ; but *Kalimat* is full of Arabic texts, highly condensed in style and cryptic as regards sense and context, while *Ahkam* is much simpler in style and its meaning is often quite plain. *Kalimat* contains only notes dictated for letters to be drafted in full on the basis of them, *i.e.*, the mere *precis* of official letters. They are highly condensed and the context or occasion being in most cases omitted, their sense is very obscure. It is only a minutely detailed knowledge of the events and persons of the reign that can enable us to understand the writer's meaning. But these 'hints', when interpreted in the light of such knowledge, are of supreme value as showing the man without disguise,—his character, its greatness and failings, his tastes and policy.

Kalimat-i-Tayyibat contains short notes for 676 letters. Good manuscripts of it are often met with; the one I have used belongs to the Asiatic Society of Bengal (Old No. F. 27), and the Sova Bazar Raj library has a very neatly written copy. Of *Ahkam-i-Alamgiri* only two manuscripts are known to exist; one, which evidently belonged to the Delhi palace, is now in the Rampur State library, the other, copied in Delhi on 31st Oct. 1736, evidently for some Mughal noble, was afterwards acquired by Safdar Nawab of Patna and presented by his family to the Oriental Public Library of that city. It contains 609 pages of 15 lines each, with about 1½ letters on a page. As this work is unknown to the outer world, I give a brief synopsis of its contents here: Letters to Shah Alam (*f* 1*b*), Azam Shah (4*a*), Bidar Bakht (27*a*—116*a*), Muizzuddin (116*a*), Azim-ush-shan (116*b*), Nusrat Jang (123*b*—180*a*), Firuz Jang (180*a*), Chin Qilich Khan (184*b*—202*b*), Zabardast Kh, Dildar Kh, Munim Kh, Murshid Quli Kh. (219*a*—225*a*), Nazar Beg Kh, Rustam-dil Kh, Sipahdar Kh, Mukhtar Kh., Md. Yar Kh, Mansur Kh, Sayyid Ahmad Kh., Numan Kh, Amanat Kh, Itibar Kh, Md. Aslam Kh, Wazir Kh, Nejabat Kh, Kifayet Kh, Haji Abdur Rahman Mufti, Shaikh Abdul Hafiz, Ahsan Kh, Khan-i-Alam Deccani, Qazi and Bayutat of Ahmadabad (285*a*) and some other minor officials.

But there is another letter-book of this type which presents a puzzling problem. The only complete manuscript of it is to be found in the Rampur State library (my transcript running to 379 pages of 14 lines each); and a small fragment, containing only 153 short letters, occurs in India Office MS. 3301, ff. 33-60 (bound up with a different work.) The India Office MS. bears the title of *Kalimāt-i-Aurangzib,* but the fuller Rampur copy reproduces the preface of *Kalimāt-i-Tayyibāt* and gives itself the latter name! Its contents are mainly taken from the other two compilations of Inayetullah, but several letters are original. Towards the end of the Rampur manuscript the copyist inserted letters from elsewhere that he had been able to get hold of. It, therefore, represents no definitive work of Inayetullah, but is a hash of several earlier collections by an editor who was certainly not Inayetullah and had no access to any correct and complete copy of Inayetullah's known collections.

Other collections of his letters

Sayyid Ashraf Khan, Mir Muhammad Al-Husaini, edited a small collection of Auragzib's letters under the title of *Raqāim-i-Karāim*, so named because it contained (but not exclusively) the letters written by Aurangzib to the editor's father Mir Abdul Karim, Amir Khan. This Abdul Karim Amir Khan (not to be confounded with the Amir Khan *bin* Khalilullah, who was Aurangzib's most famous governor of Afghanistan from 1678 to 1698), was the youngest son Mir Abdul Baqā (surnamed Amir Kh. by Shah Jahan, and died in 1647.) The family was known as Sindhi, because it was settled at Bhakkar, but it originally formed a branch of the Husaini Sayyids of Herat. Abdul Karim was very close to Aurangzib's person, being the officer in charge of his personal attendants (*khawās*), the superintendent of his chapel, and the *āmin* of his daily palace-guard (1682.) As controller of the grain marts during the Golkonda campaign of 1687-88, he greatly distinguished himself by his success in bringing in provisions and lowering prices, so that he was raised to the peerage as Multafat Khan in June 1689, later Khanahzad Khan (1701) and finally Amir Khan (15 March 1704.) His devoted attendance on the Emperor during his severe illness at Devapur (1705) and gentle soothing of the aged sufferer form a touching story, which I have told in my *History of Aurangzib*, Vol. V, Ch. 57 §8. He died about 1719, soon after his appointment as Chief *Sadr*.

This particular collection is best represented by British Museum MS. Additional 26239. It contains 116 letters, out of which only 49 (namely Nos. 48—94 and 115 and 116) are addressed to Abdul Karim.

Rajah Ayā Mal, the Delhi Court agent and afterwards prime minister of the Rajahs of Jaipur, caused two series of Aurangzib's letters to be collected and edited by his learned clerks. The first, compiled by Siddh Mal (misspelt as Budh Mal in Elliot vii. 205) was completed in 1738 with the title of *Ramz-wa-Ishara-i-Alamgiri*, and is best represented by Br. Mus. MS. Addl. 26240 ; it has been repeatedly lithographed in India under the name of *Ruqat-i-Alamgiri*. The second, named *Dastur-ul-aml-i-Agahi*, was completed in 1743, Agahi being the pen-name of Ayā Mal. Both these books have abstracted from the earlier collections and contain hardly any letter not included in the latter. India Office Library MS. 1344, though called *Dastur-ul-aml-i-Agahi* in the preface, is really a fusion of Br. Mus. 26239 and 26240, *i.e.*, of *Raqaim* and *Ramz*, with a few additions from other sources at the end.

A very interesting but incomplete work named *Ahkam-i-Alamgiri*, of which I have printed both the text and an English translation (*Anecdotes of Aurangzib*), contains many highly characteristic anecdotes, answers, repartees and orders of this Emperor, some of which are in the form of letters or rather notes for letters. But these are not cryptic like Inayetullah's collection of notes; here in every case the occasion that called forth the remark or reply is explained, and the Emperor's words are in the direct speech. If these are not true reports they are certainly *ben trovato*. This work has been found only in three MSS, all incomplete, only partly overlapping, and in each case wanting the preface and the colophon. On the cover of one of the MSS it is ascribed to Hamid-ud-din Khan Bahadur Nimcha-i-Alamgiri, (life in *Masir-ul-umara*, i. 605—611), who must not be confounded with an earlier Hamid-ud-din Khan of this reign, whose letter-book has been preserved. This last-named person was originally a servant of Aurangzib's mother-in-law, Nauras Banu, and rose to be *faujdar* of the Jalandar Doab, *qiladar* of Raisin fort (1677), and deputy governor of Malwa under prince Muhammad Akbar.

UNEDITED OR STRAY LETTERS.

We shall now describe some other groups of Aurangzib's letters, which do not form any definite book solely confined to his correspondence. The most important of these is his correspondence with Mirza Rajah Jai Singh of Jaipur. A large number of Aurangzib's letters to Jai Singh are preserved in the Jaipur State archives and eleven of them in the Bibliotheque Nationale, Paris (MS. Pers. Suppl. 476), and two others in a Delhi manuscript found by me. Most of these royal letters, especially after Aurangzib's accession, are in reply to the Rajah's despatches, and therefore the two have to be studied together. Jai Singh's secretary Udirāj (who after his master's death in 1667 turned Muslim under the name of Tāla-yār) left a collection of the letters which he had written for the Rajah and certain other persons. These were edited by the secretary's son in a book entitled *Haft Anjuman*, of which two complete copies exist in India and a fragment in Paris (Suppl. 476.) None of these letters *from* Jai Singh is preserved in the Jaipur State record office. This *Haft Anjuman* is a work of the greatest importance to the history of the times, as it gives almost daily despatches of the pursuit of Dara Shukoh, Jai Singh's Purandar campaign against Shivaji (1665), and his abortive invasion of Bijapur (1666.)

Next in volume, but of the highest importance historically, are the instructions, administrative orders and regulations sent by Aurangzib to the governors and *diwans* of Gujrat, all the examples of which surviving in 1750 have been incorporated in *Mirat-i-Ahmadi*. They afford the best and most indispensable material for a study of the Mughal administrative system in its actual working and the economic and social conditions of the country in that period. No other province of Mughal India, not even the metròpolis, affords any material of this class.

Aurangzib's letters to his rebel son Muhammad Akbar are given in several manuscripts of miscellaneous contents, such as *Khatut-i-Shivaji* (R.A.S. MS.), and *Zahir-ul-insha* (lithographed), &c. These letters, as well as Akbar's replies, have been translated by me in this volume of *Studies*, Ch. VI.

Faiyyaz-ul-qawanin, a large miscellaneous collection of letters of different ages, contains several letters of Aurangzib, especially his letters to Murad Bakhsh on the eve of the war of succession (which are repeated in a Rampur State library manuscript of another work.) These last supplement *Adab-i-Alamgiri*.

It is impossible to enumerate all the stray letters of Aurangzib that have come to my notice. Some of them occur in other peoples' letter-books, as if the editors considered them too precious to be lost.

Letters to Aurangzib

The letters written by different persons *to* Aurangzib or to his highest ministers form the natural complement to the letters written *by* that Emperor, as they help us to understand the occasion and aim of the latter class of documents. In fact the two are often inseparably related together. I shall here give a list of the persons whose letters to Aurangzib or to his chief ministers (the latter written when an officer was too humble to address the sovereign directly) I have been able to obtain:

1. Mirza Rajah Jai Singh and his successors,—Jaipur State archives, *Haft Anjuman*, and other sources.
2. Abdul Ali Tabrizi (a Golkonda State *munshi*),—Br. Mus. Add 6600.
3. *Muraqat-i-Hasan*, the letters of Abul Hasan, secretary to the subahdars of Orissa, 1655—1667,—Rampur MS.
4. *Bahar-i-sakhun*, I.O.L. MS.,—Aur. to Shah Abbas II,—imperial farman abolishing two taxes, &c.
   Also Letters of Tahir Wahid, Persian king's correspondence.
5. *Khatut-i-Shivaji*,—R.A.S. MS.
   Also Parasnis MS. giving Shivaji's correspondence with Murad and Aurangzib in Shah Jahan's reign.
6. A.S.B. MS. old No. F. 56.
7. *Faiyyaz-ul-qawanin.*
8. Letters of Hamid-ud-din (formerly servant of Nauras Banu Begam, and latterly officer in Malwa, *c.* 1677), —two MSS, only partly overlapping.
9. *Riāz-ul-widād*, by Yezid Bakhsh Rasā,—O.P.L. MS.
10. I.O.L. MS. Pers. 2678.
11. Correspondence of prince Md. Akbar,—in *Khatut* and *Zahir-ul-Insha* (Nos. 5 and 21, also 19), Br. Mus. Add. 18,881 &c.
12. Surat Factory Persian correspondence during 1695-96, —I.O.L. Pers. 150.
13. Br. Mus. Sloane MS. 3582, (eastern Karnatak, *c.* 1692.)
14. *Insha-i-Madho Ram* (litho.)

15. *Majmua-i-Insha wa Ghaira*,—Rampur MS., especially Bidar Bakht, Mukhlis Kh, &c.

16. *Karnamah-i-Hindu*, the letters of Matabar Kh (governor of Kalian), written by his munshi Jethmal,—I.O.L. MS.

17. Letters of Nawazish Khan, son of Islam Kh. Rumi; he served long in Malwa.

18. *Nigar-namah-i-Munshi*, by Munshi Malikzada, letters of Aur's grandsons and certain officers,—Br. Mus. Or. 1735, daftar 1.

19. A MS. purchased by me, 106 pages.

20. William Irvine's fragmentary MS., numbered by him 371, now in I.O.L., party covered by *Faiyyaz* (No. 7.)

21. *Zahir-ul-Insha* (litho.)

Also many isolated pieces.

Published by S. C. Sarkar of Messrs. M. C. Sarkar & Sons Ld., 15, College Square and Printed by P. C. Ray at SRI GOURANGA PRESS, 71/1, Mirzapur Street, Calcutta.

State papers and reports preserved in the Imperial Record Office, more than 70 volumes of Marathi documents and biographies, Hindi and Rajasthani histories (in verse), besides Persian manuscripts (some of them discovered by him.) A synthesis of the information thus supplied enables the history of this momentous period of India's destiny to be put in the correct light and invested with flesh and blood. Errors which had so long held the field can be now dispelled with convincing certainty.

BIHAR & ORISSA DURING THE FALL OF THE MUGHAL EMPIRE

128 pages. **Re. 1. 8 as**

This is a minutely detailed special study of the affairs of Bengal, Bihar and Orissa during 1742-1752, and gives the fullest and most correct account of the **Maratha raids** into these provinces. Material in six languages has been utilised here, and the chronology of events correctly established for the first time. The same subject has been treated in a condensed form in the larger work, *The Fall of the Mughal Empire*.

A SHORT HISTORY OF AURANGZIB

511 pages, with a large map, Rs. 5.

This book contains nearly one-half of the material of the larger work in five volumes. Besides, a chronology, an Index, a large map and a chapter on the "Empire of Aurangzib, its extent, revenue, army, trade, and administrative system" are entirely *new additions*. The narratives of campaigns and the chapters dealing with Aurangzib's career before his accession to the throne have been greatly compressed while character-sketches, reflections, survey of progress decline or fall, and generalisations,—*i.e.*, all matters pertaining to the philosophy of history,—have been given almost as fully as in the larger work.

J. R. A. S.—"The narrative is clear and orderly, the characterization of individuals is excellent, and, while the book is not short by present-day standards, there is very little indeed that could be spared. The best proof of the author's power of presentation is the fact that even battles are rendered intelligible without the aid of diagrams . . . The book can be recommended with confidence to any readers who have not time or opportunity to study the author's larger work, that well-known classic, *The History of Aurangzib.*"